JAMES JOYCE
and the Making of Ulysses

JAMES JOYCE
From an oil painting by the author
By kind permission of Mrs. Louis Sargent

JAMES JOYCE
and the
Making of Ulysses

BY FRANK BUDGEN

Spencer Curtis

With a portrait of James Joyce

and four drawings to Ulysses

by the author

INDIANA UNIVERSITY PRESS

BLOOMINGTON & LONDON

PR6019
.O9 U 433
.O9 U 433
1967

FOURTH PRINTING 1967
Copyright © 1960 by Indiana University Press
Manufactured in the United States of America

CONTENTS

ILLUSTRATIONS

INTRODUCTION

THIS book, first published in 1934 and long ago out of print, easily holds after more than a quarter of a century its unique place of virtue amid the copious and often futile literature that has grown up around the name and legend of James Joyce. It remains, for one thing, the best possible introduction to the Joyce world, an unpretentious, reliable, highly animated guide to what the new reader will find in *Ulysses*. If this is its least spectacular virtue, it is an indispensable one. Thousands of readers every year make the acquaintance of the Bloomsday chronicle, a book no one, least of all the author, expected us to absorb casually. A mentor is advisable: not an unreasonable prerequisite for one of the key books of the space-time age. Here Mr. Budgen is unexcelled. Episode by episode runs his intent exposition of a book he first saw unfolded, as it were in slow-motion, during its years of composition; and if quotation is frequent and the pace tranquil, we may thank the censorship which at the time Mr. Budgen was writing had still not permitted *Ulysses* to be legally available in Anglo-Saxonry. Not many mentors are as reliable as he, and none stays out of the reader's light more tactfully.

His second cardinal virtue follows from this one: he does not sluice our minds with irrelevant ideas generated by the technical novelties of Joyce's text. His training in Impressionist painting accustomed him to the notion that the man who is fabricating a work of art employs deliberate procedures, expends pains on small areas, and dedicates his full attention to a taut internal economy. It is never necessary for Mr. Budgen to evade the naive supposition that there is a normal way to write, which consists merely in setting down what one has to say "in plain language which cats and dogs can read," and opposed to this a Joycean or abnormal way which conceals the meaning behind technical devices and needs to be elaborately explained away with reference to Joyce's enigmatic temperament. The Impressionist painters were living comfortably with the idea that pictures are made of paint some decades before it occurred to the bolder critics of the novel that books are made of words. Hence the ease with which Mr. Budgen installs his reader in a world where the bizarre modes of presentation *are* the book, and at the same time signify more than an exercise in mechanics, opening as they do on every province of human life. Consider his comparison of Joyce's way of working with Rembrandt's:

Rembrandt seemed to his neighbours to be a great harbourer of junk for junk's sake in the shape of odds and ends picked up in the market-place. Until, behold, the useless antique helmet, the strange unwearable eastern gown, the odd-shaped sword reappeared, flooded with light, in a picture, clothing and adorning a brace of his neighbours, true-to-life portraits yet with all the significance of religious symbols. And in Joyce's case the word that fell from the lips of the car-driver or convive would be noted on the waistcoat pocket-block, receive its shape and setting and be heard again with a new intonation in the mouth of one of the personages of his invention—wandering Jew, troglodyte or bartender, but for sure a phantom portrait of one of his neighbours.

This isn't an academic analogy trumped up to edgelight idiosyncrasy by a man hunting something to say. It is an unpretentious comparison of two areas of knowledge. It keeps such topics as Joyce's use of living models in a proper professional light, never suggesting with a snicker that we might like to know who some of them really were, and it refrains from suggesting that Joyce was perversely aping Rembrandt as yet another way of complicating the trail. For Mr. Budgen there is no trail, no secret, simply a book to explore. He has no filing cards, he is not a specialist, he is simply the intelligent, curious, uncommitted man, that ideal reader for whom Joyce was writing. He lets Joyce himself explain his devotion to the written word:

I once alluded to one of his contemporaries as a great writer.

"Is he?" said Joyce. "What has he written?"

I began to describe a dramatic scene in a provincial hotel when Joyce interrupted:

"Tell me something of it in his own words."

"Ah, the words. I can't remember the actual words of the book."

"But why can't you?" said Joyce. "When you remember a scene or a sonnet of Shakespeare you tell me about it in the words that conveyed it to you. Why can't you do so in this case? Some one passage ought to stick."

"Do you think that is necessary?"

"I do. When you talk painting to Taylor, Sargent or Suter you don't talk about the object represented but about the painting. It is the material that conveys the image of the jug, loaf of bread, or whatever it is, that interests you. And quite rightly, I should say, because that is where the beauty of the artist's thought and handiwork become one. If this writer is as good as you say he is, I can't understand why some of his prose hasn't stuck in your otherwise excellent memory."

It was his never merely technological acceptance of technique that enabled Mr. Budgen to utilize as he did his unique opportunity. Beginning in the early summer of

1918, he was intimate with Joyce for almost a year and a half while the composition of the middle part of *Ulysses* was going on, and after Joyce's removal from Zürich he continued to receive explanations, confidences, and progress reports by post, and to be loaned sections of new typescript for his candid opinion. He paid Joyce the rare and simple compliment of trusting what his Irish drinking companion had to say about the nature and intention of the book, and Joyce repaid him with a confidence and an easy intimacy that one does not discover him to have shown anyone else. So it was natural for him to think of *Ulysses* as process rather than as artifact, and to describe its composition rather than enumerate static features. Thus he can note how

Joyce wrote the "Wandering Rocks" with a map of Dublin before him on which were traced in red ink the paths of the Earl of Dudley and Father Conmee. He calculated to a minute the time necessary for his characters to cover a given distance of the city.

and having noted this he can reflect on its meaning instead of standing arrested before its piquancy. The modern urban world, he reflects, is time-ridden:

All their yesterdays, that in an earlier age would have been quietly buried in the hope of a glorious resurrection as myth, lie embalmed in the files of newspapers and snapshot albums. They have suffered the influence of the penny post, telegraph and telephone, all social institutions working to a close timetable. But the principal element in forming that social timesense is the means of locomotion. The discoveries of the astronomer and the mathematician have less immediate effect on this sense than the electrification of the suburban lines. . . .

The effect of such passages is to put the technique in touch with something other than itself. For Mr. Budgen, indeed, the technique, whether it involves red lines on a map or the arrangement and rearrangement of fifteen words, is the deliberate means by which Joyce places himself in contact with his subject, and with the historical process that contains his subject, at as many points as possible, and sets a modern urban community free from contingency to speak in its multiple voices. Approached in this way, obscurities vanish; and when Mr. Budgen gives us an impression of some total effect, for instance the completeness with which Bloom is presented—

There are innumerable changes of key and scale. Sometimes he is a dark phantom in the middle distance and then he suddenly dominates the foreground plane. He may stand like a floodlit building, stark and flat against the sky or he may be entirely built up out of reflections of his surroundings. Now a searchlight illuminates violently some part of him and now normal daylight flows over him from head to foot.

—we recognize, through analogies with contemporary visual arts, a contemporary man. No one can miss the ease with which he perceives Bloom and Stephen, as human beings moving through a kaleidoscope that was urban and not unfamiliar before Joyce, transposing it into literature, let it turn rich and strange. Method follows subject, and Joyce's subject is men in a city.

Which brings us to Mr. Budgen's third cardinal virtue: his wholly unembarrassed awareness of Joyce as a human being. If *The Making of Ulysses* is one half of his subject, *James Joyce* is the other half, and no one else has succeeded so completely in bringing together in our imaginations the fabulous artificer and the man who "on festive occasions and with a suitable stimulus, beribboned and wearing a straw picture hat (Autolycus turned pedant and keeping school, Malvolio snapping up unconsidered trifles) . . .

would execute a fantastic dance." He gives us the only coherent image we possess of any portion of Joyce's life; the only one, that is, in which the man we are shown seems compatible with the major fact, the facts that justifies our interest in him: the fact that he was a very great writer. The whoring intransigent of one account, the egoistic philanderer of another, the rigid graduate-school dean of a third, could scarcely have written a page of more than clinical interest.

The secret of Mr. Budgen's presentation is simple: he merely does not feel that he must apologize for Joyce's humanity when he has brought it into the presence of his artistry, because the artistry is always, in his vision, human, as much so as singing folksongs.

One of the aspects of *Ulysses* that always pleases me is its popular character. It bears a resemblance to those old popular songs which tell of tragic happenings to a jolly tune and a ringing chorus of tooralooralay. The clock strikes four in the Ormond Hotel, Blazes Boylan licks up his sloe gin and hurries off to keep his appointment with Bloom's wife. Bloom sees him go and decides not to interfere. It was a momentous decision, the situation is tragic; yet this is the brightest and gayest episode in the whole book. The action is told in words that flutter past like gay-coloured butterflies. Bloom eats his liver and bacon, drinks his cider, talks to his fellow diner, looks at the barmaids and leaves with a tremulous murmur of wind among the reeds of his inside.

Mr. Budgen brings this sort of perception to bear even on the artistry of *Finnegans Wake* ("In modifying the shapes and sounds of words he has but followed popular usage"). On the *Wake,* though by that time his intimacy with Joyce had ceased, he remains amazingly perceptive. There are stranger things in it, he notes, than the words out of which it is made. "That which continually astonishes me is its constant and even gaiety," a phenomenon of which the Paris prophets of the Revolution of the Word, from whom our seminal attitudes to Joyce's last book still come, were not especially aware. Myth, symbol, doctrine, device, scheme, key, correspondence, all these components of Joyce's work enter Mr. Budgen's reckoning, and all of them turn out to be necessary details in a human enterprise dominated, for him, by a human being of genius. So every man calculates, every man codifies, every man mythologizes when he must; and Joyce did these things when, and because, the work in hand demanded it. Mr. Budgen's unique sympathy for the man, and the unique apprehension of the work which, along with Joyce's esteem, that sympathy earned him, flowed into this remarkable book. It is the pleasantest and most rewarding of all the books that have been devoted to Joyce, and for anyone whose interest in Joyce is not clinical nor pedantic nor vengeful, but focused on the riches Joyce made available to twentieth-century readers, it is perhaps the one indispensable supplement to the Canon itself. How stilted, petty, nasty, rigid, foolish, solipsistic and vacuous have biographers and commentators (with a little effort) succeeded in making him seem! And how incomprehensible. Mr. Budgen wrote out of an affection which preceded and guided his urge to understand: *Ubi amor, ibi oculus est.*

HUGH KENNER

January, 1960

PREFACE

This book may be said to owe its existence to a conversation that took place one Sunday afternoon during the winter of 1931-32 at the home of my friend Patrick Kirwan, novelist, writer for stage and screen, and at that time reader for the publishing house of Grayson and Grayson. We were at tea when Mr. Rupert Grayson called and joined us. The conversation turned on Joyce. Kirwan said that I ought to write a book about Joyce and that Grayson and Grayson ought to publish it. Rupert Grayson tentatively fell in with the suggestion. I agreed and said I would begin right away, for it seems to be an occupational illusion of most painters that they can write a book if they care to turn their hands to it. I very quickly realized, however, that the first thing to do was to write to Joyce and, if possible, get his blessing for the project. It would have been very difficult in any case to get far if he expressly disapproved.

As may be seen from his correspondence, Joyce was at that time greatly worried about his daughter's health and his own, and was also trying to get *Ulysses* published and on sale in England. His reaction to my project appears in a letter dated March 1, 1932, the relevant passage of which reads:

Now as regards your projected book, if Gorman and Louis Golding finish their biographies of me and if Harmsworth publishes Charles Duff's J.J. and the plain reader with a preface by Herbert Read yours will be the seventh book mainly about a text which is unobtainable in England. (*Letters of James Joyce*, ed. by Stuart Gilbert, New York, Viking Press; London, Faber and Faber.)

A reasoned skepticism is always a little discouraging, but Joyce went on to say that he thought my method of approach would probably be an original one, so that the green light was just visible.

A blank white canvas and a palette set with bright colors have always been for me provocative and stimulating objects, whereas white paper, pen and ink have always had upon me a benumbing effect. I had never looked upon myself as a Boswell or an Eckermann, and therefore it had never occurred to me during my almost daily contact with Joyce in Zürich to take notes of his conversation or indeed to keep a written record of any kind. All that I had to supply both material content and form for my own text was a copy of *Ulysses*. Joyce had at first a reasoned objection to my using the letters I had received from him, except indirectly. With a number of false starts in front of me I began to wonder if Joyce's confidence in my original method of approach were not a little too optimistic. Then out of the fog I was moving in I saw emerging the shapes of a man, a book, a place, a time. I was able to begin at the beginning and my memory was set free. It is remarkable how much hindsight it takes to perceive the self-evident.

On the two occasions on which I was able to go to Paris during the composition of the book I found Joyce most cooperative. We swapped stories of the old days in Zürich and I was helped with many valuable comments. In the spring of 1933 Joyce very generously commissioned me to paint a picture at Chapelizod near Dublin so that I might get the sight and the sound and the feel and the smell of the Town of the Ford of Hurdles and its people. In the autumn of 1933 the galley proofs arrived from the printers. I sent them on to Paris and as soon as I could do so followed in their wake on my way to Ascona. Joyce and Stuart Gilbert had already begun to read and correct them. (See Joyce's letter to me dated September 10, 1933 in *Letters of James Joyce.*) Joyce's attitude had changed from that of benevolent skepticism to one of enthusiastic approval. During my short stay in Paris he gave me many suggestions for improving and enriching my text and when I moved on to Ascona letters dictated to Paul Léon followed in the same strain. Some of these are incorporated in the text of the present book, and two of them of considerable length appear in the final section, under the title "Further Recollections of James Joyce." The one is a comment on the Altkatholische Kirche—the church that broke away from Rome on account of papal infallibility being proclaimed a dogma—and the other is an account of a performance of Rossini's *Guillaume Tell* at the Paris Opera House with Joyce's admired compatriot, Sullivan, singing the tenor role of Arnold.

James Joyce and the Making of Ulysses was published in Great Britain by Grayson and Grayson and in the United States by Harrison Smith and Haas, Inc., simultaneously in 1934. Ever since its publication it has enjoyed a considerable *succès d'estime* and many students of and commentators on Joyce's work have written to me expressing their appreciation of the book. Largely for this reason it is offered to the reader in this new edition practically without revision. The only major change has been the addition of "Further Recollections of James Joyce" as an appendix, reprinted here by courtesy of the editors of *Partisan Review.* I am grateful to the Viking Press, Inc., New York, for permission to reprint passages from *Dubliners* and *A Portrait of the Artist as a Young Man,* and to Random House, Inc., for permission to quote extensively from *Ulysses.*

FRANK BUDGEN

London, 1959

AUTHOR'S NOTE

The texts of the quotations in the present volume are from *Dubliners* (Jonathan Cape, Ltd., London), *A Portrait of the Artist as a Young Man* (Jonathan Cape, Ltd., London), *Ulysses* (The Odyssey Press, Hamburg, Paris, Bologna). As regards the book at present known as *Work in Progress*, the quotations from fragments published separately are: *Anna Livia Plurabelle* (Faber & Faber, Ltd., London), *Haveth Childers Everywhere* (Faber & Faber, Ltd., London), *Two Tales of Shem and Shaun* (Faber & Faber, Ltd., London), *The Mime of Mick, Nick and the Maggies* (Servire Press, The Hague), and for the complete Part I and Part III of the same work the text published serially by *Transition,* Paris. I wish to express my thanks to Mr. Eugene Jolas, Editor of *Transition,* and to the respective publishers, for permission to use the texts quoted.

The reader who decides to examine for himself more closely the Homeric correspondences and details of technical construction cannot do better than consult Mr. Stuart Gilbert's exhaustive work on that subject, *James Joyce's "Ulysses"* (Faber & Faber, Ltd., London, and Alfred A. Knopf, New York).

F. S. C. B.

Ascona, Switzerland,
   1933.

CHAPTER I

One afternoon in the early summer of 1918 I was sitting at my work table in the commercial department of the British Consulate in Zürich. Taylor stood by the window. He had just come in.

"I met James Joyce to-day," he said.

I looked past the dark blue silhouette and profile of King George V at the yellow, white and blue sky, green lime trees, trickling Sihl and dark railway sheds.

"Yes," I said.

"Yes. It was in the Stadttheater. Kerridge is chorus master there, you know. Joyce came in to ask Kerridge something and then he sat at the piano and sang to us."

Taylor stretched out hands to a keyboard and turned his head to an audience.

"He has a fine tenor voice and he knows it."

Taylor sings and is a judge of singing.

"But who is James Joyce?" I asked.

"He's a writer," Taylor said. "You've never heard of him? People think an awful lot of his book, *A Portrait of the Artist as a Young Man*. Do you never read? Anything but newspapers, I mean?"

He waved his hand in the direction of the office newspaper files.

"Very little," I said. "And that little not English. What do you expect? I haven't even time to paint."

"It doesn't matter," said Taylor. "I want you to meet Joyce."

"Why?"

"Because I think you'd get on well together. Of course he's Irish. You can tell that by his name. And somehow he hasn't hit it off with the C.G."

I tried without much success to make some sort of shape out of the material Taylor had given me: well-known writer, tenor singer, Irishman who couldn't get on with the Consulate-General. Still, there was friend Blaise Cendrars, also a well-known writer. August Suter and I stood godfathers to his son Odilon in the Mairie of the 14th arrondisment. His polychrome *Transsibirien.* Now he has lost an arm in the war. One mustn't label people in advance. Taylor must have read something negative in the pause. He broke in on my image building.

"Don't be lazy and standoffish," he said. "Joyce is dining with me at my pension the day after to-morrow. You can manage that, can't you?"

"I don't see what I have to do with well-known writers," I said, "or they with me. Still, I'm free, and if you think . . ."

"I do," said Taylor. "Half past seven, if we don't go up together."

Taylor was in Zürich on a cultural mission. Enemy countries were being bombarded with shot and shell, neutral countries with propaganda of all sorts designed to prove that it was both interesting and agreeable to be friends with the triple entente and its allies. A collection of modern British pictures had been got together for exhibition in the principal towns in Switzerland and Taylor was in charge of it. The show was good enough of its kind, but in the matter of painting the French and Germans had already queered the pitch. The French had shown some of the dazzling best of their nineteenth century masters, and the Germans had sent a less brilliant, but vastly interesting collection, covering the efforts of a century. On account of transport dangers and difficulties, the British collection was limited to the work of living painters, so that those who expected to see Constables and Turners were disappointed. Both Taylor and myself were painters and both of us were working for the Ministry of Information. My own job was to survey the Swiss press, translate letters and make myself generally useful.

Taylor's pension was high up on the Zürichberg beyond the Fluntern tram terminus. That his guest was delayed was of no consequence. We sat in the gravelled garden under a tree, drinking our aperitif and occasionally striking too short at wasps. The daylight began to fail. In the restaurant they switched on the lights. Taylor broke off a sentence with: "Ah, here's Joyce."

Following Taylor's look I saw a tall slender man come into the garden through the restaurant. Swinging a thin cane he walked deliberately down the steps to the gravelled garden path. He was a dark mass against the orange light of the restaurant glass door, but he carried his head with the chin uptilted so that his face collected cool light from the sky. His walk as he came slowly across to us suggested that of a wading heron. The studied deliberateness of a latecomer, I thought at first. But then as he came nearer I saw his heavily glassed eyes and realised that the transition from light interior to darkening garden had made him unsure of a space beset with iron chairs and tables and other obstacles.

Joyce's greeting to us is of elaborate European politeness, but his manner I think is distant, his handshake cool. Close up he looks not so tall though he is well above average height. The deception is due to his slender build, his buttoned coat and narrow cut trousers. Then he listens to, not looks at, his man. The form of his head is the long oval of heads of the Norman race. His hair is dark enough to look black in this light. His beard is much lighter, orangey-brown and cut to a point—Elizabethan. Behind the powerful lenses of his spectacles his eyes are a clear, strong blue, but uncertain in shape and masked in expression. I notice later that in a moment of suspicion or apprehension they become a skyblue glare. The colour of his face is a bricky red, evenly distributed. The high forehead has a forward thrust as it issues from under the front rank of hair. His jaw is firm and square, his lips thin and tight, set in a straight line. Something in Joyce's head suggests to me an alchemist. It is easy to imagine him moving around in a room full of furnaces, retorts and books full of diagrams. And something in his poise suggests a tall marshfowl, watchful, preoccupied. But I feel reassured. What I had imagined under a well-known writer is not there. He might easily be a painter.

At dinner Joyce told us of his departure from the Habsburg Empire after Italy's entrance into the war and praised the generosity of the Austrian authorities, who had allowed him to leave the country and who had even taken his word for the contents of his luggage. The war itself and its progress were left alone by common consent, but war literature was mentioned, and in this connection Joyce said that the only poem on the subject that at all interested him was one by the Viennese poet, Felix Beran, a friend of his in 'ürich.

> *Und nun ist kommen der Krieg der Krieg*
> *Und nun ist kommen der Krieg der Krieg*
> *Und nun ist kommen der Krieg*
>   *Krieg*

Nun sind sie alle Soldaten
Nun sind sie alle Soldaten
Nun sind sie alle Soldaten
Soldaten
Soldaten müssen sterben
Soldaten müssen sterben
Soldaten müssen sterben
Sterben müssen sie
Wer wird nun küssen
Wer wird nun küssen
Wer wird nun küssen
Meiner weissen Leib

The word "Leib" (body) moved him to enthusiasm. It was a sound that created the image of a body in one unbroken mass. From liquid beginning it passes over the rich shining double vowel till the lips close on the final consonant with nothing to break its blond unity. He spoke of the plastic monosyllable as a sculptor speaks about a stone.

He asked us if we knew the painting of Wyndham Lewis. He had read some of Lewis's writings and seen some of his drawings. Neither Taylor nor myself knew Lewis's work sufficiently well to talk about it with assurance. Joyce said he had read a story of Lewis's that had pleased him. It was the story *Cantelman's Spring Mate*. One of us, it must have been myself, referred to Shelley's *Prometheus Unbound*.

"That seems to me to be the Schwärmerei of a young Jew," Joyce declared bluntly.

And when I, apropos of some love affair or other, used the conventional word, heart, he said in the same tone:

"The seat of the affections lies lower down, I think."

His meaning, I thought, was clear. He objected to the sentimental convenient cliché. The allusion that prompted his remark I learned only some time later when, at his instance, I read Phineas Fletcher's *Purple Island or the Isle of Man.* The Norfolk Rector in describing the provinces of the human body says the following:

> *The sixt and last town in this region,*
> *With largest stretcht precincts, and compass wide,*
> *Is that where Venus and her wanton sonne*
> *(Her wanton Cupid) will in youth reside.*
> *For though his arrows and his golden bow*
> *On other hills he friendly doth bestow,*
> *Yet here he hides the fire with which each heart doth glow.*

So far, in spite of all politeness and conventional amiability, I had felt aware of something watchful and defensive in Joyce's attitude. But on leaving our host we walked down the hill together to the Universitätstrasse where Joyce lived, and I experienced a sense of relief, due I feel sure to a sudden expansiveness and cordiality on Joyce's part. He asked about my work, my stay in Zürich, and suggested future meetings. Some time afterwards he said to me:

"You remember that evening at Taylor's pension on the Zürichberg?"

"Yes," I said, "of course I do."

"Well, I went up to Taylor's to dinner with a mind completely made up that you were to be a spy sent by the British Consulate to report on me in connection with my dispute with them."

Joyce laughed a clear long laugh of full enjoyment at his mistake. A laugh is a significant gesture. Joyce's laughter is free and spontaneous. It is the kind of laughter called forth by the solemn incongruities, the monkeyish trickeries and odd mistakes of social life, but there was no malice in it or real Schadenfreude. His is the kind of laugh one would expect to hear if the president of the republic took the wrong hat, but not if an old man's hat blew off into the gutter.

"And what good reason had you," I asked, "for coming to the conclusion that I wasn't a spy?"

"Because," said Joyce, "you looked like an English cricketer out of the W. G. Grace period. Yes, Arthur Shrewsbury. He was a great bat, but an awkward-looking tradesman at the wicket."

It was shortly after our meeting at Taylor's pension that I again met Joyce, by chance this time, and we strolled through the double avenue of trees on the Utoquai from Bellevue towards Zürich Horn. To the left of us were the solid houses of Zürich burgesses, on our right the lake and on the far shore of the lake the green slopes and elegant contours of the Uetliberg ridge.

"I am now writing a book," said Joyce, "based on the wanderings of Ulysses. The Odyssey, that is to say, serves me as a ground plan. Only my time is recent time and all my hero's wanderings take no more than eighteen hours."

A train of vague thoughts arose in my mind, but failed to take shape definite enough for any comment. I drew with them in silence the shape of the Uetliberg-Albis line of hills. The Odyssey for me was just a long poem that might at any moment be illustrated by some Royal Academician. I could see his water-colour Greek heroes, book-opened, in an Oxford Street bookshop window.

Joyce spoke again more briskly:

"You seem to have read a lot, Mr. Budgen. Do you know of any complete all-round character presented by any writer?"

With quick interest I summoned up a whole population of invented persons. Of the fiction writers Balzac, perhaps, might supply him? No. Flaubert? No. Dostoevski or Tolstoi then? Their people are exciting, wonderful, but not complete. Shakespeare surely. But no, again. The footlights, the proscenium arch, the fatal curtain are all

there to present to us not complete, all-round beings, but
only three hours of passionate conflict. I came to rest on
Goethe.

"What about Faust?" I said. And then, as a second shot,
"Or Hamlet?"

"Faust!" said Joyce. "Far from being a complete man,
he isn't a man at all. Is he an old man or a young man?
Where are his home and family? We don't know. And he
can't be complete because he's never alone. Mephistopheles
is always hanging round him at his side or heels.* We see
a lot of him, that's all."

It was easy to see the answer in Joyce's mind to his own
question.

"Your complete man in literature is, I suppose,, Ulysses?"

"Yes," said Joyce. "No-age Faust isn't a man. But you
mentioned Hamlet. Hamlet is a human being, but he is a
son only. Ulysses is son to Laertes, but he is father to Telemachus, husband to Penelope, lover of Calypso, companion in arms of the Greek warriors around Troy and King
of Ithaca. He was subjected to many trials, but with wisdom and courage came through them all. Don't forget that
he was a war dodger who tried to evade military service
by simulating madness. He might never have taken up
arms and gone to Troy, but the Greek recruiting sergeant was too clever for him and, while he was ploughing
the sands, placed young Telemachus in front of his plough.
But once at the war the conscientious objector became a
jusqu'auboutist. When the others wanted to abandon the
siege he insisted on staying till Troy should fall."

---

* This sentiment is apparently shared on the other side of the footlights. Many years afterwards I asked Joyce why his friend Sullivan,
the Paris-Kerry tenor, was so loth to sing in an opera that has become
the standby of the Academie Nationale, and he replied: "That Samson
of the land of Dan has told me that what bothers him is not so much
the damnation of Faust as the domination of Mephistopheles."

PROTEUS

I laughed at Ulysses as a leadswinger and Joyce continued:

"Another thing, the history of Ulysses did not come to an end when the Trojan war was over. It began just when the other Greek heroes went back to live the rest of their lives in peace. And then"—Joyce laughed—"he was the first gentleman in Europe. When he advanced, naked, to meet the young princess he hid from her maidenly eyes the parts that mattered of his brine-soaked, barnacle-encrusted body. He was an inventor too. The tank is his creation. Wooden horse or iron box—it doesn't matter. They are both shells containing armed warriors."

History repeats itself. The inventor of the tank also found his Ajax at the War Office in the shape of Lord Kitchener.

It seems to me to be significant that Joyce should talk to me first of the principal character in his book and only later of the manifold devices through which he presented him. If the two elements of character and material can be separated this is the order in which he would put them. On the home stretch back to Bellevue a question grew in my mind.

"What do you mean," I said, "by a complete man? For example, if a sculptor makes a figure of a man then that man is all-round, three-dimensional, but not necessarily complete in the sense of being ideal. All human bodies are imperfect, limited in some way, human beings too. Now your Ulysses . . ."

"He is both," said Joyce. "I see him from all sides, and therefore he is all-round in the sense of your sculptor's figure. But he is a complete man as well—a good man. At any rate, that is what I intend that he shall be."

The talk turned on music, and I mentioned that Taylor had heard him singing in the Stadttheater.

"Yes, I remember," said Joyce. "I went there to ask Kerridge something about the disposition of the instruments in the orchestra, and to put him up to some of the commoner mistakes his chorus was likely to make in singing Italian. What I sang was the tenor Romanza 'Amor Ti Vieta' from Giordano's *Fedora*. I wanted to show the vocal necessity for putting an atonic vowel between two consonants. Listen."

And he began to sing:

"Amor ti vieta di non amar la man tua lieve che mi respinge."

He turned to me again:

"You hear," he said. "It would be impossible to sing that 'respinge' without interpolating a vowel breath between the 'n' and the 'g.' "

When I first called on Joyce and his family they were living at No. 38 Universitätsstrasse. There were two guests besides myself. It was after these had gone and Joyce had asked me to stay for a final half-hour's chat that we fell to talking about religion. Being an orthodox agnostic I saw nothing illogical in admitting that what are called miracles might occur. I had no satisfactory evidence that any ever had occurred, but on my limited experience I felt I couldn't rule them out. Perhaps I didn't succeed in defining my position too well, for when I rose to go Joyce laughed and said:

"You are really more a believer than is many a good Catholic."

The next day I found a packet and a letter awaiting me in my little room in the Schipfe. The packet contained a copy of *A Portrait of the Artist as a Young Man* and the letter extracts from press notices of *A Portrait of the Artist*, *Dubliners* and *Exiles*. I read the book and then the praises of Ezra Pound, H. G. Wells and others, quoted on the many-coloured leaflets. H. G. Wells wrote: "Its claim to be literature is as good as the claim of the last book of Gulliver's Travels. . . . Like Swift and another living Irish writer, Mr. Joyce has a cloacal obsession. . . . Like some of the best novels in the world, it is the story of an education. . . . One conversation in this book is a superb success. I write with all due deliberation that Sterne himself could not have done it better." And Ezra Pound and a dozen others to the same purpose, each in his own way. I remember very well my own impression. The affirmative young man, the terror-stricken and suffering adolescent were but timebound phases of a personality the essence of which was revealed in the boy Stephen Dedalus. He is like a young inquisitive cat taking stock of the world and of himself: climbing, hiding, testing his claws. This bold, sensitive, tenacious, clear-seeing boy is the essential artist. There comes a moment when hostile forces—cramping poverty and the tyrannies of Church, nation and family —threaten him with loss of freedom, with extinction as an artist, and he must mobilise all his forces of defence and attack to save himself. "Silence, exile and cunning," says Stephen himself, and he uses those arms and more besides before the battle is won.

A cold wind was blowing when I met Joyce one evening on the Bahnhofstrasse. The brown overcoat buttoned up to his chin lent him a somewhat military appearance.

"I'm glad you liked the 'Portrait,'" said Joyce. I had returned the book with a letter recording some of my impressions of it.

"That simile of yours, 'a young cat sharpening his claws on the tree of life,' seems to me to be very just applied to young Stephen."

I enquired about *Ulysses*. Was it progressing?

"I have been working hard on it all day," said Joyce.

"Does that mean that you have written a great deal?"
I said.

"Two sentences," said Joyce.

I looked sideways but Joyce was not smiling. I thought
of Flaubert.

"You have been seeking the *mot juste?*" I said.

"No," said Joyce. "I have the words already. What I
am seeking is the perfect order of words in the sentence.
There is an order in every way appropriate. I think I
have it."

"What are the words?" I asked.

"I believe I told you," said Joyce, "that my book is a
modern Odyssey. Every episode in it corresponds to an
adventure of Ulysses. I am now writing the *Lestrygonians*
episode, which corresponds to the adventure of Ulysses
with the cannibals. My hero is going to lunch. But there
is a seduction motive in the Odyssey, the cannibal king's
daughter. Seduction appears in my book as women's silk
petticoats hanging in a shop window. The words through
which I express the effect of it on my hungry hero are:
'Perfume of embraces all him assailed. With hungered
flesh obscurely, he mutely craved to adore.' You can see
for yourself in how many different ways they might be
arranged."

A painter is, perhaps, more originality proof than any
other artist, seeing that all recent experimental innovations in the arts have first been tried out on his own. And
many a painter can labour for a day or for many days on
one or two square inches of canvas so that labour expended
on achieving precious material is not likely to surprise
him. What impressed me, I remember, when Joyce repeated the words of Bloom's hungrily abject amorousness
to me, was neither the originality of the words themselves
nor the labour expended on composing them. It was the

sense they gave me that a new province of material had been found. Where that province lay I could not guess, but as our talk proceeded Joyce spoke of it himself without question of mine. We were by this time sitting in the Astoria Café.

"Among other things," he said, "my book is the epic of the human body. The only man I know who has attempted the same thing is Phineas Fletcher. But then his *Purple Island* is purely descriptive, a kind of coloured anatomical chart of the human body. In my book the body lives in and moves through space and is the home of a full human personality. The words I write are adapted to express first one of its functions then another. In *Lestrygonians* the stomach dominates and the rhythm of the episode is that of the peristaltic movement."

"But the minds, the thoughts of the characters," I began.

"If they had no body they would have no mind," said Joyce. "It's all one. Walking towards his lunch my hero, Leopold Bloom, thinks of his wife, and says to himself, 'Molly's legs are out of plumb.' At another time of day he might have expressed the same thought without any underthought of food. But I want the reader to understand always through suggestion rather than direct statement."

"That's the painter's form of leverage," I said.

We talked of words again, and I mentioned one that had always pleased me in its shape and colour. It was Chatterton's "acale" for freeze.

"It is a good word," said Joyce. "I shall probably use it."

He does use it. The word occurs in *The Oxen of the Sun* episode of *Ulysses* in a passage written in early English, describing the death and burial of Bloom's son Rudolph: ". . . and he was minded of his good lady

Marion that had borne him an only manchild which on his eleventh day on live had died and no man of art could save so dark is destiny and she was wondrous stricken of heart for that evil hap and for his burial did him on a corselet of lambswool the flower of the flock, lest he might perish utterly and lie akeled. . . ."

In leaving the café I asked Joyce how long he had been working on *Ulysses*.

"About five years," he said. "But in a sense all my life."

"Some of your contemporaries," I said, "think two books a year an average output."

"Yes," said Joyce. "But how do they do it? They talk them into a typewriter. I feel quite capable of doing that if I wanted to do it. But what's the use? It isn't worth doing."

CHAPTER II

The town clusters round the horseshoe end of the lake. Bright villages, Zollikon, Kilchberg, Ruschlikon, Erlenbach, flicker along its shores. The Glarus mountains rise orange-white in the distance. Supple contours of hills accompany the lake's flight south-eastward. Stand on the Quaibrücke on a summer day, and the lake, tilled slopes, villages and far-off mountains, absorbed by the air, become unsubstantial colour essences, but when the Föhn wind blows, bringing malaise, migraine or exhilaration to the Züricher, the high hills on the right move towards the town, heavy, hard-featured, in sullen green and leaden ultramarine. Under the Quaibrücke the Limmat runs out of the overfull lake silkily and swiftly through the town. Big Snake (*Lindemage*) is the name under which the Helvetians and Alemannen veiled her divinity, and that is her name to this day. The sons of her right and left bank hug tightly the mother river. Up the steep right bank the houses rise thickly, tier on tier, to the pine woods. The left bank goes flatly away over the shallow Sihl to the working-class suburbs of Aussersihl. Tucked away in their sheds near the bridge are the slim shells of Seeclub eights and fours. The Tonhalle brightens the quai on the left bank with its minarets. Out of the dense mass of the town rise the heavy twin towers of the Grossmünster, built by Charlemagne over the graves of SS. Felix and Regula (Prosperity and Order), the slender spire of the Fraumünster, the clocktower of the Peterskirche, the yellow renaissance façade of the Polytechnic, and the white walls and tower of the university. The Stadttheater stands on the Utoquai, right bank of the Limmat, a stone's throw from the lake. There is an open space in front of it whereon, every third Monday in April, is lit the Beltane fire of Zürich. "Sechseläuten," they call the feast, and the name of the demon of winter is the "Bögg." Guildsmen in burnous, in rococo plumed hat and gay cloak, gallop round the bonfire of the winter bogeyman. And there is no restriction, except that of good manners, placed upon them who want to drown the memory of the winter and greet the spring in wine.

From Zollikon, Meilen, Herrliberg, down the Seefeld-strasse, past the Stadttheater and the place where they burn the Bögg in spring, come in autumn, heavy country carts laden each with an immense barrel made gay with country flowers. The barrels contain Sauser, new wine, still fermenting, from the lakeside vineyards. There is no drink more full of uplift and downfall than Sauser, but it must be, as they say, "im Stadium," for it soon loses its quality. Therefore, while the elder brothers await the precious beverage in their favourite Wirtschafts in town, energetic youth goes out along the lake to drink it at the source. From village to village they go on their Sauser-bummel, and from vintage to vintage as far as their legs will carry them.

The earliest Zürichers lived in stilthouses on the lake where now the roadmaker has effaced their marshy no-man's-land. Helvetians made themselves a strong place on the left bank of the Limmat; Romans and Alemannen took it in turn; Charlemagne dispensed justice there, and there the Zürichers of 1898 swore allegiance to their brand-new constitution. But now the Lindenhof is a pleas-ant grove of lime trees garnished with convenient seats on which it is very pleasant to sit on summer evenings with Brissago and *Neue Züriche Zeitung*. The Guilds, whose young men now head the Sechseläute procession and gallop round the Beltane fire, shared the rule of the town for three hundred years with aristocrat and merchant. They stood by Zwingli in the Reformation and fought at his side at Kappel, where the militant reformer fell, sword in hand. That cross-hilted sword now lies in the Landesmuseum in a glass case. Protestant Zürich was enriched by the arts of Locarner and Huguenot weaver. They brought silk to Zürich as the Huguenot brought silk to London and poplin to Dublin. Unemployed worker and work-despising aristocrat combined in renaissance Zürich to sell their strong arms for what they would fetch to foreign princes at war. Söldner mercenaries: "Wir zogen in das Feld." The conscience of the burgess, loss to the state, with Zwingli as spearhead of their attack, put an end to the inexpedient commerce in armed fighting men. The trade of the Lanzknecht came to an end, but his military virtue is still admired. Hodler has celebrated in paint the retreat of the Lanzknecht from Marignano. Massena crushed Suvaroff at Zürich when the French Revolution was making new laws and constitutions for Europe, and humane Lavater, admired by Blake, fell while succouring the wounded when the soldiers of the year VI took the town.

Giants of German literature, Klopstock, Wieland, Goethe, Kleist, knew Zürich and praised her. Wozzeck's poet, in love with death, quitted life with the image of Zürich in his eyes. Wagner roamed the shores of the lake, head full of harmonies of Tristan and Isolde. "Tristan's Ehre." None knew land, people and legend better than the Züricher, Gottfried Keller, poet, novelist and state secretary. He wrote of his townsmen with shrewd wit and profound humanity. Nietzsche proclaimed that Swiss a master among prose writers. His seat and table are piously preserved in the "Apfelkammer." Conrad Ferdinand Meyer wrote his novels and poems in quiet Kilchberg. Pestalozzi was Zürich born and bred. His Argovian farm has been bought with the pennies of Swiss school children.

In Meilen lives Dr. C. G. Jung, curer of sick and harassed souls. He added to the doctrine of psychoanalysis, and made the Zürich school of adepts in that science. The studio of my friend August Suter, sculptor, stands in the neighbouring village of Zollikon. He has made a series of figures for the Amtphäuser in Zürich. Harmoniously yoked to his plastic vision are the forces of temperament and high intelligence. Now he has made for Liestal, native town of Carl Spitteler, poet of Prometheus, a Prometheus with counselling angel in bronze—the poet's vision made three-dimensional. Architect Karl Moser built the art gallery and the university. Crowds pack the aula to hear Professor Fleiner on constitutional history, so rare it is that so much learning and sanity are served by such persuasive eloquence. The Tonhalle overlooks the lake. When Feruccio Busoni is to play he walks thither from the Bahnhof buffet in the company of an enormous hound. Citizen and stranger throng the Bahnhofstrasse on their evening promenade. All know him and his errand, and respect his solitude. D'Albert is a citizen of Zürich and plays in the Tonhalle. Clouds are descending upon the spirit of Lehmbruck, most sensitive of German sculptors, where he works in the Seefeldstrasse. The Dadaists are planning yet another revolution in the arts over Sprüngli's tea-shop. The waiter at the Odeon will tell you discreetly which of the guests is Leonhard Frank, famous for *Der Mensch ist Gut*. He will tell you too where sat Lenin, calmly, confidently awaiting the call that came in 1917. Vladimir Ilytch was a silent listener here and zur Linde to hot word battles they say, but his was the last word when the conflict of half-truths had shaped the conclusion he desired. To another guest of Zürich, Willy Münzenberg, legend ascribes the organisation of Lenin's departure in the famous locked train. Münzenberg organised his own departure from Germany just as efficiently and his Mercedes Luxuswagen has been seen waiting for its master outside the Casino de Paris.

There is no street in London that can equal the Bahnhofstrasse for metropolitan smartness. But let the smart shops and broad pavements go as a matter of course. Its crowning glory is its avenue of lime trees that on summer evenings enrich the air with a delicious scent of lime blossom. Gottfried Keller celebrated perhaps just these lime trees in one of his loveliest verses. The trams that pass on the other side of the tree trunks are painted bright cobalt blue and white, colours of the town of Zürich, colours of the Greek flag, colours of the covers of *Ulysses*. No town in Europe is more cosmopolitan than Zürich in war time, and of all streets in Zürich the Bahnhofstrasse is the most cosmopolitan. And it is everybody's promenade, stranger and citizen, millionaire silk merchant and Aussersihl proletarian. Conspicuous among the business foreigners, legitimate and illegitimate, among the spies and propagandists, deserters and refractaires, poor and rich, were a number of young men of olive complexion, black hair and assured mien, wearing khaki gaberdine suits tightly and coquettishly cut. They were well nourished, for the half-belt at the back of their coats was overlapped in both senses by a roll of fat. They puzzled an observer of social phenomena.

"Who are these people?" I asked of a Züricher.

"They are garlic millionaires from the Balkan States," he said promptly.

At the lake end of the Bahnhofstrasse is visible the hotel

Baur au Lac, first hotel in Zürich. Mrs. MacCormick has
a suite of rooms there. She is daughter of a king, an oil
king, born Edith Rockefeller, and one of the richest
women in the world, therefore in Zürich supremely rich.
Fantastic, distinguished, benevolent, she walks the town
scattering right and left charities, houses and yachts. She
is a believer in psychoanalysis and all its prophets and disciples, and did much to spread a taste for its culture. She
has founded the MacCormick Stiftung, which will acquire
the pictures of the impecunious painter if a committee
considers them worthy. The fund should be for Zürich
painters only, but as I am an Anglo-Saxon, needy, and my
work not unworthy, I am allowed to participate. Mr. Rawson, a friend of Joyce, taught Mr. MacCormick to whistle
"It ain't gonna waltza no more."

Here and there about the town one sees a tall bearded
man of royal carriage. An exiled king? They are becoming
common. No, a reigning monarch. His realm is called the
"Meierei," a grill-room in Niederdorf, where every week
in their day Keller and Böcklin met. His name is Oom
Jan. With kingly air he asks if the beefsteak grilled by him
is to his guest's liking and, sure of the enthusiastic "Ja,"
passes on to another table. Perfection must please.

"I should like to go to England," said a Züricher to me.
"The beefsteaks there must be wonderful."

"Stay in Zürich," I counselled him. "In the world are
no better beefsteaks than those grilled by Oom Jan in the
Meierei."

I heard with grief of the death of that great Dutchman.
Où sont les biftecks d'antan?

Robed in fine linen, with canary gloves and patent
leather shoes, another Dutchman walks the town, sometimes in the company of James Joyce. He is dentist, cinema producer, dealer in shirtwaists, synthetic pearls and

synthetic bouillon. His name is Juda Devries, alias Joe Martin, alias Jules Moreau. He has written a film scenario entitled *Wine, Woman and Song,* and he writes letters on pink notepaper headed with the crossed flags of the allied nations. His father is the venerable gynæcologist of Amsterdam. Joyce was once instrumental in getting him out of jail into hospital, and he, being as ingenious as he was enterprising, made a wooden money-box in the form of a Bible for his serviable friend. It bore, by way of title, "My First Success," by James Joyce. One time professor in the higher school of commerce in Vienna, Sigmund Feilbogen haunts the Café des Banques, with an eartrumpet which he orients and occidents night and day to catch rumours of peace anywhere at any hour. Butcher Lenz, in girth surpassing Velasquez's actor, takes up all the platform of a tram designed for five and a conductor. L'homme qui rit walks round the bourse with a copious English newspaper held up to his face. He has a lion's mouth that stretches from ear to ear. In the Olivenbaum restaurant a swarthy, diminutive young man, his breast pocket full of pens and pencils, evidently a Levantine, goes from one Zürich working-man to the other talking to them all with an air of authority, making notes the while with one of his fountain pens. He doesn't look like a trade union leader, and is not a working-class party leader. Is he tallyman or conspirator? But you can't conspire in crowded teetotal restaurants, and the tallyman comes, according to tradition, on the family doorstep. We gave it up. "He's Füllfederowski, and up to some mischief," said Suter. Occasionally during the day, but for sure at about six o'clock in the evening, from the corner of the Usteristrasse to the Paradeplatz, a young man, shoulders bunched, oblivious of his surroundings, walks with long eager strides, and now and then breaks out into a stiff-legged trot. He has the great dark eyes of a sensitive intelligent deer and the combative jaw of a terrier. Steadily marching Eidgenossen wonder who the preoccupied young man may be. It is my chief. Often his staff gathers at the corner of the street to watch with wonder his erratic progress lakewards. All the British soldiers in khaki doing light work in the Consulate are invalided out of Germany in exchange for an equal number of Germans out of British hospitals and prison camps. Whitcomb is a Gloucestershire man badly knocked about at Ypres. He attends a machine in a coal mine in South Wales and in his spare time carves figures in wood. Tennant is one of the hundred and fifty lucky ones of the South African brigade to escape out of Delville Wood with their lives. All through the war the newspaper seller outside the central railway station, his chest plastered with telegrams of all nations, Reuter, Wolff, Havas, Stefani—pay your money and take your choice—cried monotonously: "Zürizitig Extrablatt!" with Vierwaldstätter je m'en foutisme.

Switzerland in war time had some of the character of a beleaguered town, although all belligerents found it expedient to respect her neutrality. All foreign and overseas supplies had to be borne over the territories of nations at war, and these could give only a minimum of transport material. The produce of Swiss orchards and pastures had to be bartered for the indispensable supplies of coal and iron for her railways and industries. This painful necessity was mother to the electrification of the federal railway system, carried through with resolute efficiency as soon as the war was over. "Moppa necessity mother of injuns." Life was a thing of Ersatz and Zusatz and doing without. Bread was rationed to a minimum. There was a great planting of maize and potatoes all along the lake shore. The potato crop failed. Boiled chestnuts became a staple dish. Frogs' legs appeared on meatless days. Saccharine pills replaced the usual sugar-lumps alongside the coffee cup. Next to every item on the menu stood a warning numeral and fraction. This was the amount of fat involved in the dish, and the waitress tore the like ciphers off the fat card. Who counted them afterwards? Butter was a grievous question. It was debated with no less ardour than the war situation, politics and psychoanalysis. About a quarter of a pound a month was our ration. Not worth scraping or saving, thought some of us, and we ingeniously contrived to eat our ration on the first day so that for the rest of the month we had neither butter nor worry. Irksome all this, and for the weak and sick probably distressing, but those of us who could put up with what came along suffered no real harm.

The perpetual neutrality of Switzerland was guaranteed by all the powers, but so was that of Belgium. And scraps of paper were at a discount at the time. Anyway, perpetual neutrality was merely an extra piece of frontier to be defended. All frontiers and fortresses had to be manned, a task which involved keeping the fighting forces of the country on a war footing. There was a perpetual ebb and flow of grey blue men of all military ages between the interior and the frontiers. One look at the map of Europe is enough to convince the intuitive observer that Switzerland is a sceptical country. It is a small country with a long frontier and a long memory. At every point of the compass stands a powerful and dangerous neighbour. During the war all Swiss talked war strategy and politics, and in general all were pacifists. The working class of Switzerland, outnumbered as it is by bourgeois and peasants, is inclined to be revolutionary in the Central European manner. Their pacifism was of a plague on both your houses kind. Swiss pacifism did not rule out preference, and preference took the line of language cleavage, with this modification, that the West Swiss, French-speaking, were more pro-French than the German-speaking Swiss were pro-German. This was expressed in popular wit: "Paris wants to make peace, but Lausanne won't hear of it." The sympathy of the German-speaking Swiss for the countries nearest of kin was tempered by a jealous fear of the over-mighty neighbour. I always felt that the Swiss knew the Germans more intimately than we. In his hostile moments the German is to him a "chaibe Schwob," in which phrase, with appropriate intonation, he expresses his resentment and mistrust for the rich, pushing and cunning neighbour. To the Englishman the Germans were Huns, a numberless horde of cruel and rapacious marauders coming from a far-off place, or (to the soldiers in the trenches) they were Jerry or Fritz, just as he was Tommy or Taffy, Jock or Pat. This was trade union familiarity. When the Frenchman said "Boche," the term indicated a rude uncultivated lout. The patriotism of the Swiss was intense, but not aggressive. Their perpetual neutrality barred all thought of territorial expansion, but there was in them a certain tendency to spiritual expansionism. The world should admire and copy their admirable institutions. Expressed with emphasis in a students' debate: "Wir müssen die ganze Welt helvetisieren."

There are probably more local differences of character in Switzerland than in most countries. Take the two opposite numbers, the Züricher and the Basler. The Züricher is robust, independent, optimistic, go-ahead. Unlike the Basler, he has his own hinterland. Basel is a frontier town, hemmed in on two sides by Alsace and the Grand Duchy of Baden, and frontier towns have always their own state of nerves, racial and cultural admixtures, and the many customs barriers cramp their economic style. Therefore the Basler is sceptical, ironical, watchful. And no wonder, for in Basel the war was at the gates. Cannonades on Hartmannsweiler Kopf and on the bridgehead at St. Louis rattled the Basler's windows, and from his streets he could see the shrapnel of anti-aircraft guns bursting and their cotton-wool clouds drifting over his town. The Züricher could rarely hear cannonades, and there were no customs barriers at the gates of his town. Owing to its commercial eminence and its distance from inconvenient and dangerous frontiers, Zürich was one of the most cosmopolitan towns in Europe during the war. I once heard that the floating population of foreigners was equal to forty per cent of the native population. Any big town with foreign business relations and a central position has its quota of foreign business men, agents, travellers and so on. But the great mass of foreign residents in Zürich in war time was made up of deserters, refractaires, and political agents of all kinds, and the legitimate business agent was reinforced by a much larger element whose house of business was any quiet corner of any convenient café on the Bahnhofstrasse, and whose business consisted in trading in contravention of war time regulations. Zürich was the Schiebers' paradise, and the headquarters of spies of all nations. The trade of the spy seems to me to be no worse than that of the combatant soldier. It has always been a part of wartime service as essential as the firing of a gun, or the making of a bullet, or the making of bread for the man who makes the bullet or for the man who fires it. But the awkward thing in a town like Zürich is that when spies are around in great numbers nobody knows who is a spy and who isn't, with the result that everybody is likely to think that everybody else is a spy unless there is clear evidence to the contrary. One relatively harmless instance of this distorting spy atmosphere is Joyce's mistaking me for a consular spy. Austrian spies had watched him closely in his early Zürich days.

Another category of foreigners were those on neutral soil for the purpose of national propaganda. The Ministry of Information, in which I was employed at the time I met Joyce, was an institution for the spread of British propaganda in neutral countries. They found me unemployed in Zürich and gave me a job. The idea was to convince the Swiss that it was pleasanter and more profitable to be friends with the Allies than with the Germans. The printed word was our principal instrument. There was a rare scramble amongst all belligerent propaganda agencies for Swiss newsprint. As they were debarred from founding newspapers themselves, the next best thing for the foreign propagandists was to get as much space as possible in newspapers already existing. It was generally believed that the *Zürich Post* was under German control. Whether from sympathy or interest, it was certainly Germanophile. The newsvendors in their local patois called it the *"Züri Boche,"* and the passer-by smiled approval. Generally speaking, however, the method was to send out articles and pars of all kinds, and on their own merit, or with the aid of a friend at court, they would usually find a place in some paper or the other. To aid us in our enterprise the M. of I. in London sent us from time to time big bundles of articles written somewhere in Whitehall or the Strand. One of the best was a carefully written study on bent wood furniture, but unfortunately we couldn't place it. Our difficulty was that if we wanted an English newspaper more or less up-to-date we had to go and buy it at the station kiosk like anybody else. Still, considering the lack of straw, our output of bricks was as good as that of the rival firms. France and Germany had the best of the cultural propaganda. Germany scored heavily with music, and France with the pictorial and plastic arts. They had the cards and were in a position to play them. The only attempt to make the Swiss public acquainted with English dramatic art in the English tongue was made by Joyce himself who, with the assistance of Mr. and Mrs. Claude Sykes, founded the English Players.

Rising steeply and elegantly out of the Limmat there is a flight of seventeenth-century houses, one of the architectural glories of the town. It is called the Schipfe and is now, I understand, condemned by a progressive municipality. I had a top room in the corner house, No. 23. Joyce had a flat in the Universitätsstrasse. From No. 38, where he lived when I first met him, he soon moved to No. 29 over the way, to remain there until he left for Trieste at the end of 1919. For some reason that she could never successfully define, my landlady, a Bavarian woman married to a Liechtensteiner stonemason, was afraid of Joyce. The chorus girls in the Stadttheater were more definite. They nicknamed him "Herr Satan." One evening on my return from the consulate she handed me a small parcel.

"Your friend, the tall gentleman with the beard, left this for you," she said with awe.

It contained *Dubliners* and those copies of the *Little Review* in which fragments of *Ulysses* had appeared. Six episodes were there. These were to be followed by another six, and then the *Little Review* was to fall beneath the effective wrath of outraged American propriety. The *Nausikaa* episode was more than the American censor could stand. That which to do is no crime, although by many serious judges thought inadvisable, that which may be discussed by word of mouth, frivolously or seriously according to taste, may not in print be hinted at, such potency for corruption resides, apparently, in the written word.

Joyce's flat was in a modernish house of no particular character. Mrs. Joyce complained that a superfluity of mice and a shortage of culinary utensils cramped her style in the kitchen, but, apart from that, it seemed to me not a bad apartment as apartments go. Joyce's own furniture was, of course, left in Trieste. At the door of the flat one heard the clear shapes and metallic tones of the Italian language. Italian was the house language, and for the children, Giorgio and Lucia, the mother tongue. At that time they spoke English hardly at all and in talking to each other used mainly the Zürich dialect, Züridütch. In about a year at school in Zürich they had learned it, so astonishingly quick are the young on the linguistic uptake. Lucia was a dark-haired, blue-eyed girl, slenderly and elegantly built; Giorgio a dark boy, built on more powerful lines. He was an excellent swimmer, champion at his age amongst Zürich schoolboys over a distance of two miles. Such were his natural aptitudes for this exercise that two or three years later in Paris he proposed entering for the annual *traversée de Paris* from Charenton to Auteuil. Mrs. Joyce was a stately presence, but what most impressed on acquaintance was her absolute independence. Her judgments of men and things were swift and forthright and proceeded from a scale of values entirely personal, unimitated, unmodified. In whatever mood she spoke it was with that rich, agreeable voice that seems to be the birthright of Irish women. Generally at the time I arrived it was the children's bedtime. To Giorgio was said, "Porta del legno"; to Lucia, "Vade a letto"; and when Mrs. Joyce came in with a carafe of the always desirable Fendant we were already talking, usually about Joyce's *Ulysses*.

"Now that's too bad," said Mrs. Joyce, as she set down the wine. "And is he talking to you again about that old book of his, Mr. Budgen? I don't know how you stand it.

Jim, you ought not to do it. You'll bore Mr. Budgen stiff."

Any disparaging remarks of Mrs. Joyce about *Ulysses* always made Joyce's eyes glitter with suppressed laughter. He protested mildly.

"If I bore Budgen," he said, "he must tell me. But he has the advantage of me. He can understand and talk about my book, but I don't understand and can't talk about painting."

Mrs. Joyce turned to me in the same vein of mocking disparagement.

"What do you think, Mr. Budgen, of a book with a big, fat, horrible married woman as the heroine? Mollie Bloom!"

I said I thought there was nothing wrong with being fat and married. Anyway a fat, married woman is a change from the sylph-like sweethearts we usually read about.

Strolling through the street one day Joyce laughed and said to me:

"Some people were up at our flat last night and we were talking about Irish wit and humour. And this morning my wife said to me, 'What is all this about Irish wit and humour? Have we any book in the house with any of it in? I'd like to read a page or two.'"

Joyce and his family settled in Zürich right away on coming from Austria, and stayed there about four years. From Basel I came to Zürich and outstayed Joyce there for the greater part of a year. Their flat in 29 Universität-strasse was the fourth of their Zürich habitations. Previously they had lived in the Seefeldstrasse, sharing a flat first with Philip Jarnach, Busoni's secretary and assistant Kapellmeister at the Stadttheater and later the same flat with Charlotte Sauermann, one of the leading sopranos of the Zürich opera. We both watched the fortunes of war change for the combatants (Joyce more objectively than

I), celebrated the armistice, experienced the grippe epidemic, the Swiss general strike of 1918, many Föhn winds, much good wine (for noble Turricum, in spite of rationing, abounded in all manner of goodly merchandise) and many fluctuations of our own personal fortunes. And it was in Athens on the Limmat that Joyce wrote the half of *Ulysses*.

CHAPTER III

I sat up reading the first three episodes of *Ulysses* in the *Little Review*. Joyce wanted them to pass on to someone else. These three episodes form an introduction to the main theme equivalent to the first books of the *Odyssey* wherein the situation in the household of Ulysses is described and young Telemachus sets forth to gain news of his father. The Telemachus of Joyce's book is Stephen Dedalus, whose childhood, boyhood and adolescence are narrated in *A Portrait of the Artist as a Young Man*. From the date of the last entry in Stephen's diary at the end of *A Portrait of the Artist* to the beginning of *Ulysses* there is a gap of about six months. Stephen has been in Paris. A telegram called him back to the bedside of his dying mother. She died, and now he is living in the Martello tower at Sandycove with his friend, Buck Mulligan, a medical student. They pay twelve pounds a year rent for the tower to the Secretary of State for War. Every reader of *Ulysses* is captivated from the start with the wit and high spirits of Buck Mulligan, but there is an atmosphere of hostility between him and Stephen. He reproaches Stephen with failing to humour his mother's last wish and pray at her bedside, and criticises generally "the cursed Jesuit strain" in him. Stephen resents the native and habitual mockery of the Buck. He instances the overheard remark of Mulligan to his aunt: "O, it's only Dedalus whose mother is beastly dead." In reality, however, it is not one remark or another that hurts him, but it is that

Mulligan is of "the brood of mockers" whose mockery is a blighting negative force. They have a guest in the tower, Haines, an Englishman—a somewhat dull, complacent individual, but fairminded and, like many Englishmen, a collector of Irish folklore. Haines had dreamed of a black panther during the night and his nightmare cries had waked Stephen.

The action that takes place is of the simplest kind. Just out of bed, Mulligan and Stephen appear on the gun platform of the tower. Mulligan shaves while Stephen looks on. They talk and in their talk their conflict of character is revealed. Then they go down into the tower and Mulligan prepares the breakfast of rashers, eggs and tea for them and for their Sassenach guest. After breakfast they go to the forty-foot hole to bathe. Mulligan strips and goes in at once. The prudent Haines sits on a rock smoking a cigarette and waiting for his breakfast to go down. Stephen doesn't bathe at all. Mulligan asks for the key of the tower and of Stephen's remaining fourpence twopence, for a pint. Stephen throws the key and the coppers on Mulligan's shirt, turns and walks away. He feels that the end of his friendship with Mulligan is near. He resolves not to sleep in the tower another night and turns away from the seated Haines and the swimmer out in the sea, uttering to himself the word, "Usurper."

The real action takes place within the mind and conscience of Stephen. His mother had begged him on her deathbed to kneel and pray for her. He refused and she died without the comfort of his prayers. It is a good thing to renounce a corrupting and destroying doctrine, and a good thing to solace the last hours of a sick mother. There would be no conflict in life at all if the choice of action lay always between good and evil. Stephen chooses what seems to him to be the greater good. If offered the choice again he would choose the same, but that he chose rightly fails to shield him against remorse of conscience—his "Agenbite of Inwit." One brought up in an atmosphere of rationalist indifferentism might have prayed and come to no harm, but Stephen was an ardent believer and holds his freedom only by dint of constant combat. He has a theologian's logic and a churchman's conscience. To pray or not to pray is a grievous question. If he refuses he must be tortured; if he consents he is lost. That is to say, he loses his feeling of integrity, his sense of direction. He knows too well the mysterious potency of words and gestures "behind which are massed twenty centuries of authority and veneration." He has proclaimed his freedom, but he is not free. His negation takes on the character of a religion of which he is the visible head, priest and communicant. The situation and the problem are not new. It is recorded that Jesus Christ was offered a choice between inclining to his mother's wish and following his own spiritual welfare and that he chose the latter.

All this is the inevitable loss and pain of war but it is no problem. It is memory, past time, and his problem is a present one. He has said his "No" to the "thou shalts" and "thou shalt nots" of the Irish Roman Catholic Church, one of the least accommodating of the churches of Christendom, and to the claims of Irish politics, most tyrannical of all oppressed nation politics. But one more chain still binds him—his associations. Stephen believes himself capable of the greatest things and this is an offence against the easy-going egalitarianism of youth. He must constantly suffer the, to him, exasperating experience of being too lightly valued. He is surrounded by those who doubt and by those who mock and others who are indifferent. Of all these his friend, Mulligan, is in some way the epitome. Every word, every action of the light-hearted Buck arouses in him mistrust and hostility. Further, he envies Mulligan his carefree soul, his physical courage and strength. One feels that the Stephen of *Ulysses* is riding for a fall. His friends have become obstacles to his progress and he must break with them. That in him which is amiable and that in him which is artist are by themselves not capable of the operation, therefore he must call to their aid all the negative qualities of his nature as the armourer makes also the kick of a gun serve his purpose. Only one of the social ties does he recognise. He will have nothing to do with religion and country, but he accepts the family. His family may call on him for physical help and service if it demands no spiritual servitude. That help and service he will give if he can.

But there's the rub. Stephen is entirely without means. He stands in boots and clothes that were given him by Mulligan. He has a job as teacher at Mr. Deasy's school but his salary is barely sufficient for drinks. He owes bits of money all round the town. Let an individualist artist deny religion and politics as vehemently as he will, economics is something he cannot deny. He will take his chance with heaven and hell; with a little luck and some judgment he will avoid the police and the firing squad; but he must eat the bread, wear the clothes and shelter under the roof made by others, and pay for these privileges. Some misguided people have at times affirmed that the stimulus of poverty is useful to the artist and it may be darkly hinted that one day one of these misguided individuals will come to an untimely end. Poverty was never any good to anybody. Starving a racehorse and doubling his handicap doesn't help him to win a race, so in what way is an artist or any inventor advantaged by being starved and overhandicapped? Not all Stephen's trouble of mind but all his problem is economic. His poverty has conditioned his relations to women and is in fact at the root of all his distress. He has never been loved by any woman, for the love of good women is more expensive than that of the other sort. What love he had he bought and he had what he paid for, but no more.

With the word "Usurper" on his lips, Stephen turns his back on Mulligan and Haines and goes on to Mr. Deasy's school. Interpreting the meaning of the word in the light of the sentence he utters a few hours later, "Ireland is important because she belongs to me," we can take it to signify that they who should serve him demand of him services, and that his rightful heritage of opportunity is being enjoyed by the undeserving. He partly escapes from this bitter and hostile mood in Mr. Deasy's school. Here he is not provoked by Mulligan's overbearing wit or irritated by the complacency of the Sassenach, Haines. He has a job to do and does it at least as well as anybody else. Roman history and English literature are the lessons. The boys, one imagines, are the sons of fairly well-to-do, middle-class Dubliners. With one exception (the dullest and weakest boy in the school), Stephen has no kindly feelings towards them. They also are usurpers. From the sly whisperings and titterings of back row boys at the mention of Kingstown pier he knows that they share experiences of pierhead flirtations. "With envy he watched their faces." His own sexual experience was a sudden plunge from romantically innocent longings into the promiscuity of bought love. Tittering flirtation with agreeable flappers was to him an unknown province. But he notes a witty phrase that occurs to him in the course of the lesson: "Kingstown pier is a disappointed bridge," and he resolves to work it off on Haines over drinks that evening, despising himself at the same time for playing the jester to people whom he despises.

History, for the boys, is a struggle to learn the record of past events; for Stephen it is a struggle against the past as it is recorded in his body and mind and in the social element in which he lives. History would present him with his life task ready made. He has inherited a religion, a national cause, a social position—all tyrannical agencies jealous of his life and time. Their demand for sacrifice must be continually disputed. It is a wearying struggle, and a mood of weariness dominates the *Nestor* episode, matching the mood of bitterness and resentment that dominated the preceding one. A running speculative commentary, unspoken, accompanies his teaching of the lesson. Why do some things escape recognition while others, not necessarily the most important, obtain a permanent place in the memory of man? Why did this thing happen instead of that other which, before the moment of time in which it happened, was among the many things that might have happened? "Had Pyrrhus not fallen by a beldam's hand in Argos or Julius Cæsar not been knifed to death." A comment more charged with the passion of his own conflict with the church occurs when young Talbot, repeating *Lycidas,* comes to the lines:

> *Through the dear might of him that walked the waves.*

"Of Him that walked the waves. Here also over these craven hearts his shadow lies and on the scoffer's heart and lips and on mine. It lies upon their eager faces who offered him a coin of the tribute. To Cæsar what is Cæsar's, to God what is God's. A long look from dark eyes, a riddling sentence to be woven and woven on the church's looms. Ay."

For ever on the defensive with his equals, Stephen has pity for weakness. It is Thursday, hockey at ten, and the boys rush eagerly out of the classroom to the playing field.

One boy, the awkward, backward, weedy Cyril Sargent, stays behind. He is in distress with his algebra and Mr. Deasy has ordered him to come to Stephen for assistance. Stephen explains, demonstrates, encourages. Something in the boy recalls to him his own youth.

"Like him was I, these sloping shoulders, this graceless-ness. My childhood bends beside me. Too far for me to lay a hand there once or lightly. Mine is far and his secret as our eyes. Secrets, silent, stony sit in the dark palaces of both our hearts: secrets weary of their tyranny: tyrants willing to be dethroned."

Mr. Deasy returns from the playground and takes Stephen to his study to pay him his salary. He is a shrewd, brave old man. As in the case with all old men in *Ulysses*, his portrait is painted with delicate sympathy. Joyce reserves his satire and caricature for the younger generation. With such a difference of age, temperament and social outlook it is necessary that they shall talk past each other but they do so with an instinctive sympathy each for the other's worth. Stephen is as deferential with Mr. Deasy as he is cantankerous with his own contemporaries. In these days of "youth" movements (generally started by some juvenile man past middle age to instil, with some profit to himself, a little youth into his gravely senile juniors) this unforced respect for age on the part of Stephen seems worth noting. Mr. Deasy is a just man, careful of money because he knows its value, and he counsels a like respect for this powerful instrument to Stephen, well knowing that his wise words will be disregarded. His view of national character is sounder than Stephen's for when he asks if Stephen knows "what is the proudest word you will ever hear from an Englishman's mouth?" Stephen replies: "That on his empire the sun never sets." No doubt Mr. Deasy knows better. "I will tell you," he said solemnly, "what is his proudest boast. *'I paid my way.'* " He was right. There never has been an English empire. It was always British, which is to say that at least four nations collaborated in the making of it. And the boast about paying their way certainly had, perhaps still has, a great vogue among Englishmen. But Stephen is wiser and fairer than his senior when they speak of the Jews.

Mr. Deasy thinks the Jew merchant is working the destruction of Old England.

" 'A merchant,' Stephen said, 'is one who buys cheap and sells dear, Jew or Gentile, is he not?'

" 'They have sinned against the light,' Mr. Deasy said gravely. 'And you can see the darkness in their eyes. And that is why they are wanderers on the earth to this day.' "

To Stephen, who wills his own personal freedom, history is a nightmare from which he is trying to awake. Mr. Deasy accepts all the obligations imposed upon him by the past of his race and believes that all history is moving forward to one great goal, the manifestation of God. But what is God?

"Stephen jerked his thumb towards the window, saying:

" 'That is God.'

" 'Hooray! Ay! Whrrwhee!'

" 'What?' Mr. Deasy asked.

" 'A shout in the street,' Stephen answered, shrugging his shoulders."

There is an outbreak of foot and mouth disease in Ireland and Mr. Deasy believes the disease to be curable if the right treatment is adopted. It can be cured, he thinks, with Koch's preparation which has been used with success by Austrian cattle-doctors. His advocacy of the Koch treatment in official quarters has failed, as he darkly hints, on account of intrigues and backstairs influence, so now he will try publicity. While Stephen waits, he types a letter to the press and asks Stephen to use his influence with his journalist friends to get it printed. Stephen promises that he will do what he can, takes the letter and leaves.

In the quieter, early episodes of *Ulysses* motives are given out that with variations recur constantly in the orchestration of the later episodes. When he takes Mr. Deasy's letter Stephen coins for himself the Mulliganesque nickname, "bullockbefriending bard"; history is a "nightmare"; God a "shout in the street"; faithless wives who brought strife into the world are mentioned by Mr. Deasy; the identity of Shakespeare in his plays is first mentioned on the walk to the bathing cove, the mystery of father and son kinship as well. Verbal pattern and plot are fused together in one.

Before Stephen was out of earshot at the bathing cove, Mulligan called out to him the rendezvous—"The Ship, half twelve"—and Stephen assents. Presumably he intended at the time to go there, but he changes his mind and sends instead a cryptic telegram, a quotation from Meredith's *The Ordeal of Richard Feverel:* "The sentimentalist is he who would enjoy without incurring the immense debtorship for a thing done." Then, glad to be alone, he goes for a walk on Sandymount shore. The morning is bright and clear but not cloudless. The third episode is a record of Stephen's thoughts and sensations during his stroll. The character of his thought has changed. He is no longer on the defensive as he was with Mulligan and Haines in the tower, or weary and dispirited as he was in Mr. Deasy's school. He is free and alone with a vast, bright space around him. This is incomparably the richest, the most musical of all the earlier episodes.

I went to 29 Universitätsstrasse one evening, after reading the three episodes, for a chat and to return the *Little Reviews.*

"You have read them?" said Joyce. "What do you think of them?"

"I like them all," I said. "But I found the third one so exciting, and I've just finished reading it, that I can hardly think of the rest. I think I'm right in calling it the best. No?"

Joyce picked up the slim paper-covered volume.

"I think you are," he said. "It's my own preference. You understand that this is the opening of the book? My Ulysses appears in the next episode. What is it you like about this one?"

"It is rich," I said, "and full of light and colour. But apart from the colour and material I like the Stephen in it. He has the freshness of the schoolboy Stephen in *A Portrait of the Artist*. And then I like the seashore. And I've painted a lot on seashores, Cornish mainly, between St. Ives and Land's End, so I know something about them."

Does any other prose writer know and enjoy his own work as Joyce knows and enjoys his? We expect the poet to recognise and place any one of his lines, but it must be a rare thing for the writer of prose to be able to do as much. He would need first to compose with as much care and to be very satisfied with the result. Joyce composes with infinite pains, but he looks on his handiwork when he has done it and finds it good.

"You catch the drift of the thing?" said Joyce. "It's the struggle with Proteus. Change is the theme. Everything changes—sea, sky, man, animals. The words change, too."

He began to read the episode from the beginning in a smooth, easy way, without emphasis, which is his normal manner of reading the unspoken thoughts of his personages. Emphasis and the normal speaking voice too much suggest the normal spoken word. There is nothing from beginning to end of *Proteus* that is not thought or sensation. Other characters who come into the picture do so only as part of the content of Stephen's mind. Through his senses the seashore comes to life. The natural abode of change is that area between low water and high water mark. It is easier to believe that life began here than that it began in a garden. Tides ebb and flow, cheating the clock every day, lagging behind. The volume of water changes, spring to neap and neap to spring again. Cold water flows over hot sand. Sea breeze and land-wind alternate. The colour of sea and sky changes like shot-silk. The sea makes and unmakes the land. Steel-hard rocks are broken up, firm contours of land are dissolved and re-made. A sea-town drifts inland and the houses of an inland town topple into the sea. Yellow sand, lying neatly round rocks, is taken away by an overnight storm and a floor of black boulders appears. Then with the smooth lapping of the next calm the yellow carpet is laid again. There is a whole population of plants and animals here and of living things that are neither plant nor animal. Carcasses of man, beast, bird, fish, washed ashore, decompose. Sea and sand bury them. Wreckage rots and rusts and is pounded to pieces and every tide brings new flotsam and jetsam, lays it on other ribbed sand, other stones. The seashore is never twelve hours the same.

To this Protean province comes Stephen. With open eyes he walks through space. In it things lie *nebenei-nander*. He calls it the "ineluctable modality of the visible." With eyes shut he walks through space in time. "Time is the ineluctable modality of the audible." One happening follows the other *nacheinander*.

"My definitions of space and time are good. What?" said Joyce.

Stephen has suffered a sea change. There is nothing in him sullen, listless, bitter, resigned, weary. With no half hostile friends to force him into a defensive watchfulness, no longer performing wearily an uncongenial task, he is free, alone, essentially himself. He is a magician's apprentice experimenting with new magic. Whatever images are shown him by his memory they can cause him no remorse, no shame, no regret. They are material for his poetic improvisations like the sights, sounds and smells of land and sea around him. His invention, humour and sensibility are memory proof.

He sees two old midwives come down to the beach with a bag to gather cockles and, with the humour of fantastic association, imagines a telephone cable of navel-cords trailing back through time to Eden garden and himself ringing up our first parents through his own navel.

His feet seem to be conveying him to the house of Richie Goulding, his maternal uncle, but his mood is too rich to waste upon a visit, the nature of which he knows beforehand. He remembers a typical reception in the house of uncle Richie. It is, like his own, a house in decay.

Without wincing, he remembers pages of his follies. "You prayed to the devil in Serpentine Avenue that the fubsy widow in front might lift her clothes still more from the wet street. *O si, certo.* Sell your soul for that, do, dyed rags pinned round a squaw. More tell me, more still! On the top of the Howth tram alone crying to the rain: *naked women.* What about that, eh?

"What about what? What else were they invented for?"

His conscience has no better luck when it reminds him of his before-the-mirror vanities and fantastical literary projects. He mimics himself gaily:

"You bowed to yourself in the mirror, stepping forward to applause earnestly, striking face. Hurray for the Goddamned idiot! Hray! No-one saw: tell no-one. . . ."

Sight of the Pigeon-house reminds him of Paris and of

Kevin Egan's son, who introduced him to the blasphemies of M. Leo Taxil.

"Qui vous a mis dans cette fichue position?"

"C'est le pigeon, Joseph."

Joyce stopped often to laugh at his own composition as he read through Stephen's recollection of his Paris exploits.

"Proudly walking. Whom were you trying to walk like? Forget: a dispossessed. With mother's money-order, eight shillings, the banging door of the postoffice slammed in your face by the usher. Hunger toothache. *Encore deux minutes.* Look clock. Must get. *Fermé.* Hired dog! Shoot him to bloody bits with a bang shotgun. Bits man spattered walls all brass buttons. Bits man khrrrlak in place clack back. Not hurt? Oh, that's all right. Shake hands. See what I meant, see? Oh, that's all right. Shake a shake. Oh, that's all only all right.

"You were going to do wonders, what? Missionary to Europe after fiery Columbanus. Fiacre and Scotus on their creepystools in Heaven spilt from their pintpots loudlatinlaughing: Euge! Euge! Pretending to speak broken English as you dragged your valise, porter threepence, across the slimy pier at Newhaven. *Comment?* Rich booty you brought back; *Le Tutu,* five tattered numbers of *Pantalon Blanc et Culotte Rouge,* a blue French telegram, curiosity to show:

" 'Mother dying come home father.' "

Joyce looked up and said:

"I haven't let this young man off very lightly, have I? Many writers have written about themselves. I wonder if any one of them has been as candid as I have?"

Yellow sunlight on sand and boulders reminds Stephen of the lemon streets and houses of Paris. The same sun is shining there, too. For himself he sees nothing in Irish nationalism but an authority to make his art tonguetied, but he is Irish enough when in Paris to seek out the exiled Fenian, Kevin Egan, forgotten at home mourning his exile in café, restaurant and printing shop. "Weak, wasting hand on mine. They have forgotten Kevin Egan, not he them. Remembering thee, O Sion."

He turns and scans the shore. Southward he sees the tower, his home, and foresees his messmates, Mulligan and Haines, waiting for him that night in vain. He has told them nothing, but he has resolved not to go to the tower that night. He sits on a rock, watching the tide flow, rocks all round him.

"Sir Lout's toys. Mind you don't get one bang on the ear. I'm the bloody well giant rolls all them bloody well boulders, bones for my steppingstones. Feefawfum. I zmellz de bloodz oldz an Iridzman."

Joyce read this with stammering, cluttered utterance, then stopped with a laugh at the odd sounds he made.

"Who are Sir Lout and his family?" I said. "The people who did the rough work at the beginning?"

"Yes," said Joyce. "They were giants right enough, but weak reproductively. Fasolt and Fafnir in Das Rheingold are of the same breed, sexually weak as the music tells us. My Sir Lout has rocks in his mouth instead of teeth. He articulates badly."

A dog appears and runs towards Stephen, barking. Stephen fears dogs and remembers Mulligan laughing at his fear. A gay pretender: but he reflects that Ireland was ever a Paradise of pretenders. He can't, however, escape the comparison: Mulligan saved a man from drowning at the risk of his own life, while he shakes at a cur's yelping. Would he do what Mulligan did? No twisting and turning help him. He is forced to confess that he would not. He pictures to himself the horror of death by water and the

vision fades into that of his mother's death agony. Th
dog's master and mistress appear at the surf edge, looking
for cockles. Stephen's attention is fixed on the dog.

"Did you see the point of that bit about the dog?" said
Joyce. "He is the mummer among beasts—the Protean
animal."

"Weininger says something about the imitative nature
of the dog in his *Uber den letzten Dingen,*" I remembered.

"He does?" said Joyce. "This one mimics the other animals while Stephen is watching him. Listen."

" 'The dog ambled about a bank of dwindling sand,
trotting, sniffing on all sides. Looking for something lost
in a past life. Suddenly he made off like a bounding hare,
ears flung back, chasing the shadow of a lowskimming
gull. The man's shrieked whistle struck his limp ears. He
turned, bounded back, came nearer, trotted on twinkling
shanks. On a field tenney a buck, trippant, proper, un-
attired. At the lacefringe of the tide he halted with stiff
forehoofs, seawardpointed ears. His snout lifted, barked
at the wavenoise, herds of seamorse. . . . The dog
yelped, running to them, reared up and pawed them,
dropping on all fours, again reared up at them with mute,
bearish fawning. Unheeded, he kept by them as they came
towards the drier sand, a rag of wolf's tongue redpanting
from his jaws. His speckled body ambled ahead of them
and then loped off at a calf's gallop. The carcass lay on
his path. He stopped, sniffed, stalked round it, brother,
nosing closer, went round it, sniffling rapidly like a dog all
over the dead dog's bedraggled fell. . . . Along by the
edge of the mole he lolloped, dawdled, smelt a rock and
from under a cocked hindleg pissed against it. He trotted
forward and, lifting his hindleg, pissed quick short at an
unsmelt rock. The simple pleasures of the poor. His hind-

paws then scattered sand: then his forepaws dabbled and delved. Something he buried there, his grandmother. He rooted in the sand, dabbling, delving and stopped to listen to the air, scraped up the sand again with a fury of his claws, soon ceasing, a pard, a panther, got in spouse-breach, vulturing the dead.' "

"There he is," said Joyce. "Panther: all animals."

"I don't know a better word-picture of a dog," I said. "English and Irish, we are all dog-lovers. But when we write about dogs or paint them we sentimentalise them. Landseer."

"This certainly wasn't done by a dog-lover," said Joyce. "I don't like them. I am afraid of them."

The word "panther" brings to Stephen's mind first Haines's dream and then his own.

" 'After he woke me up last night, same dream, or was it? Wait. Open hallway. Street of harlots. Remember Haroun al Raschid. I am almosting it. That man led me, spoke . . .' "

"Almosting!" I said.

"Yes," said Joyce. "That's all in the Protean character of the thing. Everything changes: land, water, dog, time of day. Parts of speech change, too. Adverb becomes verb."

The dog's owners are gypsies. Stephen sees them go, picturing to himself their strange existence in dark lanes, under archways at night. He remembers fragments of gypsy speech. All words are precious to the poet, gypsy words no less than those of Aquinas. "Monkwords, mary-beads jabber on their girdles: roguewords, tough nuggets patter in their pockets." He watches the gypsy woman's receding back on which her spoils are hung. "She trudges, schlepps, trains, drags, trascines her load." Joyce repeated the sentence.

"I like that crescendo of verbs," he said. "The irresistible tug of the tides."

Tides of another blood move in the gypsy woman's veins. A god comes to her in the shape of death.

"He comes, pale vampire, through storm his eyes, his bat sails bloodying the sea, mouth to her mouth's kiss.

"Here. Put a pin in that chap, will you? My tablets. Mouth to her kiss. No. Must be two of 'em. Glue 'em well. Mouth to her mouth's kiss."

He fumbles in his pocket for paper to hold the words, finds only the banknotes of his salary, curses himself for having forgotten to take slips from the library counter and finally tears off the half blank last page of Mr. Deasy's letter on the foot and mouth disease, to serve as tablets for his inspiration. He lies on his back, his mind full of memories. The noise of the moving sea breaks in on them and his thoughts turn outwards again. He makes speech for the rocks and water.

"Listen: a fourworded wavespeech: seesoo, hrss, rsseeis ooos. Vehement breath of waters amid seasnakes, rearing horses, rocks. In cups of rocks it slops: flop, slop, slap: bounded in barrels. And, spent, its speech ceases. It flows purling, widely flowing, floating foampool, flower unfurling."

Out at sea they are dragging for a drowned man. He heard at the bathing pool that the drowned man would rise that day and he pictures the bloated carcass being dragged over the gunwale of the boat.

"A seachange this, brown eyes saltblue. Seadeath, mildest of all deaths known to man. Old Father Ocean. *Prix de Paris:* beware of imitations. Just you give it a fair trial. We enjoyed ourselves immensely."

But now he must go. He dallies yet awhile among rocks, sand and seashells. The seashells remind him that his teeth are hollow like them. Shall he go to the dentist with Mr. Deasy's money? It isn't enough. Mulligan threw his handkerchief to him after using it as a razorwipe, but he left it lying and must use his fingers. He lays dry snot from his nose on a ledge of rock and looks round to see if he is observed.

"He turned his face over a shoulder, rere regardant. Moving through the air high spars of a three-master, her sails brailed up on the crosstrees, homing, upstream, silently moving, a silent ship."

Joyce laid down the *Little Review*. At times, in reading the long monologue, he had sunk his voice to a talking-to-himself murmur so that only precise articulation and a silent room allowed it to be audible. But inside this small scale of tones and with a minimum of emphasis he expressed all the moods of reverie, mockery, perception.

I stopped at the door as I was about to leave.

"You know, Joyce," I said, "when Stephen sees that three-masted schooner's sails brailed up to her crosstrees."

"Yes," he said. "What about it?"

"Only this. I sailed on schooners of that sort once and the only word we ever used for the spars to which the sails are bent was 'yards.' 'Crosstrees' were the lighter spars fixed near the lower masthead. Their function was to give purchase to the topmast standing rigging."

Joyce thought for a moment.

"Thank you for pointing it out," he said. "There's no sort of criticism I more value than that. But the word 'crosstrees' is essential. It comes in later on and I can't change it. After all, a yard is also a crosstree for the onlooking landlubber."

And crosstree does recur in the pattern in that episode where Stephen discusses Shakespeare with some Dublin scholars. ". . . Who, put upon by his fiends, stripped and whipped, was nailed like bat to barndoor, starved on cross-tree. . . ."

Joyce told me that some admirers of *A Portrait of the Artist as a Young Man*, Americans, I understood, had expressed disappointment at the way *Ulysses* was shaping.

"They seem to think," he said, "that after writing *The Portrait* I should have sat down to write something like a sermon. I ought to have a message, it seems."

A conflict of direction would be no new thing in an artist. Religion and politics are the most frequent rivals of words, paint and stone. It isn't necessary, one supposes, that the victory of one side shall mean the annihilation of the other, but it must mean that it has won the direction. Stephen first appears as a named person in *A Portrait of the Artist as a Young Man* but there is no doubt that he is the unnamed narrator of the first three studies in *Dubliners*. The story of Stephen's early years has one peculiarity that marks it off from the general experience of boys, sensitive or insensitive, weak or strong: that is his intense preoccupation with words. To most boys words are convenient counters and no more. When you are hungry, words like "bread" and "butter" provoke pleasant thoughts and are useful if you say them to the right person. And you have to say the right words at games or the other fellows laugh at you. Again, they are troublesome and slippery things in lessons, with spellings and logical relations specially devised to make them as difficult as possible. But to Stephen they were mysteriously alive. In a sense, they were much more potent than the objects, actions and relations they stood for. You say a word or think of its shape and sound and it makes you unhappy or afraid. You say another and a feeling of peace and joy comes to you. The child narrator in the story, *The Sisters*, says: "Every night I gazed up at the window I said softly to myself the word paralysis. It had always sounded strangely in my ears, like the word gnomon in the Euclid or the word simony in the Catechism. But now it sounded to me like the name of some maleficent and sinful being." And Stephen, in *A Portrait of the Artist:* "Suck was a queer word. . . . But the sound was ugly. Once he had washed his hands in the lavatory of the Wicklow Hotel and his father pulled the stopper up by the chain after and the dirty water went down through the hole in the basin. And when it had all gone down slowly the hole in the basin had made a sound like that: suck. Only louder."

There came a time when the storms of puberty, his care for the state of his soul, his preoccupation with religious experience and church doctrine and ritual, poverty, youthful rivalries displaced temporarily his interest in his predestined material. But the storms die away and the dominant interest returns, enriched, stronger. It is a tenacious growth that no painful experience can kill. It seems like an inversion of normal values, yet while Stephen felt himself to be lost in mortal sin and despaired of pardon, when he obtained pardon and peace and resolved to devote his life to the service of the church he was not undergoing an experience more formative, more fruitful than when, as a boy, he stood before the hotel lavatory basin listening to the last handful of soiled water say "suck" as it went down the waste-pipe.

CHAPTER IV

There is a sudden break with Stephen after the end of the third episode. The clock is put back to eight in the morning, but the scene changes from the Martello tower at Sandycove to the kitchen of a house in Eccles Street. A man of different race, age and character comes into the foreground of the book and almost without a break stays there till the end. He is Joyce's Ulysses, the Jew, Leopold Bloom. Bloom and Stephen are opposites. Bloom *is* while Stephen is becoming. He leans to the sciences, Stephen to the arts. He is by race a Jew, is equable in temper, humane and just, whereas Stephen, the Gentile, is egotistical, embittered, denies his social obligations and can be generous but is rarely just. But there is a difference of dimension and substance as well as of character. Stephen is a self-portrait, and therefore one-sided. Bloom is seen from all angles, as no self-portrait can be seen. He is as plastic as Stephen is pictorial.

The question, is this or that character in fiction good or bad, sympathetic or unsympathetic ought to be aesthetically immaterial and the answer unimportant; yet there is something in us that asks it. Mr. Wyndham Lewis considers Stephen a priggish, mawkish and altogether objectionable young man, but why should that matter if he is presented with force enough to make him organic and memorable? On this logic a Christian Scientist ought to turn down a picture of a hospital ward, a vegetarian one of a butcher's shop and both of them would refuse to enter a

gallery where a picture of a bullfight was hung even if
Goya painted it. If in the world of imagination we allow
only such characters as would make good neighbours and
club-mates there would be no room in it for Iago, Macbeth, Madame Bovary and Cousine Bette. However, putting Stephen to the social and moral test, is he really such
a priggish and detestable person? His mood for the first
hour of *Ulysses* is a weary and embittered mood, but then
Stephen is a Dubliner and what Dubliner, or for that
matter what Londoner, is at his bright best at eight o'clock
in the morning? That mood changes in the schoolroom.
There he is sympathetic to the backward schoolboy and,
without malice behind his manner, he is deferential to a
man three times his age. When he walks on the seastrand
his mood is one of bright, elfin, poetic humour. Later in
the day he is delicate and tactful with his sister, and, still
later, he forgets his own existence in philosophical discussion. Although not in funds he stands many rounds of
drinks for his friends. Humanly considered, Stephen is
certainly as sympathetic as Stavrogin and there is no doubt
that he much more resembles a possible human being.

Joyce said to me once in Zürich:

"Some people who read my book, *A Portrait of the
Artist* forget that it is called *A Portrait of the Artist as a
Young Man.*"

He underlined with his voice the last four words of the
title. At first I thought I understood what he meant, but
later on it occurred to me that he may have meant one of
two things, or both. The emphasis may have indicated that
he who wrote the book is no longer that young man, that
through time and experience he has become a different
person. Or it may have meant that he wrote the book looking backwards at the young man across a space of time as
the landscape painter paints distant hills, looking at them

through a cube of air-filled space, painting, that is to say, not that which is, but that which appears to be. Perhaps he meant both. However, it led me to ask myself if the writer, representing his own past life with words, is subject to the same limitations as the painter representing his physical appearance with paint on a flat surface. How near can each one get to the facts of his own particular case? Their limitations cannot of course be the same, but they are equivalent, and on the whole, the painter has the lighter handicap and is the likelier of the two to produce a true image of himself in his own material, although the extra difficulties that confront him are considerable. His first limitation is the inevitable mirror. The best of quick-silvered glass gives an image that is less true than an unreflected one, and the size of that image is by half smaller than it would be, were the same object standing where stands the mirror. He sees in the mirror a man holding in his left hand brushes and in his right hand a palette and he paints right-handedly this left-handed other self. Then he is fatally bound to paint himself painting himself. His functional, his trade self is in the foreground. The strained eye, the raised arm, the crooked shoulder may be ingeniously disguised (they generally are) but something of objective truth gets lost in the process. And he is not only painting himself painting himself; he is also painting himself posing to himself. He is painter and model, too. The painter may be pure painter, but the model may be a bit of a poet or half an actor, and this individual will slyly present to his better half's unsuspecting eye something ironical, heroic or pathetic, according to the mood of the moment or the lifetime's habit. The limitation of viewpoint is obvious. The painter's two-dimensional mode of presentation limits him to one view of an object whatever he paints. He chooses that view and must abide by his choice. All that he can do is to convey the impression in painting one side of an object that the other side exists. In the case of any other object but himself he has at any rate the whole compass to choose from. He can walk round any other model but not round himself. So that, unless he resorts to one of those cabinet mirrors in which tailors humiliate us with the shameful back and side views of our bodies, he can see nothing of himself but full face and three-quarter profile. All this has to do merely with the getting to grips with what is usually called nature. The resulting picture, as all the galleries of Europe testify, may be as good as any other. Are there any Rembrandts we would change for the best self-portraits? One difficulty or limitation more or less among thousands is of no consequence.

And the writer's self-portrait? Goethe subtitled his own, *Dichtung und Wahrheit*. Did he mean that he consciously mixed fiction and fact to puzzle, delude or please, or did he mean that some Dichtung would be there by sleight of memory or because there were many true things better left unsaid? All the psychological inducements to fictify his portrait are present in greater measure for the writer than for the painter. A painter will rather paint the wart on his nose than the writer describe with perfect objectivity the wart on his character. All the posing that the painter does for himself the writer must do also. If he has a passion for confession he will exaggerate some element or other—make the wart too big or put it in the wrong place. He has his favourite rôle too—villain, hero or confidence man—and he would be more than human if he failed to act it. But, worst of all, his medium is not an active sense, but memory, and who knows when memory ceases to be memory and becomes imagination? No human memory has ever recorded the whole of the acts and thoughts of its possessor. Then why one thing more than another? Forgetting and remembering are creative agencies performing all kinds of tricks of selection, arrangement and adaptation. The record of a man's past is inside him and there he must look with the same constancy as the painter looks at his reflection in the mirror; only he is not looking *at* something (still less *round* something like a sculptor) but *into* something, like a mystic contemplating his navel. He can as little walk round his past life psychologically as the painter can walk round his reflected image. Between the moment of experiencing and the moment of recording there is an ever-widening gulf of time across which come rays of remembered things, like the rays of stars long since dead to the astronomer's sensitive plate. Their own original colours have been modified by the medium through which they passed. The "I" who records is the "I" who experienced, but he has grown or dwindled; in any case, he has changed. The continuous present of the painter is the writer's continuous past. No doubt, the most fervently naturalistic painter paints from memory, for there is a moment when he turns his eye away from the scene to his canvas and he must remember what he saw, but for practical purposes his time may be regarded as present time. Interpretation in material, words, pigment, clay, stone, is equivalent in all arts and all have the same aesthetic necessities. One other thing: if the writer cannot see the other side of himself, by a still more elementary disability he cannot see the outside of himself in action at all. He knows what he does as well as any, and why he does it better than any, but how he does it less than any.

Does he even, for example, know the sound of his own voice? If he is a singer he may, after long practice, get to know the sound of it when he is singing, but he will certainly not know how it sounds when he is arguing with a taxi driver. He knows the inside of himself and the outside of everybody else. He supplies other folk with his inner experiences and motives, and himself, by judgment and comparison, with the visible outward of their actions. The mimic among our friends will show the assembled company how we walk or talk. It seems strange and unbelievable to us, but from the laughter and "just like him"s of the others we know that it must be reasonably like. The essence, however, of this comparison is to show that all self-portraits, whether painted or written, are one-sided— that they are pictorial in character, not plastic.

Stephen Dedalus is the portrait and Bloom the all-round man. Bloom is son, father, husband, lover, friend, worker and citizen. He is at home and in exile. One morning he leaves his home and after a time returns. True, he is absent from home only about seventeen hours, but one day or many: it is of no consequence. If a thousand years may be as a day, why not a day as a thousand years? The same elements are present in them all. Bloom's wanderings do not take him outside the city boundaries; but it is enough. Blake said that he could touch the ends of space with his walking stick at the end of his garden. Dublin is the locality, and the day on which the action takes place is the 16th of June, 1904. Nothing is recorded that did not take place or might not have taken place on that day.

Rodin once called sculpture *"le dessin de tous les côtés."* Leopold Bloom is sculpture in the Rodin sense. He is made of an infinite number of contours drawn from every conceivable angle. He is the social being in black clothes and the naked individual underneath them. All his actions are meticulously recorded. None is marked "Private." He does his allotted share in the economic life of the city and fulfils the obligations of citizen, husband and friend, his body functioning meanwhile according to the chemistry of human bodies. We see him as he appears to himself and as he exists in the minds of his wife, his friends and his fellow citizens. By the end of the day we know more about him than we know about any other character in fiction. They are all hemmed in in a niche of social architecture, but Bloom stands in the open and we can walk round him. His past is revealed in his own memory and in the memories of others. He is a Jew of Hungarian origin. The family name was Virag but Leopold's father changed it to Bloom. Leopold was baptised a Protestant and later a Roman Catholic. His wife, Marion, is the daughter of Major Brian Tweedy and a Gibraltar Jewess. There were two children of Bloom's marriage, one of whom, Rudolph, died on his eleventh day. The other, Millicent, is just fifteen and works as a photographer's assistant in Mullingar.

The completeness with which Bloom is presented is at times bewildering. There are innumerable changes of key and scale. Sometimes he is a dark phantom in the middle distance and then he suddenly dominates the foreground plane. He may stand like a floodlit building, stark and flat against the sky or he may be entirely built up out of reflections of his surroundings. Now a searchlight illumines violently one part of him and now normal daylight flows over him from head to foot. But always he is the same kindly, prudent, level-tempered, submissive, tragically isolated, shrewd, sceptical, simple, uncensorious person, with an outward seemingly soft and pliant but with a hard inner core of self-sufficiency.

His wife, Marion, is a onesidedly womanly woman. She is unfaithful, but her infidelities are not the furtive, conscience-stricken infidelities of average life. They are the actions of a body that refuses to accept the rules of custom, and therefore has no need of duplicities. She is proof

against all doubts of the mind and all remorse of conscience, because, according to her own scale of values, she
does no ill. She is a shrewd, humorous, wilful personage,
who might perhaps, except for a sisterly quarrel or two,
get on very well with the Wife of Bath. In person she appears only twice in the book, once in the first episode and
again to speak the epilogue at the end, but she is ever
present in the thoughts of her man as he pursues his wanderings throughout the day.

A host of minor characters throng the pages of *Ulysses*
—two hundred, perhaps. Most of these are present in the
flesh, but those absent or dead become known to us
through the minds of those living and present. Of the
dead the most important are Bloom's father and son and
Stephen's mother. Through the conversation of the mourners at his funeral we become acquainted with Paddy Dignam, a friend of Bloom. Bloom's earlier friends, Apjohn
and Meredith, now dead, have a ghostly yet amiable existence. His daughter, Millicent, is absent in Mullingar
but she writes home; we meet her friend, Alec Bannon,
and we hear a great deal about her from her father and
mother. Not all the population of the book is accorded
the same measure of attention and seriousness of treatment. Some of them, notably those of the older generation, are portrayed with a certain humorous and touching
intimacy. Stephen's father, Simon Dedalus, is the principal example, but with him might stand Martin Cunningham, Jack Power, Ben Dollard and others. They seem to
be portrait studies conveying all the illusion of character
and experience. Others, as, for example, Professor Mac-
Hugh, Haines the Englishman, young Dignam, Tom
Rochford, are drawn on the flat with a few suggestive
lines. Yet others, and these are of the most enjoyable, are
vital, grotesque types—caricatures as a Rowlandson might

have conceived them. The Nameless One and the Citizen in the *Cyclops* episode are examples. Blazes Boylan, Marion Bloom's impresario and lover, can hardly be classed in any of these categories, but in the main he is a caricature of the overbearing blond beast, who gets the better of his neighbour in bed and business, who thinks himself a hero, but who in reality is a comic automaton.

Most of the people belong to the poorer class of Dublin citizen. Hardly any of them are what might be called working people; that is to say, there are no plumbers, carpenters or railway guards in regular employment among them. Nearly all are of the lower middle class, in dire poverty if they have lost their jobs or property, but a shade above the well-paid workingman if things are going well with them. The comfortably-connected Buck Mulligan is an exception. Apart from Mulligan all the students are of the hard up or stony-broke variety. Bloom canvasses for advertisements; Tom Kernan is a traveller in tea; Martin Cunningham has a good job in Dublin castle; Simon Dedalus, without property or position, can only with difficulty give his daughters a shilling for food; Cowley is dodging the bailiffs, and Dollard lives in a home for gentlemen who have seen better days. The rich bourgeois and governing patrician, as also the pure and simple wage worker play no great part in the book. About ninety per cent of the people in George Moore's Dublin are of the Irish literary movement. That movement, in the persons of some of its most distinguished representatives, figures also in *Ulysses* but in a proportion equal to its importance in the life of the city.

One important personality that emerges out of the contacts of many people is that of the city of Dublin.

"I want," said Joyce, as we were walking down the Universitätstrasse, "to give a picture of Dublin so complete that if the city one day suddenly disappeared from the earth it could be reconstructed out of my book."

We had come to the university terrace where we could look down on the town.

"And what a city Dublin is!" he continued. "I wonder if there is another like it. Everybody has time to hail a friend and start a conversation about a third party, Pat, Barney or Tim. 'Have you seen Barney lately? Is he still off the drink?' 'Ay, sure he is. I was with him last night and he drank nothing but claret.' I suppose you don't get that gossipy, leisurely life in London?"

"No," I said. "But then London isn't a city. It is a wilderness of bricks and mortar and the law of the wilderness prevails. All Londoners say, 'I keep myself to myself.' The malicious friendly sort of town can't exist with seven million people in it."

But it is not by way of description that Dublin is created in *Ulysses*. There is a wealth of delicate pictorial evocation in *Dubliners*, but there is little or none in *Ulysses*. Streets are named but never described. Houses and interiors are shown us, but as if we entered them as familiars, not as strangers come to take stock of the occupants and inventory their furniture. Bridges over the Liffey are crossed and recrossed, named and that is all. We go into eating-houses and drinking bars as if the town were our own and these our customary ports of call. Libraries, churches, courthouses, the municipal government, professional associations function before us without explanations or introductions. The people are being born, dying, eating and drinking, making love, betting, boozing, worshipping, getting married and burying their dead. Politics, especially the politics of Irish nationalism, and economic questions, such as the cattle trade with England, are being fiercely debated. The history of Dublin and of the Irish nation is served up piping hot in the speech of living patriots. Young men are struggling for bread and a place in the sun; prudent middle age is doing what it can to keep what it has; and the old are scheming for a little peace and quietness away from the hungry generations. Women of all ages aid, thwart, distract, criticise, and comfort them in all their enterprises. Sex, in all its normal manifestations, is ever present together with the solidarities and disputes of families. There is much in *Ulysses* that, in the normal acceptation of the word, is obscene, but very little that is perverse. The cultural life of Dublin is revealed to us in discussions on music and literature. It is a thirsty day and any moment of it seems to be a suitable moment for having a drink. At times the reader so acutely realises the existence of Dublin that Dublin's sons and daughters, even including Bloom and Stephen, become by comparison unimportant.

How do we come by our vision of place for the happenings in books? Some pagelong, meticulous descriptions are lost on us and we place the action in a setting we know. I have often been obliged to do this for Balzac; and Borrow's fight with the Flaming Tinman I always place on a certain roadside patch between Godstone and Lingfield. But in reading Tolstoy, George Moore, Kipling and Henry Handel Richardson, to mention only four, I see places in my mind that I never saw with my eyes. Writing descriptively, Joyce created a pictorial Dublin in *Dubliners*. The slow train in *Araby,* creeping "among ruinous houses and over the twinkling river"; the truant schoolboys in *An Encounter,* wandering aimlessly among the scattered slums, along the Dodder bank, through dismal suburbs and meeting with the sinister pervert; Dublin under snow as the guests return from the party in *The Dead.* There is another way, and that is not to describe the place at all.

"A platform in front of a castle"; "A Heath"; "Before Prospero's Cell" tell us nothing in particular. The persons when they possess our imaginations do all that is required. We lend them freely their ambient of material and colour; and we have no special instructions in the matter. One blasted heath, one beetling crag will do as well as another. But it is essential to Joyce that we shall not substitute our own home town for his, and yet in *Ulysses* he neither paints nor photographs it for our guidance. It must grow upon us not through our eye and memory, but through the minds of the Dubliners we overhear talking to each other. They must make us guests or adopted citizens of their city. Names of streets and suburbs, allusions to the intimate life of the place, are constantly on their lips. Here and there we get a clue to the shape and colour of this place or that, but in the main Dublin exists for us as the essential element in which Dubliners live. It is not a décor to be modified at will, but something as native to them as water to a fish. Joyce's realism verges on the mystical even in *Ulysses*.

The Dublin of *Dubliners* is seen piecemeal as a series of isolated happenings. The sky is overcast. An air of corruption and frustration hangs over the city. The people are frail human beings and even when they are corrupt we are made to feel a human pity for their weakness. Individual, obscure human destinies are isolated and endowed with special importance apart from their place in the mass of human experience. They are gravely and gently regarded, without irony, condemnation or any tendencious contrast. But a hard, bright light floods the Dublin of *Ulysses* and the air is a quickening, tonic air. We see the city as a whole, in a wide sweep, so that the individual destiny is merged in the mass of experience. Death and decay are robbed of their sting, for they are never isolated, but a part of the texture of life, continuing always. Thus Paddy Dignam's death is balanced by his son's growth. An act of adultery is seen as a mechanical and grotesque incident in marriage. The cries of a woman in childbirth and the cries of her newborn child mingle with the shouting and laughter of young men drinking ale. Perhaps it is because the tempo of *Ulysses* matches the tempo of our own lives and repeats their texture in its manifold balances and compensations that the reading of it is a tonic experience. Fifty years of life, as in *The Old Wives' Tale,* is depressing because the funerals follow too quickly one upon the heels of the other and people grow old and die before our eyes as if in a nature-film such as *The Life and Death of the Nasturtium,* only minus the dance-like grace of such a spectacle.

And the attitude of the writer towards the world that he sees? Some human mood must invest the work of every poet, for every poet is himself a human being. Joyce is a keen-sensed stranger, a delicate recording instrument, an artificer as ingenious, patient and daring as the hawklike man whom Stephen invokes at the end of *A Portrait of the Artist.* It is not easy to define the mood of *Ulysses,* but it seems to me that Joyce neither hates nor loves, neither curses nor praises the world, but that he affirms it with a "Yes" as positive as that with which Marion Bloom affirms her prerogative on the last page. It is not to him a brave new world, about to set forth upon some hitherto unattempted enterprise. Rather is it a brave old world, for ever flowing like a river, ever seeming to change yet changing never. The prevailing attitude of *Ulysses* is a very humane scepticism—not of tried human values, necessary at all times for social cohesion, but of all tendencies and systems whatsoever. There are moods of pity and grief in it, but the prevailing mood is humour. Laughter in all tones and keys, now with the world and now at it, is heard continually. The laughter reminds us often of the bright, mocking laughter of Sterne of whom Nietzsche wrote that he, "the freest of all free spirits," resembled a squirrel flying from tree to tree, bewildering the eye with his agility. But then it often resembles the louder laughter of a Shakespeare or a Dickens, delighting in the over-lifesize caricature of human types, the political windbag, the snarling, scurrilous man, the monumental liar. There is, too, that rarer grim, noiseless laughter which shines out through the eyes of a mask. The relation of woman to man is presented as one of mighty importance but, in its essence, of lapidary simplicity. That of man to man is presented as one full of subtleties and fine shades. Of mother love not much is said. To father love is ascribed a significance rarely admitted. Sometimes a faint note of condemnation of his characters is heard, as in the case of Mulligan or Lynch, but Joyce looks on the doings of men, in the words of Blake applied to Chaucer, "oftener with joke and sport."

CHAPTER V

In Part Two of *Ulysses* begin the adventures of Mr. Bloom. "Don't tell me what happens," says the novel reader, "or I shan't want to read the book." But some people have found that nothing, or very little, happens in the 735 pages of the book. Dr. Jung, of Zürich, the famous psychoanalyst, is one of them. He finds Thursday, June 16th, 1904, in Dublin an unimportant sort of day on which, in reality, nothing at all occurs. It is adways difficult to agree with anybody about what is important, yet if we enumerate the things that happen in *Ulysses* most human beings will agree that of themselves, apart from the manner of the presentation, these happenings are important. Included in them are a funeral, a fight, political discord, an act of seduction, one of adultery, the birth of a child, a drunken orgy, a rupture of friendship and the loss of a position. A new theory as to the character and dominant motive of a great poet is expounded. Domestic beasts, on which the life of human society largely depends, are smitten with a dread disease and the community brings its varied intelligence to bear on a means to end that plague. Acts of charity, both public and private, are performed and acts of treachery as well. True, there is no declaration of war with proclamations and the calling out of fighting men, no revolution with conspirators issuing from cellars to take command of the state, but war and revolution are present in the memories and aspirations of the characters of the book. The Boer War and the Russo-

Japanese War are living memories and the Sinn Fein Party is actively organising the citizens of Ireland for rupture with Great Britain and the setting up of a separate state.

Alongside these larger actions there are actions that may be called common only because they are being constantly performed by many people all over the world. They are not and never were unimportant. Thus the preparing and eating of a breakfast, a bath, looking at bookstalls, wandering round the town, looking in shop windows, buying odds and ends of things in shops, lunch, a stroll through a museum, short talks in the street, the singing of a few songs, a practical joke, stray drinks here and there: all the things, in short, that somebody is doing all the time and everybody does sometimes. If the experience is common why does Joyce narrate it? Because he is building with an infinite number of pellets of this clay of common experience the character of Leopold Bloom.

In the course of many talks with Joyce in Zürich I found that for him human character was best displayed—I had almost said entirely displayed—in the commonest acts of life. How a man ties his shoelaces or how he eats his egg will give a better clue to his differentiation than how he goes forth to war. This must be true, for a man goes forth to a war so seldom that he has no scope for individuality in the doing of it. On this heroic occasion he must do as others do. His dress is ordered for him. His careless shoestring brings down on him wild incivility. Cutting bread displays character better than cutting throats. Neither homicide nor suicide can be as characteristic as the sit of a hat. Character, in short, lay not in the doing or not doing of a grand action, but in the peculiar and personal manner of performing a simple one. It lay also in a man's preferences. Does he prefer dogs to cats or does he detest or like both equally? Is he an amateur of beefsteaks, or does he, like Mr. Bloom, eat "with relish the inner organs of beasts and fowls"? Oranges or lemons? Apples or pears? Mozart or Wagner? Women or men, thin or fat? And how dressed? What colour? On which side of a companion does he prefer to walk? These are socially not weighty matters, but from the point of view of character differentiation they are more important than a man's veiws on relativity or the Russian Revolution. There is a further element of character, often lost sight of, and that is what happens to a man, his destiny. Is he lucky or unlucky? Do chimney pots fall on his head in a high wind or do people leave him fortunes?

Before 1918 an article on Joyce, by the late Mr. Clutton Brock, appeared in the *Times Literary Supplement*. This was a critic whose work Joyce respected, and it appears that he greatly appreciated Joyce's writings, but in this article he reproached Joyce for the lack of distinction in his subject matter.

"What do you think he means?" said Joyce.

"From what you tell me," I said, "I suppose he means that the persons in your book are undistinguished—socially or spiritually—both, perhaps—and that their actions and destinies are not important."

"Very likely you are right," said Joyce. "Clutton Brock has always treated my writings generously and with understanding, but if that is what he means he is certainly wrong. In fact he wrote to me about it also. He is stating the English preference for tawdry grandeurs. Even the best Englishmen seem to love a lord in literature."

Distinguished or not, Mr. Bloom is a singular person. We are introduced to him as he potters about the kitchen of 7 Eccles Street, preparing breakfast for his wife and himself. The street is wide, its houses sizeable. The red

brick façades form an architectural unit and have an air
of being good early Victorian. No doubt it was originally
a street of well-to-do bourgeois. Now it has an air of being
inhabited by working class people. But it is well-kept and
exhibits none of the dilapidation of the more magnificent
Mountjoy Square. The kitchen where Mr. Bloom is busy
is below the street level, but for a basement is light and
airy. Breast-high railings protect the passer-by from the
drop into the area and mark the property off from the
pavement. The ground floor of No. 7 is now a tobacconist's
shop and small general store. At the back of the house is
what house agents would call a good garden, which runs
down to a lane or mews.

While he is preparing the tray for his wife's breakfast
Mr. Bloom is pondering a kidney for his own. "Kidneys
were in his mind as he moved about the kitchen
softly. . . ." The cat calls for attention and he, a Jew,
pauses to admire the clean, fierce enemy of rats and mice,
the protector of granaries, worshipped by the taskmasters
of his forefathers. On his way out to get his kidney he
stops at the bedroom door to ask Marion if she also would
like something tasty. He hears her sleepy negative and the
brass quoits of the bed jingle as she turns over. The jingle
of this second-hand bed is one of the musical refrains of
Ulysses. He crosses to the light side of the street, enjoying
the happy warmth. As with half-shut eyes he walks, visions
of the Orient, the sun's home, home, too, of his race, come
to him. In rapid association the Oriental images pass and
merge into the headpiece over the leader in the *Freeman's
Journal.* Arthur Griffith's witticism, "Home rule sun rising up in the north-west from a laneway behind the Bank
of Ireland" ends the chain of associations to Bloom's
pleased smile.

Larry O'Rourke's pub provokes another train of

thought. The business position is good, that of M'Auliffe's is bad. "Of course, if they ran a tramline along the North Circular from the cattle market to the quays values would go up like a shot." Simon Dedalus can mimic O'Rourke wonderfully. He passes the time of day with the publican, who is leaning against the sugarbin in his shirt-sleeves, and goes on, musing on the mystery of the licensed vintner's business. How is it that a red-headed barman can come up from County Leitrim and in a short time blossom out as a complete publican? Tricks known only to the trade, perhaps. He passes a school and hears the mass product education being produced. It is a geography lesson which reminds him of the mountain that bears his own name: Slieve Bloom.

He arrives at the window of Dlugacz's pork-butcher's shop. Only one kidney is left on the willow patterned plate. The general servant from the house next door just heads him off at the counter. Her coarse, muscular body pleases him. He has looked at it often from his back window, vigorously whacking carpets on the line. But will she take the only remaining kidney? To still his mind he takes up a piece of Dlugacz's wrapping-up newspaper from the counter and begins to read. "A model farm at Kinnereth on the shores of Lake Tiberias . . . Moses Montefiore. I thought he was." The ad. is adorned with a photograph of a farmhouse with cattle cropping round it. That reminds him of the job he once had as sales clerk to the cattle salesman, Joe Cuffe. The servant girl departs with her sausages, leaving his kidney unbought. "Mr. Bloom pointed quickly. To catch up and walk behind her if she went slowly, behind her moving hams." But she turns in the other direction and, baffled, he disparages to himself those charms he is baulked of enjoying.

Walking home with his kidney he reads the advertisement carefully. "Agendath Netaim: planter's company." The project is to found an earthly paradise on land to be bought from the Turkish Government. The reader is invited to pay ten marks down and his name is entered in the book of the Union and at once they begin to plant his land with olives, oranges, almonds or citrons. "Bleibtreustrasse 34, Berlin, W.15. Nothing doing. Still, an idea behind it." His mind wanders again to the sunlit east, its scented fruits, the growing, plucking and grading of them, till a cloud over the sun of Dublin darkens his vision of the Orient. Agendath Netaim is one form of the Orient motive of *Ulysses*.

Two letters and a postcard have been delivered in his absence. One of the letters is addressed to Mrs. Marion Bloom. "His quick heart slowed at once. Bold hand. Mrs. Marion." He takes it to his wife and when, a few minutes later, he takes in her tea, he sees a strip of torn envelope peeping from under her pillow.

"Who was the letter from?" he asked.

"Oh, Boylan," she said. "He's bringing the programme."

"What are you singing?"

"*La ci darem,* with J. C. Doyle," she said, "and *Love's Old Sweet Song.*"

Marion has mislaid her book and Bloom finds it "sprawled against the orange-keyed chamberpot." A word is bothering her, "metempsychosis," and Bloom is trying to explain the meaning of it to her when her sensitive woman's nose smells burning in the kitchen. He hurries back to kidney and breakfast.

While eating, he reads the letter to himself from his daughter, Milly. Her birthday was on the fifteenth and she thanks him for the birthday present. She is pleased with her job as a photographer's assistant. Among other things she mentions that a young student, Alec Bannon, is paying her attentions. Mulligan's bathing companion is mentioning the same thing at about the same time, only from Bannon's angle, at the bathing cove, a few miles away. Bloom thinks of her birth, of the birth and death of his son, of her job and her approaching sexual experience. It's good she has a job. As for her sex, she must look after herself. There is thunder in the air. "He felt heavy, full: then a gentle loosening of the bowels."

There are two toilet conveniences in Bloom's house. One of these is at the end of the garden and this he prefers. He prefers, too, the printed page to the rolled up scroll. On his way to the jakes he notices the infertility of the garden. It needs manuring. Seated, he reads the prize story in *Tit-Bits,* "Matcham's Masterstroke," by Philip Beaufoy, of the Playgoers Club. "It did not move or touch him, but it was something quick and neat." He notes that it "begins and ends morally." And, "he envied kindly Mr. Beaufoy, who had written it and received payment of three pounds thirteen and six." Could he write one himself or in collaboration with Marion? One fears that he couldn't, for his mind runs on subjects in which the public isn't interested: his wife, her sayings, her mannerisms, her impresario, Ponchielli's ballet, *The Dance of the Hours.* His sense of reality is too strong. In any case, since 1904 the verdant one has far outdistanced its golden and scarlet rivals. It is fast going highbrow. Neither Philip Beaufoy's contributions nor Bloom's would now stand a chance against those of the great names of our best sellers. "In the bright light, lightened and cooled in limb, he eyed carefully his black trousers, the ends, the knees, the houghs of the knees. What time is the funeral? Better find it out in the paper." The bells of George's Church strike three-quarters. Listening to the overtones following on through the air, Bloom says to himself, "Poor Dignam."

As this day demands of Bloom the best of his qualities the event narrated is of the highest importance. Were the state of his bowels otherwise, "the cloudie isle with hellish dreeriment would soon be filled and thousand fearful roumours." Bloom's moral staying power is rooted in his body's regularity.

The *Calypso* episode ends and *The Lotus Eaters* begins. Bloom has left Eccles Street and is walking soberly along Sir John Rogerson's Quay. Dignam's funeral is due to start at eleven from Sandymount. Bloom has to call at Westland Row post office, which lies on his way. There should be time to spare for a bath. It is a warm morning and the pores of the city exude a sickly odour of dope.

"By Brady's cottages a boy for the skins lolled, his bucket of offal linked, smoking a chewed fagbut. A smaller girl, with scars of eczema on her forehead, eyed him, listlessly holding her battered cask hoop."

Shall fatherly Bloom warn him against the evils of the toxic weed? "Oh, let him! His life isn't such a bed of roses."

The window of the Belfast and Oriental Tea Company in Westland Row reminds him that he must order some tea from Tom Kernan. He takes off his hat to the warmth of the morning and inhales the sweet scent of hair oil. His poste restante card is tucked away in the leather headband. Vaguely he remembers that he has seen somewhere the picture of a man lying on his back on the water, reading under a spanned parasol. "Couldn't sink if you tried: so thick with salt. Because the weight of the water, no, the weight of the body in the water is equal to the weight of the . . . What is weight really when you say the weight? Thirty-two feet per second, per second. Law of falling bodies: per second, per second." Tea, with its fragrant associations, hair oil perfume, and the massive formula

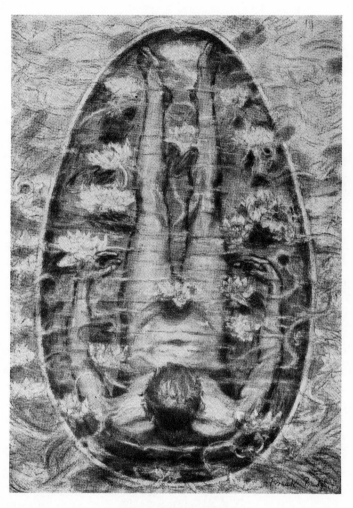

THE LOTUS EATERS

for the law of gravitation slightly numb the mind of Bloom.

He presents his card at the grille of the P.O., Westland Row, and, while waiting, looks at the recruiting posters showing soldiers in the distinctive uniforms of their regiments. The clerk hands him a letter addressed Henry Flower, Esq. He takes it and turns again to the poster. "Where's old Tweedy's regiment? . . . There he is: Royal Dublin Fusiliers. . . . Maud Gonne's letter about taking them off O'Connel Street at night: disgrace to our Irish capital. . . . Half baked they look: hypnotised like."

While he is discreetly opening the letter in his pocket outside the post office he sights M'Coy, whose wife also sings. Reluctantly he listens to the talkative man explaining at great length how he came to hear of the death of Paddy Dignam. Round M'Coy's head he sees an outsider pulled up before the door of the Grosvenor and a handsome, well-dressed woman waiting while the porter hands up the luggage and her male escort fumbles for change. Barely listening to the drone of M'Coy's voice, he watches intently for the treat of seeing the rich thoroughbred woman get up on her equipage. In spite of her aloof air she knows he is looking. But he is baulked of his vision of silk stockings and what not. "A heavy tramcar honking its gong slewed between them." He mentally curses the tramdriver for his untimeliness and turns with more polite attention to M'Coy. Attention is needed, for M'Coy begins to tell him that his wife has an engagement to sing and M'Coy is a confirmed valise borrower. Bloom defends his valise adroitly, hinting at the same time at the professional eminence of Marion. "My wife, too," he said. "She's going to sing at a swagger affair in the Ulster Hall, Belfast, on the twenty-fifth." At parting, he promises to put

M'Coy's name down on the list of mourners at Dignam's funeral. He is glad to be rid of M'Coy, but the glamour of the rich dame has drugged him into forgetting to work M'Coy for a free pass to Mullingar.

He returns to the letter, but faces an advertisement hoarding so as to be able to keep an eye on the vanishing figure of M'Coy. Advertisement is also a drug. It flatters and numbs till the victim walks meekly to the sales counter. Mrs. Bandman Palmer is playing *Leah* that night. The night before she played *Hamlet*. Ophelia's suicide reminds him of his father's death from an overdose of aconite. He is glad that he didn't go into the room to look at his father as he lay dead. He passes a cab rank where gelded cab-horses are champing their oats in patient quietism. A timber yard off Cumberland Street promises seclusion for his letter. There is no one in sight but a child playing marbles and a blinking tabby cat watching the child. He reads:

"Dear Henry,

"I got your last letter to me and thank you very much for it. I am sorry you did not like my last letter. Why did you enclose the stamps? I am awfully angry with you. I do wish I could punish you for that. I called you naughty boy because I do not like that other word. Please tell me what is the real meaning of that word. Are you not happy in your home you poor little naughty boy? I do wish I could do something for you. Please tell me what you think of poor me. I often think of the beautiful name you have. Dear Henry, when will we meet? I think of you so often you have no idea. I have never felt myself so much drawn to a man as you. I feel so bad about. Please write me a long letter and tell me more. Remember if you do not I will punish you. So now you know what I will do to you,

you naughty boy, if you do not wrote. Oh how I long to meet you, Henry dear, do not deny my request before my patience are exhausted. Then I will tell you all. Good-bye now, naughty darling. I have such a bad headache to-day and write *by return* to your longing

> "MARTHA.

"P.S.—Do tell me what kind of perfume does your wife use. I want to know."

Bloom passes on, reflecting on a probable meeting with Martha. So far the affair has been carried on poste restante, Bloom using for the purpose the "beautiful name" of Flower. The complications involved incline him to prudence. But her name recalls to him a picture he once saw of Martha and Mary. It is evening and Mary listens entranced while Martha prepares the meal. "She listens with big, dark, soft eyes. Tell her: more and more: all. Then a sigh: silence. Long, long, long rest."

He tears up the compromising envelope and throws the shreds of paper away under a dark railway arch. A goods train laden with barrels of porter clanks overhead. Musing on the fortunes of the Guinness family and on the great vats and thirsts out of which they sprang, Bloom reaches All Hallows Church. "The cold smell of sacred stone called him." The odd contrast of religious symbols strikes him: tranquil and entranced Buddha, suffering and bleeding Christ. He defends the integrity of his own mind against the mass suggestions of religion. "Shut your eyes and open your mouth. What? Corpus. Body. Body. Corpse. Good idea the Latin. Stupefies them first. . . . Rum idea: eating bits of a corpse why the cannibals cotton on to it. . . . There's a big idea behind it, kind of kingdom of God is within you feel. First communicants. Hokey-pokey penny a lump. Then feel all like one family party, same in the theatre, all in the same swim. . . . Blind faith. Safe in the arms of kingdom come. Lulls all pain. Wake up this time next year." He notes the ineffectiveness of religious observances to restrain criminals (witness Carey, the Invincible, a regular communicant), but to the Church's credit he places Benedictine and green Chartreuse and the fact that at times it has fostered the fine arts. He admires its purposefulness as a business institution.

From "the cold smell of sacred stone" to the "keen reek of drugs, the dusty dry smell of sponges and loofahs." He calls at a chemist's shop to get some skin lotion made up for Marion and buys a tablet of lemon soap, to be paid for when he comes back for the lotion. On leaving the shop he runs into Bantam Lyons, an ardent supporter of bookmakers and thoroughbreds. It is Gold Cup day at Ascot. Bass's great mare, Sceptre, is running. Lord Howard de Walden's Zinfandel is fancied. The French horse, Maximum II, is considered to have a chance. Lyons excitedly asks for a sight of Bloom's *Freeman's*. His intrusion is unwelcome to Bloom, who tells him he can keep the paper: he was just about to throw it away. The tip is clear. Throwaway is an outsider. Bantam Lyons returns the paper and rushes off. Luckily for his bookmaker he doesn't back Throwaway. He is the classic punter who always swears he will back his own fancy next time and for ever takes expert advice instead.

The warm weather pleases Bloom. "Cricket weather. Sit round under sunshades. Over after over. Out. They cant play it here . . . Donnybrook fair is more in their line." Cricket still had its agreeable lotus flavour in 1904. There was no body line or barracking dispute in those days.

As a boy Joyce ran and hurdled but I have never heard him talk of track athletics. He was never a games-playing man. The game of cricket, however, does interest him. A page of his *Work in Progress* is written in an idiom suggestive of cricket reminiscences.

"And her lamp was all askew and a trumbly wick-in-her, ringeysingey. She had to spofforth, she had to kicker, too thick of the wick of her pixy's loomph, wide lickering jessup the smoky shiminey. And her duffed coverpoint of a wickedy batter, whenever she druv behind her stumps for a tyddlesly wink through his tunnilcleft bagslops after the rising bounders yorkers, as he studd and stoddard and trutted and trumpered, to see lordherry's blackhams had read bobbyabbels, it tickled her innings to concert pitch at kicksoclock in the morm."

The dreamful suggestion to which Bloom finally succumbs is that of a hot bath. "He foresaw his pale body reclined in it at full, naked, in a womb of warmth, oiled by scented melting soap softly laved." Ink smeared newsprint, greatest dope of all, he has not looked at. He smelt it only.

Hades follows *The Lotus Eaters*. The under world into which the hero and his companions descend is Glasnevin cemetery. Dignam's house is in Sandymount, on the opposite side of the city. Here Bloom enters the mourners' coach. There are three other occupants: Jack Power, Martin Cunningham and Simon Dedalus. Simon's wife, Stephen's mother, died but recently and they are travelling to the place where she lies. Martin Cunningham is an intelligent, kindly man, whose face suggests that of Shakespeare. His wife is a drunkard and ruins him by drinking up one home after another. Together with Jack Power he figures in the story *Grace* in *Dubliners* in the friendly conspiracy against the drinking habits of Tom Kernan. Simon Dedalus is described by his son in *A Portrait of the Artist as a Young Man:* "A medical student, an oarsman, a tenor, an amateur actor, a shouting politician, a small landlord, a small investor, a drinker, a good fellow, a storyteller, somebody's secretary, something in a distillery, a taxgatherer, a bankrupt and at present a praiser of his own past." Tom Kernan, with Hynes of the story, *Ivy Day,* are following in another coach with Ned Lambert.

They are trundling along past Watery Lane when Mr. Bloom sights young Stephen and calls the attention of Simon to his son. A swerve of the carriage unsights Simon Dedalus, who falls back in his seat and begins to curse Stephen's associates, particularly Mulligan. He will write to Mulligan's aunt about it. Mulligan's aunt thinks that Stephen is leading the Buck astray and will write to Stephen's father about it. Bloom's thoughts stray to his own boy, who died, and he envies Simon the possession of such a promiseful namebearer. Grand canal, gas works, dog's home: and he remembers his father's dying wish that he should be kind to the old dog, Athos.

From his side of the carriage Martin Cunningham greets an acquaintance on the street. It is Blazes Boylan. Mr. Dedalus salutes and Boylan's straw hat flashes a reply from the door of the Red Bank. The bold hand of Marion Bloom's organiser and associate. "Mr. Bloom reviewed the nails of his left hand, then those of his right hand. The nails, yes. Is there anything more in him than they she sees? Fascination. Worst man in Dublin. That keeps him alive. They sometimes feel what a person is. Instinct. But a type like that. My nails. I am just looking at them: well pared." His momentary embarrassment thus covered, Mr. Bloom answers readily and urbanely their questions about the concert tour.

The bent form of a notorious moneylender near the O'Connell statue brings a welcome change of subject.

Bloom begins to tell the story of Reuben Dodd's son, who, when ordered by his father to go to the Isle of Man out of reach of a designing female, jumped into the Liffey. Martin Cunningham brusquely thwarts Bloom's effort and tells the story himself. The laugh gives them qualms of conscience, but they reflect that Dignam wouldn't grudge them their little joke. He was a good fellow. His death was due to apoplexy brought on by overdrinking. Bloom thinks sudden death is the best death, swift and painless, but a silence of disagreement follows his remark. His commonsense paganism shocks their religious prejudice.

"But the worst of all," Mr. Power said, "is the man who takes his own life." Martin Cunningham tries to change the subject. He is the only one of Bloom's companions who knows that Bloom's father died of aconite poisoning. In any case, he claims a charitable judgment for him who dies by his own hand. Bloom is unable to understand the harsh Christian condemnation of suicide.

Their carriage drives into a drove of cattle and Bloom comes back to his idea of running a tramline from the Parkgate to the quays by way of the North Circular. They pass over the Royal Canal, Crossguns Bridge, as a barge is being locked through. A stonecutter's yard, the turn to Finglas Road, the high railings of Prospects, flickering of tombstones through the trees, remind them that they are near the end of their journey. At the cemetery gate a general reshuffle takes place. Bloom falls back with Tom Kernan and discusses with him the destination of the Dignam children. Ned Lambert talks to Simon Dedalus of a whip-round to cover their immediate needs. A former employer of Dignam's, John Henry Menton, solicitor, present at the funeral, has put his name down for a quid.

At the door of the mortuary chapel Bloom looks down

with pity on the thin neck of Dignam's eldest boy in front of him. Inside all kneel, Bloom on one knee only and that protected from the dusty floor by his *Freeman's*. He listens unmoved to the service for the dead. His mind is proof against the pathos of religion, but, seeing that some rite is necessary, as well this as another. On the slow procession to the grave he again walks with Tom Kernan, who was once a Protestant and still prefers the more homely Protestant burial service in the language they all understand. But to Bloom's humane materialistic mind the "resurrection of the body" is a comic idea. "It may bring comfort to the living, but it brings none to the dead. Knocking them all up out of their graves. Come forth, Lazarus! And he came fifth and lost the job. Get up! Last day! Then every fellow mousing around for his liver and his lights and the rest of his traps. Find damn all of himself that morning. Penny weight of powder in a skull. . . ." John Henry Menton asks who is that man walking with Tom Kernan. He is told that it is Bloom, husband of Marion Bloom, born Tweedy.

"In God's name," John Henry Menton said, "what did she marry a coon like that for? She had plenty of game in her then."

Bloom's thoughts at the graveside are of the same shrewdly human commonsense order. He is not overmuch awed by death. It is just one of the facts of life. How all nations and races meet it with different beliefs and pieties, how dead things feed the living: all that is just natural. Dying is the difficult thing. He imagines a death-chamber, a dying man who can't believe that at last his turn has come, delirium, the priest, death. "Gone at last. People talk about you a bit: forget you. Don't forget to pray for him. Remember him in your prayers. Even Parnell. Ivy day dying out. Then they follow: dropping into a hole one after the other." Hynes, the Parnellite of *Ivy Day*, comes round to get the names of those present for the paper. He doesn't know Bloom's Christian name. Bloom supplies it and at the same time fulfils his promise to M'Coy to have his name put down. Both Hynes and Bloom have seen an unknown man in a macintosh hanging round—evidently a melancholy person who takes his morbid pleasure in graveyards and such places. He has disappeared as if by magic. Hynes asks his name.

"Macintosh. Yes I saw him," Mr. Bloom said. "Where is he now?"

"M'Intosh," Hynes said, scribbling. "I don't know who he is. Is that his name?" Bloom tries to shout a correction to his colleague, but Hynes is out of earshot.

Hynes proposes to some of the mourners a visit to Parnell's grave. Bloom, unheeded, follows on behind them. Why not put people's trades on the tombstones instead of dates and pious texts? A bird sitting tamely on the branch of a poplar reminds him that all graveyards are bird sanctuaries. And if we want to remember the dead why not supplement the photograph with gramophones of their voices? An obese, grey rat toddles among the pebbles of a crypt. Corpse is meat to him. Bloom prefers cremation to burial but "priests are dead against it." Coming to the cemetery gates he reflects that each visit brings him nearer to his own grave. But what of it? "Plenty to see and hear and feel yet. Feel live, warm beings near you. Let them sleep in their maggoty beds. They are not going to get me this innings. Warm beds: warm full-blooded life." He meets Martin Cunningham in the company of John Henry Menton. Bloom politely calls attention to a dent in the solicitor's hat and is rewarded with a hostile stare. Martin confirms Bloom's observation and at this John Henry Menton puts the matter right with a curt,

"Thank you," not addressed to Bloom. Marion's husband once had the better of a game of bowls with him and he can't forget it.

So far Bloom has prepared and eaten his breakfast, has guessed at an intrigue of his wife's and has carried on a little flirtation of his own. His body has functioned normally. He has met a few acquaintances, has had a bath and has attended a funeral. But all the time his mind has been busy. He has noted the present and reacted to it and he has remembered the past. He has walked and talked and all the while he has been thinking. What thoughts? Great or small? They were his own, the natural expression of his being. Joyce, in *Ulysses,* takes life as it is and represents it in its own material. Violences of temperament apart, his art resembles that of Rodin. He achieves the monumental through the organic, through the swift seizing of an infinite number of contours from the living model. There is a saying of Rodin's to the effect that what is visible in the human body is but a fraction of that which lies below the surface. Each undulation is a mountain peak the base of which lies below. As with the human body at rest, so with the human being in action. What a man does displays only a part, and that the smaller part, of his character. What he thinks and dreams is the greater part. That which is manifest in action is to the unacted part as the visible peak of the iceberg to the submerged, invisible mass.

The acts of the principal persons in *Ulysses* are shown with the accompaniment of their unspoken thoughts, memories, aspirations and the momentary impress of the world upon them through their senses. If we knew only their acts they would be no more to us than ingenious automatons, walking, talking, gesticulating mechanisms. They would remind us of that painting and sculpture which is a collection of gestures and grimaces. Borne along on the stream of their consciousness are all sorts of material. The present occupations of the thinker, his distant projects, recent and distant memories are supplemented by the sights, sounds and smells around him, by what he touches and tastes and by the well-being or malaise of his body. All this complicated mass of material is represented by Joyce as an impressionist painter might have rendered a view cross river—the foreground rushes, towpath and bushes, the water itself, the reflections of sky and opposite bank (church spire, roofs and trees), the boats and swans on the surface, the town and upward sweep of the thither bank and the sky over it all. It is to be noted that Bloom, Molly and Stephen, the three persons above all whose silent thoughts are recorded, each has his or her own peculiar character of thought: Stephen's, hither and thither darting, swallow-like; Bloom's, nose on the ground, like a dog on the scent; Molly's, an oleaginous, slow-moving stream, turning in every direction to find the lowest level. Not all thoughts are in words, but all other material is specialists' material. Words are the substance of everybody's thoughts.

Joyce uses the interior monologue (the phrase was coined by M. Valery Larbaud) principally in the earlier episodes of *Ulysses*. Except through this device it isn't easy to see how, given the one day plan of *Ulysses,* the past life of the people could have been conveyed to us. As it is we know not only the past, but the attitude of the people towards it, the outer manner and the inner comment, social form and the kind and degree of sensibility. It has been called "a photographic representation of a stream of consciousness." Why photographic? The word looks like contraband negative. It is more like impressionist painting. The shadows are full of colour; the whole is built up out of nuances instead of being constructed in broad masses; things are seen as immersed in a luminous fluid; colour supplies the modelling, and the total effect is arrived at through a countless number of small touches. Like impressionist art—any other art for that matter— it is an effort to approach reality. The conversations in *Ulysses* and in *A Portrait of the Artist as a Young Man* have been praised for their vividness. Sometimes we might think that a recording instrument had been hidden in the room or bar and whisked away when it had served the author's purpose. The Christmas dinner quarrel in *A Portrait of the Artist* is a case in point. Bloom's talk with M'Coy is another. No one said: "This is a gramophone record of a real conversation." If a dramatist is true to life it is said that the fourth wall was absent while his people held the scene, meaning to say that the matter, the tempo, the accent of life were there to perfection. The function of the interior monologue is, of course, the same as that of any monologue spoken on the stage—to make us acquainted with the persons and aware of their inner conflicts.

All writers of fiction do this in one way or another. The interior monologue is simply a convenient and intimate way. And although the device is largely associated with Joyce's *Ulysses* he never claimed any originality in the use of it. In the course of a conversation in his flat in the Universitätstrasse Joyce said to me:

"I try to give the unspoken, unacted thoughts of people in the way they occur. But I'm not the first one to do it. I took it from Dujardin. You don't know Dujardin? You should."

It was not until 1923 or '24 that Joyce met Dujardin. By that time Joyce's acknowledgment of his debt to the French writer was everywhere known. M. Dujardin presented Joyce with a copy of his book, *Les Lauriers Sont Coupés,* reprinted after thirty-five years of oblivion, containing the inscription: *"A James Joyce, maître illustre, mais surtout a celui qui a dit à l'homme mort et enseveli: Lazare lève toi."*

Some years later I called at Joyce's flat while he was writing on the flyleaf of the French *Ulysse.* He showed me the flyleaf. On it stood: *"A Edouard Dujardin, annonciateur de la parole intérieure. Le larron impénitent, James Joyce."*

Originality is in any case a much overrated quality. If Joyce began by taking the hero and incidents of the *Odyssey* as his example why should he stop at a technical device? Where Joyce took it he has said plainly enough. Who was first to invent it is still a question. Most new things turn out to be as old as the hills. All the very latest sculpture comes from past civilisations in Egypt, Central Africa and Yucatan. Dutch painters for a century produced immortal paintings without inventing anything new. And our great national poet beautified himself and our tongue with stories and technique taken wherever he could find them.

From Glasnevin cemetery Mr. Bloom goes to the offices of the *Freeman's Journal.* He is what is known in our day as a spacehound, an advertisement canvasser. Really it should be spacetimehound, seeing that he sells quantities of space for periods of time. This is the *Aeolus* episode. The newspaper office is the Cave of the Winds and Myles Crawford, editor-in-chief, is the god in charge of all the zephyrs, breezes, gales and hurricanes of hot air that blow out of it. It is squally weather. Mr. Bloom is blown out of his course by head winds, but with good seamanship keeps off a lee shore, and the calm finds him in deep water with all spars and sails intact. The episode is written in a style of all winds except the reliable trade wind. Mainly it is puffy and gusty. The whole is cut up into short fragments, each one being headlined in the breezy manner of an American sub-editor.

Alexander Keyes, tea, wine and spirit merchant, has an ad. in the *Freeman's Journal* and he has promised Bloom a renewal on condition that the design is changed. He wants an allusion to his name in the shape of a drawing of the crossed keys, emblem of the Manx Parliament. To get as much as possible for his money he wants also a par. in the Saturday pink *Telegraph*, an associated journal. Bloom's present task is to get consent to the change from all concerned. He takes a cutting of the *Freeman's* ad. from the advertisement clerk (who, having no responsibility in the matter, says they can do Keyes a par. if he wants one) and makes for the office of the foreman printer, Councillor Nannetti. On the way he meets Joe Hynes, from Nannetti's office, outward bound, and hails him. He tells Hynes that the cashier is just going to lunch but that if he hurries he'll catch him. This was not so altruistic as it looked. Hynes owes Bloom three shillings and Bloom's advice was intended as a hint. Hopes of a sub filling Hynes's sails, he vanishes in the direction of the cashier's office. The hint was lost.

Bloom explains the idea to Nannetti amid the clanking and roaring of the machines. Long use has made them noiseless to the foreman printer.

"We can do that," he said. "Let him give us a three months' renewal." Bloom will get the design of the crossed keys which has already appeared in a Kilkenny paper, but is not too pleased with the job of persuading Keyes to a three months' renewal. The time element complicates matters. "Want to get some wind off my chest first. Try it anyhow." He decides against making a tram journey to

Keyes with the chance of not finding him in. He will first
telephone in the office of the *Evening Telegraph*. Outside
the office door he hears laughter and voices. Inside he finds
Ned Lambert, Simon Dedalus and Professor MacHugh.
Ned Lambert is reading some particularly flatulent nonsense about the beauty of Ireland to the accompaniment
of his hearers' laughs and protests.

"What is it?" Mr. Bloom asked.

"A recently discovered fragment of Cicero's," Professor
MacHugh answered, with pomp of tone. *"Our Lovely
Land."*

"Whose land?" Mr. Bloom said simply.

A violently opening door hits Bloom in the back with
its knob and J. J. O'Molloy enters. He is a barrister with
a dwindling practice, failing health and many debts, come,
as Bloom shrewdly surmises, to raise the wind. The inner
door flies open, admitting Myles Crawford. "A scarlet
beaked face crested by a comb of feathery hair." Simon
Dedalus suggests a drink to wash down Dawson's super-
fatted prose and Bloom, seeing the coast clear, steers
neatly through the door of the sanctum to the telephone.
In the doorway, returning from the phone, he collides
with Lenehan entering with sports tissues. Lenehan
broadcasts his tip for the Gold Cup, Sceptre, with O. Madden up. Bloom has heard on the telephone that Keyes is
in Dillon's auction rooms and he leaves with the editor's
blessing to fix up the crosskeys ad. Newsboys follow in his
wake, mimicking his awkward walk. The four who are
left are in the middle of a discussion on Greek, Roman,
Egyptian, Hebrew and modern civilisation when Stephen
appears in the company of O'Madden Burke, an occasional contributor, and hands to the editor Mr. Deasy's
letter on the foot and mouth disease. Myles Crawford's
suggestion to Stephen that he shall write something for

the paper leads him through a conversational eddy to the great feat of journalism of Ignatius Gallagher who cabled to the *New York World* the story of the Phœnix Park murders.

Excitedly he turns over the *Freeman's* files and describes to them Gallagher's brainwave. This super journalist had used the letters of an advertisement in the *Freeman's Journal* to cable a sketch map of the scene of the crime, and the route taken by the murderers, to the New York paper. In the middle of his speech Bloom is reported on the phone and he promptly orders that Bloom shall be told to go to hell. As an epilogue to his story he pours scorn on the younger generation of journalists without flair, of orators without eloquence. His mouth, curled in disdain, reminds Stephen of his own poem composed on Sandymount Strand:

> *On swift sail flaming,*
> *From storm and south,*
> *He comes, pale vampire,*
> *Mouth to my mouth.*

Bright coloured rhymes of Italian verse—green, rose and gold—mock the heavy colouring of his own. The Italian rhymes are gaily dressed girls dancing. "But I old men, penitent, leadenfooted, underdarkneath the night: mouth south: tomb womb."

J. J. O'Molloy takes up cudgels for the younger generation. He cites the eloquence of Seymour Bushe, who defended the accused in the Childs murder case.

"He spoke on the law of evidence," J. J. O'Molloy said, "and of Roman justice as contrasted with the earlier Mosaic code, the *lex talionis*. And he cited the Moses of Michelangelo in the Vatican. . . . He said of it: *that stony effigy in frozen music, horned and terrible, of the*

human form divine, that eternal symbol of wisdom and
prophecy which, if aught that the imagination or the hand
of sculptor has wrought in marble of soul-transfigured and
of soul-transfiguring deserves to live, deserves to live."

Professor MacHugh caps his quotation of Seymour
Bushe with a speech by John F. Taylor, improvised on
the occasion of a debate on the Irish language. The subject of Bushe's eloquence was Roman and Mosaic law: that
of John F. Taylor defended the use of the Irish tongue by
reference to the Hebrew affirmation of nationhood in
Egyptian captivity. But when Professor MacHugh has
come to an end Stephen has had enough oratory. His
salary is burning his pocket. His motion that the house
do adjourn for a drink is declared by self-appointed chairman Lenehan to be carried unanimously. They went, presumably, to the Mooney's in Abbey Street. They are already under way when Bloom reappears in a great hurry.
He has seen Keyes and Keyes will renew his ad. for two
months, but wants a puff in both *Freeman's* and the *Evening Telegraph*. The lord of the airs is explosive. He
despatches Bloom to Keyes with a rude counter-message
that Bloom will not deliver. The patient vendor of space-
time allows the squall to pass, regarding with solicitude the
receding back view of Stephen's relatively new but dirty
boots. "The last time I saw him he had his heels on view.
Been walking in muck somewhere. Careless chap. What
was he doing in Irishtown?"

Stephen has also a story to tell and tells it to a full audience on the way to Mooney's. Two poor old dames on a
day's outing climb to the top of Nelson's pillar. They take
with them brawn and bread to eat and they buy four and
twenty ripe plums from a girl at the foot of the column for
their thirst. Sitting on the top platform of the monument
they look up at the statue of the "onehandled adulterer"

as they entitle the great English sea captain. But it gives them a crick in the neck, so they turn to their plums, slowly eating them and spitting the stones through the railings on to the heads of the people below, if any. "He gave a sudden, loud, young laugh as a close. . . . 'Finished?' Myles Crawford said." These are the two phases of Stephen's art, the low-toned, elegiac verse that he speaks to himself and the Rowlandsonesque sketch of the two elderly Dublin dames. It is a realistic, grotesque sketch of Dublin life and evidently it puzzles his hearers as much as it pleases them. They expect a literary point of some sort but there is none. The point lies in the seeing of it.

One of the problems that confronted Joyce continually in the composition of *Ulysses* was the spatial and psychological position of his hero, Leopold Bloom. In the first three episodes he completely dominates the foreground. In the fourth, *Aeolus,* he wanders in and out. Sometimes in the book he is right in the front of the stage. At others he is seen only indistinctly among the supers or he has vanished in the wings. In the fifth episode, the *Lestrygonians,* he again holds the centre of the stage. It is lunch time and there is no further business to be done. Keyes must be left for the moment. The greater part of the *Lestrygonians* is Bloom's unspoken thoughts on his way to lunch. It differs from the other interior monologue in substance and rhythm. Its substance is coloured by the state of his body, and the rhythm is that of the digestive organs, the peristaltic movement.

As they go east Bloom goes south, riverwards. A young Y.M.C.A. man has pushed into his unsuspecting hand a handbill announcing the visit of Dr. John Alexander Dowie. Indifferently regarding "Blood of the Lamb," Bloom notes that God is always asking for blood on some pretext or other. "Birth, hymen, martyr, war, foundation

of a building, sacrifice." Just as regularly his professed
ministers ask for money. The year before it was Torry
and Alexander of Glory Song fame. Looking along Bachelor's Walk he sees Dilly Dedalus outside Dillon's auction
rooms, waiting for her father, and pities the child for her
tattered clothes and undernourished body. She is one of
a large family, and Bloom condemns that cruel and senseless theology borrowed from the tribal necessities of his
own race, that commands the poor to bring unfeedable
mouths into the world. He flings the Dowie handbill to
the gulls off O'Connell Bridge, but they are not gullible
enough to dive for it, so he buys them a Banbury cake.
A placard pasted on a moored rowboat catches his approv-
ing publicity eye. Quack doctors' ads. pasted up in men's
urinals are also appropriately placed. Suppose Boylan
were afflicted with. . . . But he banishes the thought. A
string of sandwichboardmen heaves in sight on the other
side of the bridge. The letters on their tall white hats spell
H-E-L-Y-S. He once worked for the big Dame Street sta-
tioner and printer and remembers how his employer
turned down his excellent publicity notions. The best one
was to have a transparent showcart with two smart girls in
it writing. "Smart girls writing something catch the eye
at once." That was in the early years of his married life.
The fun they had bathing the baby daughter, the suppers
and the chats at night.

"Stream of life" recurs in one form or another throughout the *Lestrygonians* episode. Generation after generation flowing from the cradle to the grave. And the process
is repeated on a small scale by the human intestines daily
taking in nourishment and throwing out waste. In West-
moreland Street he meets Mrs. Breen, an old flame of his.
She is now married to an elderly man suffering from persecution mania. A practical joker has just sent him a post-

card, bearing the words, U.P. up, and he is running round, getting legal advice with a view to claiming ten thousand pounds damages from the unknown who sent it. To change the subject Bloom asks after their common friend, Mina Purefoy, and is told that she has been in the lying-in hospital three days expecting a baby. This is another family with religion and a high birth rate, Protestant this time. But Mrs. Breen catches sight of her husband struggling with huge law books and hurries off to look after him. Just before she goes one of the Dublin oddities of *Ulysses* passes them. It is Cashel Boyle O'Connor Fitzmaurice Tisdall Farrell, whose form of harmless idiocy consists in walking outside the lamp posts of the city at top speed, talking to himself.

Mr. Bloom passes the offices of the *Irish Times*. It was in this paper that, with ulterior motives, he advertised for a young lady to assist gentleman with literary work. The Martha correspondence is the outcome of that advertisement. He thinks with a sympathetic shudder of women's childbirth agony. Why not twilight sleep? And why not a state endowment at birth for every child as an insurance against poverty and to give them a start in life at the age of twenty-one? A squad of constables going on their beats reminds him of a students' counterdemonstration when Joseph Chamberlain was given his degree in Trinity. An innocent passer-by on that occasion, he was almost ridden down by mounted policemen. He has no patience with the rebel politics of youth. "Silly billies: mob of young cubs yelling their guts out. Vinegar Hill. The Butter exchange band. Few years time half of them magistrates and civil servants. War comes on: into the army helter-skelter: same fellows used to whether on the scaffold high." Another aspect of the stream of life is suggested by the constant procession of trams before Trinity's surly front.

"Trams passed one another, ingoing, outgoing, clanging. Useless words. Things go on same; day after day:
squads of police marching out, back: trams in, out. Those
two loonies mooching about. Dignam carted off. Mina
Purefoy swollen belly on a bed groaning to have a child
tugged out of her. One born every second somewhere.
Other dying every second. Since I fed the birds five minutes. Three hundred kicked the bucket. Other three hundred born, washing the blood off, all are washed in the
blood of the lamb, bawling maaaaa."

He had just been thinking about Parnell in connection
with nationalist demonstrations and the brother of the
great chief passes on the other side of the street. How like
in form; in action how unlike. The chief used men as
pawns for his cause. His brother plays chess in a teashop.
Another famous Dublin figure passes: A. E. the poet. In
homespun tweeds he is pushing a bicycle with an ill-
dressed literary-looking lady at his side. Another coincidence: one of the replies to his ad. in the *Irish Times*
came from Lizzie Twigg. Her literary efforts, she said, had
met with the approval of Mr. Russell. Might this lady
with the loose stockings be Lizzie Twigg? He is now at
the corner of Nassau Street and Grafton Street and stops
to look into the window of Yeates and Son. Astronomy is
Mr. Bloom's hobby. He thinks of sunspots and of the
eclipse due later in the year. Parallax is a word that bothers him. He might go out to Dunsink and talk to the professor about it. A fortnight ago was new moon and that
was the night he was walking by the Tolka with Marion
and Boylan. No doubt they were already flirting with
touches of hands. He sees Bob Doran (hero, timid and
trapped, of the story, "The Boarding House," in *Dubliners*) sloping into the Empire pub. M'Coy told him earlier
in the day that Doran was on one of his periodical binges.

Some years back the Empire was a theatre. "I was happier then. Or was I? Twenty-eight I was. She twenty-three. When we left Lombard Street West something changed. Could never like it again after Rudy. Can't bring back time. Like holding water in your hand. . . ."

He is now in Grafton Street, smartest of the shopping thoroughfares of Dublin. A shop window dressed with women's silk petticoats and stockings fills his mind with amorous longings and he turns Combridge's corner still pursued by perfume of embraces. Entering the Burton Restaurant, a mixed stink of food and clatter of hurried eating shatters his luxurious vision of silk-clad, perfumed women's bodies. Lunchers are perched on high stools at the bar, sitting at tables in the body of the room. Bloom is appalled by the stink, clatter and messiness of man-filled eating houses and, with a face-saving pantomime of looking for a friend, turns at the door and goes away. He almost becomes a convert to vegetarianism. It is clean, causes no pain to animals and is more aesthetic. ". . . Poor, trembling calves. Meh. Staggering bob. Bubble and squeak. Butcher's buckets wobble lights. Give us that brisket off the hook. Plup. Rawhead and bloody bones. Flayed, glass-eyed sheep hung from their haunches, sheepsnouts bloody-papered snivelling nosejam on sawdust. . . ." Bloom turns into Davy Byrne's pub in Duke Street.

Davy Byrne's is still going strong and is the same "moral pub" it was on June 16, 1904. The amiable proprietor still "stands a drink now and then" but, well advanced in years, is no longer to be seen behind the bar in shirt sleeves, serving and counting. The bar, too, is the same "nice piece of wood" on which Bloom gazed with quiet admiration, except that it has been shortened by a foot or two to make room for a private bar at the Duke Street end. Bloom calls for a Gorgonzola sandwich and a glass of

Burgundy. While he is dabbing mustard on his cheese, Nosey Flynn, sitting at the counter, asks him about the concert tour.

"Ay, now I remember," Nosey Flynn said, putting his hand in his pocket to scratch his groin. "Who is this was telling me? Isn't Blazes Boylan mixed up in it?"

"A warm shock of air heat of mustard hauched on Mr. Bloom's heart."

A sip of wine steadies him and he replies with composure that indeed Boylan is managing the tour. Flynn goes on to laud the astuteness of Blazes as boxer manager and then proceeds to discuss the chances of the horses engaged in the Gold Cup. Bloom is no gambler and tenders no opinion. His prelunch fleshly yearnings turn to recollections of pleasures enjoyed. He remembers a day on Howth Head with Marion. "Ravished over her I lay, full lips open. Kissed her mouth. Yum. Softly she gave me in my mouth the seed cake warm and chewed. . . ." The fine curves and material of the bar woodwork fuse in his mind with the curves of women's flesh. "Curves the world admires." He resolves to call at the library museum and see for himself how the sculptor deals with the back views of goddesses. While Bloom is away in the rear of the premises, Flynn and the publican discuss him. With winks to his words Flynn tells Davy Byrne that Bloom doesn't buy cream for his wife on the commission he picks up canvassing ads. for the *Freeman's Journal*. Bloom is a Mason and the craft help him. The publican remarks that although he has seen Bloom often he has never seen him the worse for drink, and Flynn adds that when the fun gets too hot Bloom will always consult his watch and vanish.

" 'He's not too bad,' Nosey Flynn said, snuffling it up. 'He has been known to put his hand down, too, to help a fellow. Give the devil his due. Oh, Bloom has his good points. But there's one thing he'll never do.'

"His hand scrawled a dry pen signature beside his grog.

" 'I know,' Davy Byrne said.

" 'Nothing in black and white,' Nosey Flynn said.

"Paddy Leonard and Bantam Lyons came in. Tom Rochford followed, a plaining hand on his claret waistcoat."

Bloom greets all with uplifted three fingers on his way out. Bantam Lyons whispers to the others that he has a tip from Bloom for the Gold Cup, but doesn't tell them the name of the horse or how Bloom gave it. He is alluding to Bloom's remark that he was about to throw away his *Freeman's Journal.* Lyons has yet to meet the professional tipster, Lenehan, and be laughed off his fancy by the book of form. In Dawson Street, on his way to the National Library, Mr. Bloom meets a blind stripling and pilots him across the road to the corner of Molesworth Street. A post office reminds him that he must answer Martha's letter. He sees Sir Frederick Falkiner going into the Freemasons' Hall and thinks of the slating the softhearted judge gave the crookback moneylender. But then, he is "really what they call a dirty Jew." Near his goal in Kildare Street he sights Blazes Boylan. A meeting with his wife's lover would be most unwelcome, especially as his cheeks are flushed with Burgundy. To avoid the encounter he makes for the Museum with quicker, longer strides, keeping his eye from roving by searching for nothing in his pockets.

" 'I am looking for that. Yes, that. Try all pockets. Handker. *Freeman.* Where did I? Ah, yes. Trousers. Purse. Potato. Where did I?'

" 'Hurry. Walk quietly. Moment more. My heart.'

"His hand looking for the where did I put found in his

hip pocket soap lotion have to call tepid paper stuck. Ah, soap there! Yes. Gate. Safe!"

Joyce's first question when I had read a completed episode or when he had read out a passage of an uncompleted one was always: "How does Bloom strike you?"

Technical considerations, problems of homeric correspondence, the chemistry of the human body, were secondary matters. If Bloom was first it was not that the others were unimportant but that, seen from the outside, they were not a problem. At about the time of the publication of the *Lestrygonians* episode he said to me:

"I have just got a letter asking me why I don't give Bloom a rest. The writer of it wants more Stephen. But Stephen no longer interests me to the same extent. He has a shape that can't be changed."

Bloom should grow upon the reader throughout the day. His reactions to things displayed in his unspoken thoughts should be not brilliant but singular, organic, Bloomesque. Joyce delighted in many of the natural, quick sayings of his Greek friends in Zürich, but all were too imaginative for his Dublin Jew. Typical of Bloom's character is the thought that occurs to him as he looks at the cat in the kitchen in Eccles Street. He first supposes that to her he looks like a tower but corrects himself. "Height of a tower? No, she can jump over me."

An infinite number of small touches builds up Bloom's character: his guess at the sensibility of the blind, his judgment of student politics, his simple question, not ironically intended, "Whose land?" in the *Telegraph* office, his remembering how the poplin industry came to Ireland, his taking note of Stephen's relatively new but muddied boots, his sympathetic talk with Mrs. Breen, his care to avoid waking the sleeping horse, his nervous avoidance of Boylan, his calmly unresentful acceptance of John

Henry Menton's and Myles Crawford's snubs, and so on.

Joyce in Zürich was a curious collector of facts about the human body, especially on that borderland where mind and body meet, where thought is generated and shaped by a state of the body. Bloom is led on to lunch by erotic visions. After his bread and cheese and Burgundy he lives in erotic memories. "Sun's heat it is. Seems to a secret touch telling me memory. Touched his sense moistened remembered."

"Fermented drink must have had a sexual origin," said Joyce to me one day. "In a woman's mouth, probably. I have made Bloom eat Molly's chewed seed cake."

I told him I had just read a German book in which was described a tribal orgy on a South Sea island. The drink was prepared by the women of the tribe. They chewed a certain herb and spat the pulp into a huge crock out of which the men then drank.

Alluding once to the end of the first episode I said:

"You remember that H. G. Wells, in writing about *A Portrait of the Artist as a Young Man,* says you have a cloacal obsession. What would he say to this?"

"Cloacal obsession!" said Joyce. "Why, it's Wells's countrymen who build water-closets wherever they go. But that's all right. H. G. Wells is a very appreciative critic of my writings. There's only one kind of critic I do resent."

"And that is?"

"The kind that affects to believe that I am writing with my tongue in my cheek."

CHAPTER VI

"Don't you think," said Joyce, "that early afternoon is the time of greatest brain activity?"

I vaguely thought it wasn't so in my case but, besides my own experience, I had no facts on which to generalise.

"The brain," he said, "is the organ presiding over *Scylla and Charybdis*. The Aristotelian and Platonic philosophies are the monsters that lie in wait in the narrows for the thinker."

This episode is foreshadowed when, on the way to the bathing cove, Mulligan tells Haines that Stephen has a Hamlet theory all his own. Haines, ever ready to add something to his scrap book, wants to hear it at once, but Mulligan protests: "Wait till I have a few pints in me first," and calls on Stephen to affirm that he couldn't state it on less than three pints. The reason Stephen gives is: "We are always tired in the morning. And it is rather long to tell." But his theory is with him all day. Undertones of it creep into his monologue on the beach at Sandymount, and his mind constantly reverts to it in the *Telegraph* office. He has a rendezvous at the National Library, at any rate intends going there, and it is there that he will expound it. More or less subconsciously he is seeking for anything that will add to his argument or give force to his exposition. When J. J. O'Molloy commands silence to give them a taste of Seymour Bushe's oratory a line occurs to Stephen: "And in the porches of mine ear did pour . . ." He notes a lack of probability, and thinks:

"By the way, how did he find that out? He died in his sleep. Or the other story, beast with two backs?"

While Professor MacHugh is capping the eloquence of Bushe with that of John F. Taylor the spirally upcurling smoke of cigarettes brings to his mind the words from *Cymbeline:* "And let our crooked smokes . . ." A few minutes later, on the way to Mooney's: " 'You remind me of Antisthenes,' the professor said, 'a disciple of Gorgias, the sophist. It is said of him that none could tell if he were bitterer against others or against himself. He was the son of a nobleman and a bondwoman. And he wrote a book in which he took away the palm of beauty from Argive Helen and gave it to poor Penelope.'

" 'Poor Penelope. Penelope Rich.' "

The question of brain activity in the early afternoon is perhaps associated with the question of lunch. A light lunch may stimulate, and a heavy one retard it. Stephen's has consisted of the drinks he has had in Mooney's with the journalists. He has eaten nothing, and cannot have had fewer than three drinks. The episode opens in the National Library with Stephen facing an audience of four, John Eglinton, Mr. Best, Mr. Lyster and A. E., the poet, prepared to expound his theory and sparring for an opening.

If in *Hamlet* more than in any of the other plays is to be sought Shakespeare's own tragedy and personality, with which of the characters is the poet to be identified? General opinion answers: with Prince Hamlet himself. Hamlet's passion and despair are Shakespeare's own heart-cry. Stephen holds, on the contrary, that Shakespeare is to be identified with the ghost of the murdered king, the part that, as actor, he himself played; Hamlet, the prince, with young Hamnet Shakespeare, who died at the age of twelve; Ann Shakespeare, born Hathaway, with the guilty queen;

and Gilbert, Richard and Edmund, the poet's brothers, with the murderous usurper. Ann Hathaway was eight years older than William Shakespeare, and Stephen assumes that she took the initiative in their love. Under pressure probably from down Shottery way, William did the right thing by Ann, but left her after three years of domesticity to seek his fortune in the capital. While he was away his brothers became his wife's lovers. The poet never forgot Ann's victory over himself—he is the Adonis overborne by the aggressive Venus—and he never forgave Ann's marital infidelity. The birth of their granddaughter, Elizabeth Hall, brought about a reconciliation, but that reconciliation was neither deep nor lasting enough to prevent his shaming her in his will with the legacy of his second-best bed.

After two false starts John Eglinton gives him an opening of which he takes advantage.

" 'He will have it that Hamlet is a ghost story,' John Eglinton said for Mr. Best's behoof. 'Like the fat boy in Pickwick he wants to make our flesh creep. . . .'

" 'What is a ghost?' Stephen said with tingling energy. 'One who has faded into impalpability through death, through absence, through change of manners. . . .' "

Stephen captures his hearers' imagination with a picture of Shakespeare walking from the Huguenot's house in Silver Street to the theatre and in the rôle of the spectre, addressing Burbage, who is playing Hamlet, bidding him list.

". . . To a son he speaks, the son of his soul, the prince, young Hamlet, and to the son of his body, Hamnet Shakespeare who has died in Stratford that his namesake might live for ever.

"Is it possible that that player Shakespeare, a ghost by absence, and in the vesture of buried Denmark, a ghost

by death, speaking his own words to his own son's name
(had Hamnet Shakespeare lived he would have been
Prince Hamlet's twin)—is it possible, I want to know, or
probable that he did not draw or foresee the logical conclusion of those premises: you are the dispossessed son:
I am the murdered father: your mother is the guilty
queen, Ann Shakespeare, born Hathaway."

A. E. objects. The plays are there and they are immortal. Let us enjoy and appreciate them and leave the poet's
private life alone. Stephen is hostile to A. E. and all that
he stands for and A. E. dislikes Stephen. But Stephen's
hostility cannot make him forget that A. E. lent him a
guinea and that he has no reasonable prospect of paying
it back. John Eglinton's voice recalls him from his inner
dialectic with the observation that Ann "died for literature at least, before she was born."

"The world believes that Shakespeare made a mistake,"
he said, "and got out of it as quickly and as best he could."
Stephen affirms that the man of genius makes no mistakes.
"His errors are volitional and are the portals of discovery."
There is every reason for supposing that Ann had beauty.
The poet who created the handsome shrew, Katherine,
and the much-loved Cleopatra knew what beauty was in
a woman. No doubt but that Ann was comely but Shakespeare did not choose her. She chose him.

". . . She put the comether on him, sweet and twenty-
six. The greyeyed goddess who bends over the boy Adonis,
stooping to conquer, as prologue to the swelling act, is a
boldfaced Stratford wench who tumbles in a cornfield a
lover younger than herself."

A. E. gets up to go. Contemptuous comment, unspoken,
on the mystic, his disciples, his practices patters through
Stephen's mind while the leave-taking speeches buzz in his
ear. A useful lull in the talk enables him to approach

A. E. with a copy of Mr. Deasy's letter. Will he publish it? A. E. promises with ifs that it shall be published. "The door closed behind the outgoer" and the discussion is resumed.

John Eglinton and Mr. Best note that the plays of the later period breathe a spirit of reconciliation.

"There can be no reconciliation," Stephen said, "if there has not been a sundering. . . . If you want to know what are the events which cast their shadow over the hell of time of *King Lear, Othello, Hamlet, Troilus and Cressida,* look to see when and how the shadow lifts. What softens the heart of a man, shipwrecked in storms dire, tried like another Ulysses, Pericles, prince of Tyre? . . . A child, a girl placed in his arms, Marina."

This is the birth of Shakespeare's first grandchild. Mr. Best creates a diversion by mentioning the sonnets. It proves to be a new path of approach to the seduction part of Stephen's theory. Why did Shakespeare send his fair young friend to woo for him his lady coloured ill? She was more than approachable. She was "a bay where all men ride, a maid of honour with a scandalous girlhood. . . ." Whence the feeling of inferiority evident in such a delegation of his lover's risks and privileges? Why was it not enough that he was a lord of language and successful in the affairs of the world? Stephen's answer is that it was because Ann Hathaway's conquest of him had killed his belief in himself as a lover.

"He was overborne in a cornfield first (ryefield I should say) and he will never be a victor in his own eyes after nor play victoriously the game of laugh and lie down. Assumed dongiovannism will not save him. No later undoing will undo the first undoing. . . . He goes back, weary of the creation he has piled up to hide him from himself, an old dog licking an old sore. But, because loss is his gain, he passes on towards eternity in undiminished personality untaught by the wisdom he has written or by the laws he has revealed. His beaver is up. He is a ghost, a shadow now, the wind by Elsinore's rocks or what you will, the sea's voice, a voice heard only in the heart of him who is the substance of his shadow, the son consubstantial with the father.

" 'Amen!' responded from the doorway."

It is the unwelcome Buck Mulligan come to break the force of Stephen's argument and the spell of his eloquence with a jest. There is a general dispersal of interest during which Stephen's thoughts come to rest on himself. He is poor, insufficiently esteemed, unloved, and surrounded by half friends. Mulligan comes towards him with the telegram he sent to them, the quotation from Meredith's *The Ordeal of Richard Feverel:* The sentimentalist is he who would enjoy without incurring the immense debtorship for a thing done. The Buck reproaches him in the manner of Synge for not coming to the "Ship" to stand them drinks as arranged. Then, in his own voice, he assures Stephen that Synge is out to murder him on account of a practical joke of which Stephen is innocent. Stephen had met Synge in Paris, and the clash of their temperaments had produced heat but no light.

"Harsh gargoyle face that warred against me over our mess of hash of lights in rue Saint-André-des-Arts. In words of words for words, palabras. Oisin with Patrick. Faunman he met in Clamart woods, brandishing a wine-bottle. *C'est vendredi saint!* Murthering Irish. His image, wandering, he met. I mine. I met a fool i' the forest."

Then the card of a caller is sent in to the librarian. It is that of Bloom who wants to see the *Kilkenny People* to copy the design for Keyes' advertisement. Mulligan recognises him and gleefully tells Stephen he has just seen the "sheeny" in the museum, regarding intently the back view of a plaster cast of a Venus.

John Eglinton and Mr. Best want to hear more about Ann Shakespeare. Hitherto they had thought of her as a patient Griselda, a Penelope stay-at-home. Stephen draws for them a picture of life in those days and supposes that the poet's amorous adventures were many whatever his inward grief might be. He concludes: "But all those twenty years what do you suppose poor Penelope in Stratford was doing behind the diamond panes?" Buck Mulligan challenges him to name whom he suspects. Stephen retorts that the burden of proof lies with them. If they deny that Shakespeare branded his wife with infamy in the fifth act of *Hamlet* they have to explain why there is no mention of her in the thirty-four years between the day she married him and the day she buried him. Or only one: while he was living in luxury in London she had to borrow forty shillings from her father's shepherd to pay a debt. True, his swansong, the will, exists but in the first draft of it she is not mentioned at all and when, perhaps under pressure, he includes her in the final draft, he leaves her his second-best bed. Shakespeare was a man who loved money. From his debtors he exacted the uttermost farthing, and "a man who holds so tightly to what he calls his rights over what he calls his debts will hold tightly also to what he calls his rights over her whom he calls his wife."

He brings in his mother's name in the forest of Arden, and her death inspired him to the scene with Volumnia in *Coriolanus*. We can identfy the girl women and the grown women, bold, capricious and passionate. His own name appears slily in corners of the plays and copiously in the sonnets. But there are three other members of his family, his brothers, Gilbert, Edmund and Richard. Edmund and

Richard appear in the plays as usurpers, traitors and adulterers.

Stephen's argument is complete. Brothers Gilbert, Richard and Edmund are the usurping king; the long since dead Hamnet is the young Prince Hamlet; Ann Shakespeare-Hathaway is the treacherous queen; and the poet himself is the ghost of the wronged and murdered king. Shakespeare was overborne by a woman older than himself. He left her and came to London. During his absence his brothers supplanted him. Ann Hathaway ravished him; Ann Shakespeare betrayed him. He could forget neither her victory nor her treachery. His son's death darkened his life, and the shadow of that event spread over the great tragedies. The birth of his granddaughter lightened his own darkness and illumined the later plays.

Parallel with his Hamlet theory runs Stephen's conception of the nature of fatherhood. This has its bearing on his argument and on his own family conflict. As it occurs in *Scylla and Charybdis* it is the dominant father motive of the action of the book, stated as a theological mystery. In Stephen's words:

"A father is a necessary evil. He wrote the play in the months that followed his father's death. If you hold that he, a greying man with two marriageable daughters, with thirty-five years of life, *nel mezzo del cammin di nostr vita,* with fifty of experience, is the beardless undergraduate from Wittenberg, then you must hold that his seventy-year-old mother is the lustful queen. No. The corpse of John Shakespeare does not walk the night. From hour to hour it rots and rots. He rests disarmed of fatherhood, having devised that mystical estate upon his son. . . . Who is the father of any son that any son should love him or he any son? . . . The son unborn mars beauty: born, he brings pain, divides affection, increases care. He is a male: his growth is his father's decline, his youth his father's envy, his friend his father's enemy. . . . When Rutlandbaconsouthamptonshakespeare or another poet of the same name in the comedy of errors wrote *Hamlet* he was not the father of his own son merely but, being no more a son, he was and felt himself the father of all his race, the father of his own grandfather, the father of his unborn grandson who, by the same token, never was born. . . ."

Asked by John Eglinton if he believes his own theory, Stephen promptly says "No." Something has gone wrong with the atmosphere. He came expecting, probably, to get a commission for an article in *Dana,* and now he sees that there is no chance at all. Mulligan has spoilt the *Stimmung,* and John Eglinton can't see why he should expect payment for something in which he doesn't believe. He leaves the library in Mulligan's wake. "I gall his kibe." Mulligan is in high spirits, drinks in prospect. Stephen is dull, washed out, tired. Mulligan has written a sketch of a bawdy comedy during the discussion and reads it to Stephen with gusto but without success. The only thought of which Stephen's tired mind is capable, apart from certain stairwit connected with the discussion, is prompted and shaped by enmity to Mulligan. But the Buck goes on to jape over the listeners in the library, and persists in regarding Stephen's theory as a big, colourful joke. Bloom, leaving the reading-room, doubtless with a tracing of the *Kilkenny People* design in his pocket, stares at Stephen and greets him. Mulligan bids Stephen beware, affecting to regard the "sheeny" as a pederast with designs on the youthful bard.

"What do you think of Buck Mulligan in this episode?" said Joyce when I returned the typescript.

"He is witty and entertaining as ever," I said.

"He should begin to pall on the reader as the day goes on," Joyce said.

"The comic man usually wearies," I said, "if he keeps it up too long. But I can't say that Buck Mulligan wearies me."

"And to the extent that Buck Mulligan's wit wears threadbare," Joyce continued, "Bloom's justness and reasonableness should grow in interest. As the day wears on Bloom should overshadow them all."

"But Bloom?" I said. "In this episode he hardly comes in at all."

"Bloom is like a battery that is being recharged," said Joyce. "He will act with all the more vigour when he does reappear."

The Stephen of *Scylla and Charybdis* is the Stephen of the *Telemachus* episode with which *Ulysses* begins. His unspoken thoughts reveal to us the same mood of hostility, suspicion, envy. The difference is that the bored tiredness of eight in the morning has given place to the energy and mental activity of middle day. He is stimulated, too, with the three drams of usquebaugh he has bought with Dan Deasy's ducats and with the task of expounding a pet theory to a resistant audience. His exposition is accompanied by an undercurrent of thought critical or contemptuous of his hearers. Why should he be critical and contemptuous of them? The reason seems to be that he meditates greater work than in these surroundings he can produce. He must live and learn to find himself, but not here. Early in the morning he announced to himself his resolve not to sleep in the tower that night, which means in fact that he will sleep there no more. Now he augments that resolve with another. He will leave Dublin altogether. Dublin is a round of drink, women, talk; always repetition but no growth. Even the force of his own pride is sapped when he sees himself in the mirror of his associates. Leaving the library with Mulligan, he thinks:

"Part. The moment is now." Where then? If Socrates leave his house to-day, if Judas go forth to-night. Why? That lies in space which I in time must come to, ineluctably.

"My will: his will that fronts me. Seas between."

I never knew to what extent Joyce himself was attached to the theory expounded by Stephen. Presumably if he had never at any time held to it he would not have made it the theme of an episode in *Ulysses*. In one respect the Joyce of Zürich resembled the Stephen of *Scylla and Charybdis*. Shakespeare the man, the lord of language, the creator of persons, occupied him more than Shakespeare the maker of plays. And Stephen refers to the sonnets as sugared.

So far no critic of Joyce's *Ulysses* has mentioned Stephen's theory to approve or refute it. It seems to me that as there is no direct evidence on the question of the bard's lovemaking, Stephen's hypothesis must be taken as reasonably likely, but not more so than the contrary, for the passion of the eighteen-year-old boy for the woman of thirty is common enough. However, at eighteen, though he probably had never loved a woman, Shakespeare certainly had experience of sex, eighteen years of it. Everything that he was and everything that he was to become was present in him, though he had many miles and years to go to find it. The twig was bent: the tree was inclined. If he was "overborne in a cornfield," why was he overborne? Because he willed it. In the language of Stephen, it was a portal of discovery, but a portal to which he had been advancing all the years of his life.

And what about the brothers? Here the evidence entirely contradicts Stephen's hypothesis. Richard was ten years William's junior, and Edmund sixteen, so that by the time Richard was eighteen Ann was thirty-six and by the time Edmund had reached cornfield age Ann was forty-two. It is generally supposed, too, that women aged more quickly in the sixteenth century than they do in our own day. But grant Ann exceptional vitality, and even then Richard and Edmund look very unlikely as her lovers. They seem much more probable playfellows for Susanna and Judith. Gilbert, the possible brother rival in point of age, is not mentioned in the plays. However, all men are brothers, and as symbols of universal male rivalry those of his blood might serve.

If Shakespeare neglected his family as bread provider, if he neither visited Stratford nor sent money there, how did Ann and their daughters live? Goldsmith's notes or coin of the realm, sent or taken, they must have had. If Ann really borrowed two pounds from her father's shepherd on one occasion her credit must have been sound or the good shepherd would never have lent it. Many an embarrassed woman has borrowed money rather than confess to having overspent.

Long absence, hints of poverty, second-best bed: all this has an air of complete estrangement if viewed from a certain angle, more, of absolute enmity. But Stephen says there was a reconciliation at the time Elizabeth Hall was born. It must have been a reconciliation of a very superficial order if the old grief persisted to the extent of permitting Shakespeare to disinherit Ann. But did he? Second-best bed sounds ungenerous, but was there a best bed? "It is clear that there were two beds, a best and a second-best, Mr. Second-best Best said finely." It is just possible, however, that Susannah took the best bed when she got married, and that the second-best was willed to Ann to save it from the deadly swoop of Judith.

But all this is a matter for Shakespeare scholars. What is indisputably true is the remark of John Eglinton when Stephen's exposition was ended.

" 'The truth is midway,' he affirmed. 'He is the ghost and the prince. He is all in all.' "

Stephen agrees, and in an eloquent parting speech, hat and ashplant in hand, ready to go, blows his own theory sky-high.

" 'He is,' Stephen said. 'The boy of act one is the mature man of act five. All in all. In *Cymbeline*, in *Othello* he is bawd and cuckold. He acts and is acted on. Lover of an ideal or a perversion, like José he kills the real Carmen. His unremitting intellect is the hornmad Iago ceaselessly willing that the moor in him shall suffer. . . . Every life is many days, day after day. We walk through ourselves, meeting robbers, ghosts, giants, old men, young men, wives, widows, brothers-in-love. But always meeting ourselves. . . .' "

All the persons represented, ghost king and usurper, queen and young prince as well as Ophelia, Polonius, Laertes, grave-diggers and all the rest, draw their life from the same source, the poet's imagination. If he is one of them he is all of them. He walked through himself and met them all, and in that same country he found Caliban and Ariel, witches and fairies, sluts, hoydens and fools. Had the self through which he walked been solely his own experience its population would be to others of his race incomprehensible. Imagination sees, remembers, foresees, divines. But that is not all. It is a heritage of human experience bequeathed from generation to generation and is therefore knowledge as such. If the poet had not this inheritance of race memory to draw upon he could never create a woman, so wide and deep is the gulf of desire and misunderstanding set between man and woman in the threescore years and ten of their existence. In his own life he can experience much but not everything. Life is too short. He regales us with his inheritance. His own gains would be insufficient for such a banquet. The elements of what has been are within him; he sees what is and divines what may be.

All of which leaves the riddle of *Hamlet, Macbeth, King Lear, Othello, Troilus and Cressida* still unanswered. Shakespeare was myriad-minded. Millions of strange shadows attended on him. But why so often and at one time of his life the dark shadows of betrayed king, banished lover, deserted father, disillusioned friend? And why expressed with all the force and poignancy of a personal grief? Metempsychosis, one of the recurring motives of *Ulysses,* provokes a fancy. Those whom no doubts hinder from pursuing the fancy might consider that Michelangelo died in the year Shakespeare was born. The fierce spirit who goaded him to create his despairing Titans, his prophets and race-fathers may have looked for a likely cradle when his broken instrument was carried to the grave, and disputed with the local earth gods the possession of a pen.

CHAPTER VII

To see Joyce at work on the *Wandering Rocks* was to see an engineer at work with compass and slide-rule, a surveyor with theodolite and measuring chain or, more Ulyssean perhaps, a ship's officer taking the sun, reading the log and calculating current drift and leeway. Most of the characters of *Ulysses* appear in *Wandering Rocks*. Their actions are seen separately and simultaneously. Linking them together in unity are the paths of Christ and Cæsar. Christ appears in the person of his servant, Father Conmee, and Cæsar in the person of Cæsar's servant, the Right Honourable William Humble, Earl of Dudley, Lord Lieutenant-General and General Governor of Ireland. These are the static forces of Church and State, restraining the destructive forces of wandering anarchic individualism.

Christ and Cæsar are here not in conflict—only in opposition. What is God's and what is Cæsar's has been settled for them both long ago. They are complementary and are so considered by the Dubliners who salute them and who are, in their turn, saluted or blessed by them. The one needs for the exercise of his ministry the secular peace procured by kingly authority and the other exercises his authority by virtue of institutions to be protected. We know the thoughts of Father Conmee. They are prim, clean, benevolent thoughts. He thinks hopefully of the vast number of precious souls to be saved and of the mysterious variety of God's familiar world. The cloudy summer sky pleases him and the warm air. To children and grown-ups of all classes he is equally benevolent. Of man's "tyrannous incontinence" he thinks without condemnation. The ways of God are not our ways: and how shall souls be saved if no bodies are made? Also, being a priest, he thinks with pleasure of his office and of its technical difficulties. He is God's servant, but he is also a good workman pleased with his job. The thoughts of the Right Honourable William Humble, Earl of Dudley, are not revealed to us. Both Christ and Cæsar are on errands of mercy bent. William Humble, Earl of Dudley, and Lady Dudley, accompanied by Lieutenant-Colonel Hesseltine, and with the honourable Mrs. Paget, Miss de Courcy and the Honourable Gerald Ward in attendance in another carriage, are driving to Sandymount to open a bazaar in aid of funds for Mercer's Hospital. Father Conmee is on his way to Artane at the instance of Martin Cunningham to see if he can get one of the Dignam orphans in the Artane orphanage. Father Conmee makes his way to Artane by way of Mountjoy Square, Great Charles Street, the North Circular Road, North Strand Road to Newcomen Bridge, and here takes the tram as far as the Howth Road tramstop, whence he pursues his way on foot along the Malahide Road. The Lord Lieutenant-General and General Governor of Ireland leaves the viceregal lodge with his party and passes out of the lower gates of Phœnix Park, proceeds along the north quays past the Four Courts, crosses Grattan Bridge, and so on to his destination by way of Dame Street, Nassau Street, Merrion Square North, Lower Mount Street, Northumberland Road and Landsdown Road.

Joyce wrote the *Wandering Rocks* with a map of Dublin before him on which were traced in red ink the paths of the Earl of Dudley and Father Conmee. He calculated to a minute the time necessary for his characters to cover a given distance of the city. For this is peculiarly the episode of Dublin. Not Bloom, not Stephen is here the principal personage, but Dublin itself. Its houses, streets, spaces, tramways and waterways are shown us, and the people appear as sons and daughters and guests of the city. All towns are labyrinths in which for the townsfolk there are charted fairways; but we are strangers in the town and can find our way only by the exercise of attention and caution. While working on the *Wandering Rocks* Joyce bought at Franz Karl Weber's on the Bahnhofstrasse a game called "Labyrinth," which he played every evening for a time with his daughter Lucia. As a result of winning or losing at the game he was enabled to catalogue six main errors of judgment into which one might fall in choosing a right, left or centre way out of the maze.

Dublin was said to be the cardrivingist, teadrinkingest city in the empire, and teatime, with its general reshuffle of the population on foot or on trams is approaching. Among the normal citizens drift the vague personages, freaks and naturals of the city. The irritable blind pianotuner is making his way by touch through the maze. Cashel Boyle O'Connor Fitzmaurice Tisdall Farrell, "his stick umbrelladustcoat dangling," snakes his way round lamp-posts towards an unknown destination. The melancholy man with the macintosh, thirteenth mourner at Dignam's funeral, drifts aimlessly around, gnawing dry bread. Mr. Breen, suffering from persecution mania and megalomania, is still in pursuit of legal information which shall enable him to bring an action for libel claiming ten thousand pounds damages against an unknown practical joker. His faithful wife attends him. Most of the characters move from place to place on foot, two of them, Almidano Artifoni, Stephen's music master, and Father Conmee, take the tram, and the viceregal cavalcade moves forward at a sharp trot.

Apart from Father Conmee's journey to Artane and the official viceregal drive to Sandymount, there are eighteen pictures in the episode, each one featuring the activities of one or several of the characters. According to their directions and velocities their position at any time is noted, for they are all regarded in a twofold sense. They are human souls bound together by psychological ties, as, for example, ties of family, religion, friendship, enmity, citizenship, interest; and they are also bodies, isolated masses of matter moving through space. The viewpoint changes from one sentence to another so that the reader must be continually on the alert to follow the variations of scale and angle. The view constantly changes from a close-up to a bird's-eye view. A character is introduced to us at close-up range, and suddenly, without warning, the movement of another character a mile distant is described. The scale suddenly changes. Bodies become small in relation to the vast space around them. The persons look like moving specks. It is a town seen from the top of a tower. The spiritual attributes of each person remain what they were, but all, as individuals, become small in relation to the city that contains them.

Thus, during a short talk between Corny Kelleher, undertaker and informer, and P.C. 57C, we are told without warning: "Father John Conmee stepped into the Dollymount tram on Newcomen Bridge." He had saluted the constable a few minutes previously.

Maggy Dedalus is boiling shirts, using as fuel for her copper some unpawnable books. Two hungry schoolgirls, her younger sisters, come in, and as she pours them out peasoup we read: "The lacquey rang his bell. Barang!" This brings us to Dillon's auction rooms, half an hour's

walk distant, where Dilly Dedalus hopes to meet her
father.

While Blazes Boylan is buying fruit for "a lady friend,"
"a dark-backed figure under Merchant's Arch scanned the
books on the hawker's car." Bloom is five minutes' walk
away from his rival.

While Bloom is buying for Marion the *Sweets of Sin*
under Merchant's Arch, "on O'Connell Bridge many persons observed the grave deportment and gay apparel of
Mr. Dennis J. Maginni, Professor of Dancing, etc." Professor Maginni is hardly a stone's throw away.

Mr. Simon Dedalus and his daughter Dilly meet outside
Dillon's auction rooms, and at a certain point in their
conversation, Mr. "Kernan, pleased with the order he had
booked, walked boldly along James's Street." Mr. Kernan
is twenty minutes' walk away from father and daughter.

As their conversation is about to come to an end, "the
viceregal cavalcade passed, greeted by obsequious policemen, out of Parkgate." Parkgate is about a mile and a half
from Bachelor's Walk.

Stephen Dedalus stands before a jeweller's and watch-
maker's shop: "Old Russel with a smeared shammy rag,
burnished again his gem, turned it and held it at the point
of his Moses beard. Grandfather ape gloating on a stolen
hoard.

"And you who wrest old images from the burial earth!
The brainsick words of sophists: Antisthenes. A lore of
drugs. Orient and immortal wheat standing from everlasting to everlasting.

"Two old women fresh from their whiff of the briny
trudged through Irishtown along London bridge road,
one with a sanded umbrella, one with a midwife's bag in
which eleven cockles rolled."

The two old midwives, Stephen's beach companions,

have just left Sandymount Shore. Stephen is half an hour's walk away in the centre of the town.

Mr. Dedalus and Father Cowley meet Ben Dollard on the metal bridge just as, ten minutes' walk away, "Cashel Boyle O'Connor Fitzmaurice Tisdall Farrell, murmuring, glassyeyed, strode past the Kildare street club."

The serviable Martin Cunningham comes out of Castle Yard Gate, the interests of the Dignam family in mind, when, "Bronze by gold, Miss Kennedy's head by Miss Douce's head, appeared above the crossblind of the Ormond Hotel." There is a leisurely three minutes' walk between the sympathetic Mr. Cunningham and the ladylike barmaids.

The tidal waterway, the Anna Liffey, mother of Dublin, plays as ever her part in Joyce's Dublin. As a creative force she is older and greater than Christ or Cæsar. If Christ left Dublin the city would still exist. Man can invent fresh gods as he needs them and new gods would replace the old. If the hand of one Cæsar let fall the reins, the hand of another would take them up. A committee of public safety or a representative republic can rule as firmly and well as King Edward VII. But if Anna Liffey deserted Dublin, Dublin would cease to exist. On her outgoing waters she bears the Elijah handbill thrown away by Bloom at lunchtime off O'Connell Bridge. While the Dedalus sisters are eating their peasoup, "a skiff, a crumpled throwaway, Elijah is coming, rode lightly down the Liffey, under Loopline bridge, shooting the rapids where water chafed around the bridgepiers, sailing eastward past hulls and anchor chains, between the Customhouse old dock and George's quay." And later, while Mulligan and Haines are spooning their *mélanges*, "Elijah, skiff, light crumpled throwaway, sailed eastward by flanks of ships and trawlers, amid an archipelago of corks, beyond new

Wapping Street, past Benson's ferry, and by the three-masted schooner *Rosevean* from Bridgewater with bricks." The throwaway is a further mile seaward, outward bound on the ebbtide.

As with the town, so with the people, the time, the object. An organized sensibility and a good memory go to the just recognition of identity. Similarity of names must not confuse us. Shadows must not be mistaken for substances. Past time must be recognised for past time. The same name may be used to designate different persons or things. Mr. Bloom, whose father changed his name by deed poll from Virag to Bloom must not be confused with Mr. Bloom, the dentist, nor Father Conmee with Don Jon Conmee. Ben Dollar has nothing to do with Dollard, the printer. Alderman Cowley is not the Father Cowley who stands in fear of the bumbailiffs set upon him by Reuben J. Dodd, the moneylender. Mr. Kernan thinks he sees Ned Lambert's brother over the way, but both are moving, and the sun on the windscreen of a motorcar hinders accurate observation. Bloom and Stephen are both dressed in black, and both pore over bookstalls. McCoy and Lenehan, seeing Bloom at the bookstall, conclude that he is looking for a book on astronomy, which they know to be his hobby, but Bloom in reality is looking for an erotic book suitable for the literary taste of his wife. Subsheriff Long John Fanning ascends towards Subsheriff Long John Fanning in the mirror. Young Patrick Dignam, on his way home with a pound and a half of pork steaks for the funeral guests, sees an exciting placard advertising a welterweight boxing match, Myler Keogh v. Sergt.-Major Bennett, and makes plans to evade parental control and go and see it. Then he notices that the fight has already taken place. Lenehan drops into Lynam's office to enquire about Sceptre's starting price and meets there

Bantam Lyons, who is about to back Throwaway, tipped him earlier in the day by Bloom "in the dark language of prophecy." Lenehan puts Lyons off his bet. Lyons might have followed our system with the same debit result.

Mr. Wyndham Lewis, in a brilliant but negative essay, has reproached Joyce with the vast amount of local time detail in *Ulysses*. But if the artist is not to be the abstract and brief mirror of his own time, of what time is he to be mirror and abstract? The personages he creates can hardly exist in a timeless, spaceless vacuum. All characters in fiction have appeared in the dress and social organisation of their time from Burnt Njal to Bloom. Only the fairy story begins, "Once upon a time" with people dressed in timeless garments going on from one adventure to another in unsurveyed places. The timeplace of Dostoevsky's dreams of bad consciences was tsarist nihilist Russia. Balzac constituted himself social historian of restoration France. *L'Education Sentimentale* is second republic, second empire. Dickens is mid-nineteenth century petit-bourgeois England. Ibsen's characters are as locally late nineteenth century Norwegian as they are universal. And Chaucer's pilgrims are of his own day. Time, history, define the conflict and give to character its local habitation. Joyce's time is 1904. His Dubliners wear the clothes, drink the ale, eat the bread provided by the brewer, baker and tailor of their available place and time, and they talk the politics of early Sinn Fein days. He couldn't very well make them eat, drink, and wear nameless beer, bread and clothes, and talk eternal verities homeless in time. Virtue and vice, wisdom and folly, have always worn garments woven upon time's roaring loom. The one question that matters is: Does Joyce display or hide the shapes of his figures with the time detail of his day? To me his figures stand out starkly against a background of things and happenings. It is all a question of aesthetic judgment and "how you see it," but everything depends on it.

There is a second sense in which Joyce, as in the *Wandering Rocks,* and in varying degrees in all other episodes in *Ulysses,* is greatly interested in time: that is, in the time of day. As Bloom says, "Time is the time the movement takes." And Joyce, having only seventeen hours at his disposal, was obliged to use them with the logic and economy of the dramatist. With the exception of Stephen, who is concerned with time as the medium in which his destiny unfolds and who hates past time because it would bind him with present duties, all the characters in *Ulysses* have just that social time sense that is part of the general social mentality of the period, and no more. This arises out of the necessity for co-ordinating their daily social movements. It is a purely technical thing, born of mechanical development. James Watt invented the steam engine, and the steam engine begat the locomotive, and the locomotive begat the time-table, forcing people to grapple with its complexities and think in minutes where their great-grandfathers thought in hours. All their yesterdays, that in an earlier age would have been quietly buried in the hope of a glorious resurrection as myth, lie embalmed in files of newspapers and snapshot albums. They have suffered the influence of the penny post, telegraph and telephone—all social institutions working to a close time-table. But the principal element in forming that social time sense is the means of locomotion. The discoveries of the astronomer and the mathematician have less immediate effect on this sense than the electrification of the suburban lines. Light and the heavenly bodies are doing what they always did, but the wheels of mechanical civilisation are ever accelerating. What is the difference between Dick Turpin and the modern gangster highwayman? Only a mode of transport, a tempo of gunfire, and a quickened time sense. One rides to York on Black Bess and shoots with a muzzle loader, and the other drives a stolen Bentley and carries a machine pistol. As Kipling says, transportation is civilisation. It may be a coincidence, but spacetime came in with the taximeter, which is by petrol engine out of clockwork.

Joyce took carefully into account all the mechanical conditions of his day, but those mechanical conditions never influenced him in the sense that they influenced many of his contemporaries. The cubist, for example, is stricken with dull wonder by the massive organisation of the machine at rest. The futurist is excited to frenzy by the speed and fury of the machine in motion. Both are slavishly subservient to the wheels and pistons of the engines that were created to be our slaves. Them the machine has mastered, but it has never influenced the material or outlook of Joyce in this sense. Except by way of observing its effects on the minds and movements of his characters Joyce pays mechanical development no heed. Still less does he pay heed to it in his tempo of composition.

In *Wandering Rocks* the action goes forward at clockspeed. The characters seem to be performing actions with a minimum of will-power. It is as if they were borne towards their ends floating on on invisible tide, actively swimming neither with nor against it. Bloom has done all he can do for the moment in the matter of the Keyes ad. He has copied the drawing of the crossed keys out of the *Kilkenny People,* and now it is up to his chiefs on the paper to agree to his client's terms. Stephen is at a loose end, fatigued and deflated after his talk on Shakespeare in the National Library. Marion, in 7 Eccles Street, is preparing for a serious rehearsal of *Love's Old Sweet Song.*

Blazes Boylan, not yet "Boylan with impatience," is preparing for a favourable reception with a purchase of ripe fruit. Punters are putting their last minute bets on their fancies for the Ascot Gold Cup; the horses are in the paddock, but the race is not yet run. The time employed can hardly be more than three-quarters of an hour.

No one person seems more important than another. Inasmuch as the centre of the stage is held, it is held not by an individual but by a family, a unit of social organisation. After Dublin itself comes the Dedalus family, father, daughters and Stephen. Grievous poverty that engages the mind continually in a defensive warfare against want is the keynote of their existence. Maggy, Boody, and Katey Dedalus are eating their gift of peasoup with bread, while sister Dilly is looking for their father. They are inclined to be critical of their father, but when the youngest of the three exclaims with thoughtless bitterness, "Our father who art not in heaven," Maggy rebukes her with "Bloody! For shame!" Dilly meets her father outside Dillon's auction rooms. A clever man and apt at diversions, he criticises her round shoulders and drooping carriage, but she brushes his attack aside and bluntly asks for money. He gives her a shilling, but Dilly is as tenacious as she is direct, and demands more. Two further pennies is his limit. As he walks away with the din of the lacquey's bell ringing in his ears, he mimics the mincing speech of the nuns who were responsible for his daughter's education. He meets an old friend, Bob Cowley, who is in distress on account of a couple of bumbailiffs who are hanging round his house trying to effect an entrance. More poverty. One penny of the twopence her father had given her for a bun and a glass of milk for herself she spends on culture. She buys a coverless copy of Chardenal's French primer and, prize in hand, meets and hails her brother, Stephen, at a neighbouring bookstall. She is afraid that her ambition to learn French may strike her brother as ridiculous.

" 'What did you buy that for?' he asked. 'To learn French?'

"She nodded, reddening and closing tight her lips.

"Show no surprise. Quite natural.

" 'Here,' Stephen said. 'It's all right. Mind Maggy doesn't pawn it on you. I suppose all my books are gone.'

" 'Some,' Dilly said. 'We had to.'

"She is drowning. Agenbite. Save her. Agenbite. All against us. She will drown me with her, eyes and hair. Lank coils of seaweed hair around me, my heart, my soul. Salt green death.

"Agenbite of inwit. Inwit's agenbite.

"Misery! Misery!"

Stephen has a strong sense of family solidarity. He will not serve the Christian God, and he will not serve in the tribal warfare of the Irish nation, but he would serve his family if he could. The family bond seems to be the only one of which he recognises the validity. But who would save drowning people must first be a good swimmer.

It seemed to me that no two episodes pleased Joyce more in the writing of them than *The Sirens* and that which followed, *The Cyclops*. Perhaps it was because the war ended while *The Sirens* was being written. A man may well be non-political, but he would be lacking in humanity if he felt no relief when the slaughter came to an end. *The Sirens* was written towards the end of 1918.

One of the aspects of *Ulysses* that always pleases me is its popular character. It bears a resemblance to those old popular songs which tell of tragic happenings to a jolly tune and a ringing chorus of tooralooralay. The clock strikes four in the Ormond Hotel, Blazes Boylan licks up his sloe gin and hurries off to keep his appointment with

Bloom's wife. Bloom sees him go but decides not to interfere. It was a momentous decision; the situation is tragic;
yet this is the brightest and gayest episode in the whole
book. The action is told in words that flutter past like
gay-coloured butterflies. Bloom eats his liver and bacon,
drinks his cider, talks to his fellow diner, looks at the barmaids and leaves with a troublous murmur of wind among
the reeds of his inside.

The episode falls under the bodily sign of the ear and
the art of music. For the form and technique Joyce borrowed the devices of the musician. *The Sirens* is a fugue
in counterpart. Joyce is himself a tenor singer and a lover
of music, and was well aware how far and in what way
the musician's manner would serve his turn. It is easy
even for the non-musical, myself for example, to see that
for a distance both arts—that of the musician and that of
the poet—can run together, singly or in double harness.
Both use sounds that follow one another in time, and both
use written symbols to conserve and communicate them.
Notes lie like words on paper *nebeneinander* and like
words they float in the air—or seem to float in the air—
nacheinander. Poet and musician only part company when
the musician writes his notes *übereinander* and sends them
forth on the airs in clusters and swarms. The poet is bound
to sense, and if he followed the musician here he would
leave sense behind, and then farewell to poesie. The chord
is their last point of contact. Here no doubt but that Joyce
has followed him, not in *The Sirens* episode of *Ulysses*,
but in his *Work in Progress*. Joyce can give some of the
effect of four voices singing together, but not the fact.
The reader speaks the words and the sounds fall from
his lips one after the other, for all parts must be sung
with his voice, and he has only one. The beauty of *The
Sirens* episode lies in this: that Joyce has mimicked all the

musician's mannerisms and rhythmical devices with so much fantastical humour, at the same time carrying his own narrative a most important step forward. It was a field-day for the virtuoso in Joyce.

Virtuosity! Why not! The artist is a man who can do supremely well what everybody can do to some extent. He is more, and can do more—in his own province. He is a specialist, in short. Every man or woman can write a book, paint a picture, make a tune, walk a tight rope, box a round, but when Blondin walked the tight rope over Niagara Falls strong men gasped for breath; when Pavlova danced people thought the force of gravity was vanquished; and Jim Driscoll, they say, could make a sixteen-foot ring look as spacious as a twenty-acre field. He has a wonderful technique, but he has nothing to say. He is full of inspiration, but he has no technical ability. These are mechanical antitheses. Every artist has the technical accomplishment that belongs to the character of his thought and vision. There may be mute inglorious Miltons, but the articulate Milton who was so inspired that somehow he failed to acquire the necessary organ tones is a myth.

A musical episode was easy to place in Dublin, for Dublin is, or was, a musical town, with a particular passion for vocal music. A few Dubliners of the older generation meet in the lounge of the Ormond Hotel and a couple of songs, with an improvisation on the piano, constitute the entertainment. No writer with any respect for probability would dare to make the same thing happen in London. People and pub are both lacking. The influences that limited the expression of the Irish people in sculpture and painting—poverty, politics, patriotism, whatever they were—failed to hinder expression in word and melody. In *The Sirens* the Dubliners are shown to divide their interest in vocal music between opera of the Italian school and popular ballads. What makes them good orators probably makes them good singers. Only a general cult of vocal music can produce the exceptions such as John McCormack and John Sullivan. The bar of the Ormond Hotel, where the actors of the drama enter and through which they leave, exists as it did in 1904, but the rest of the space—saloon in which Simon Dedalus sang, and dining-room in which Bloom and Richie Goulding listened and ate—has disappeared in the rebuilding and re-organising of the Ormond as the New Ormond Hotel.

The whole of the time he was writing *The Sirens* Joyce literally lived in music. There was opportunity enough and to spare in Zürich which at any time is a musical town. Its annual musical festival is a European event. Opera there is a permanent institution with a home in the Stadttheater. But just at the time when Joyce was writing *The Sirens* Austrian and German currencies were falling, while the Swiss franc was a gold franc, so that the native musicians were reinforced by a continual inflow of able performers from neighbouring countries, lured by uninflated currency. Every evening there was a concert of importance in the larger or smaller Tonhalle. Joyce attended most of them, and to one or two I went in his company. It was on one such occasion when, after leaving the Tonhalle, we were crossing the Limmat, that Joyce asked me suddenly:

"What do you think are the correspondences in the other senses for the sense of absolute pitch in music?"

I didn't know what he meant. When he explained I sought a parallel in the sense of sight and art of painting.

"What about the sense of value in painting?" I said. "Some painters have it in great measure—Corot for example—others . . ."

"No, I don't think that's it," said Joyce. "That is using the sense of sight creatively, to make something. The thing I mean is passive, but it is something inborn, intuitive. Kerridge has it. It enables the person who has it to assign to any heard sound its place in the musical scale."

"Then what about the wine-taster?" I said, "who picks out the vintage? Or the tea-taster, who knows all aromas of all blends?"

"Now that's something," Joyce said. "That's good. I have a traveller in tea in my book who is also a tea-taster. Tom Kernan. You remember? I shall probably use that."

But he didn't use it. The correspondence for the sense of absolute pitch in music in *The Sirens* is Molly Bloom's comprehension of the hurdy-gurdy boy without understanding a word of his language. Bloom, looking at one of the barmaids, reflects on the peculiar sympathy that exists between people of like sexual tempo, and his thoughts go off at a tangent to the incident of Molly and the boy. "With look to look: songs without words. Molly that hurdy-gurdy boy. She knew he meant the monkey was sick. Or because so like to Spanish. Understand animals too that way. Solomon did. Gift of nature."

Another problem of musical association prompted the question Joyce put to me one evening in the Pfauen Restaurant:

"What epithets do you think most appropriate to apply to a tenor voice?"

My own random suggestions were just such that would occur to anybody—the brighter-toned metals and colours, I think. Dramatically, however, the tenor voice in *The Sirens* is heard through the mind of Bloom, and appropriately the words used are those heard by Bloom earlier in the day when Ned Lambert read aloud the fustian speech of Dan Dawson on Our Native Land to those present in the *Telegraph* office.

"It soared, a bird, it held its flight, a swift pure cry, soar silver orb it leaped serene, speeding, sustained, to come, don't spin it out too long long breath he breath long life, soaring high, high resplendent, aflame, crowned, high in the effulgence symbolistic, high, of the etherial bosom, high, of the high vast irradiation everywhere all soaring all around about the all, the endlessnessnessness."

Joyce's vast admiration for the tenor voice always seemed to me to be somewhat one-sided, and, perhaps, that is not entirely because I am no musician, for musicians find it just as difficult to appreciate as I. But, as in the case of his original usage of words in *Work in Progress,* his worship of the tenor voice is only an exaggeration of a popular tendency that always existed. The people have always raved over a tenor voice. They queued up for hours on end, myself among them, to be admitted (at double the ordinary rates) to the comfortless gallery at Covent Garden Opera House to hear Caruso sing. When they heard the first aria it was not only the excitable Italians of Saffron Hill, but stolid Englishmen and Englishwomen too who climbed on the seats and shouted "bis" and "encore," according to how their beaks grew, at the tops of their voices. I never saw the same enthusiasm shown for, say, van Rooy, who on all hands was admitted to be at least in the same rank as a singer. And even this popular idolatry, according to an article by Count Carducci, in *Music and Letters,* October 1930, fell short of that madness for the eighteenth century "castrato" Farinelli, in whom culminated six generations of non-virile tenors. His "high sustained *points d'orgue* were of such a purity and volume from pianissimo to fortissimo and back again that after the first note of his air, which was afterwards to be

Philip of Spain's lullaby for ten consecutive years, the *son qual nave,* a theatre would jump to its feet and applaud rapturously for ten minutes on end." To acquire an archangel's voice at the expense of his sex, especially when it brought him the worship of the people, the favour of a king, a title and a pension of £2,000 a year, might be considered for a man a privileged exchange. The entirely unmusical intelligence says of the tenor: he has something wrong with his throat. By the same token the pearl is something wrong with the oyster, and the blue orchid something wrong with the tropical tree. Yet for the pearl the Ceylon diver goes all naked to the hungry shark, and for the orchid many hardy men die of fever and wild beasts. But the tenor voice is more than rare. It is high, "high in the effulgence symbolistic" as Bloom thinks. It is a goblet full of wine, atopmost deed of nature working with the material, man. When Joyce talks "tenor" one has the idea that he sees in the tenor organ not only an instrument of musical expression but also an adornment and a justification of humanity.

Joyce's brilliant burlesques of the more banal tiddleypom aspects of music pleased him, and all of us who heard him read them, immensely. I remember two in particular. This is one of them:

"Miss Douce withdrew her satiny arm, reproachful, pleased. 'Don't make half so free,' said she, 'till we are better acquainted.' George Lidwell told her really and truly: but she did not believe. First gentleman told Mina that was so. She asked him was that so. And second tankard told her so. That that was so. Miss Douce, Miss Lydia, did not believe: Miss Kennedy, Mina, did not believe: George Lidwell, No: Miss Dou did not: the first, the first: gent with the tank: believe, no, no: did not, Miss Kenn: Lidlydiawell: the tank—"

The other occurs two pages later after Bloom has written his letter to Martha:

"Bald Pat who is bothered mitred the napkins. Pat is a waiter hard of his hearing. Pat is a waiter who waits while you wait. Hee hee hee hee. He waits while you wait. Hee hee. A waiter is he. Hee hee hee hee. He waits while you wait. While you wait if you wait he will wait while you wait. Hee hee hee hee. Hoh. Wait while you wait."

To these simple rhythms on our homeways I invented appropriate dances. The steps wouldn't have satisfied Professor Maginni, but they were better than I could ever do on a dance floor to the music of drums and saxophones.

The beginning of *The Sirens* overlaps the *Wandering Rocks*. Both are treated in the same simultanist manner, but the action in *The Sirens* is brisk and voluntary, and Bloom once more dominates the scene. While Mr. Dedalus, a few paces away, is bringing his hat low to His Excellency, Miss Douce and Miss Kennedy hear the vice-regal hoofs ringing steel on the quay outside the window of their bar. Impertinent boots brings them in their tea, which they drink to the accompaniment of talk on skin treatment (Miss Douce has come back from her holidays sunburnt) and much laughter provoked by the funny looks and mannerisms of elderly men. Then Mr. Dedalus strolls into the empty bar and after him Lenehan. Lenehan is still the same tragic sponger of the story "The Two Gallants" in *Dubliners,* but in *Ulysses* he is painted in gayer colours. He is a parasite without any separate existence of his own. His life depends upon his being able to attach himself to some more robust and brutal being whom he diverts with his wit and whose spare shillings he in his turn absorbs. Boylan is to him in *Ulysses* what Corley was in "The Two Gallants." While waiting for Boylan he tries to attach himself to Simon Dedalus, and is duly cold-shouldered. The barmaids treat with disdain his efforts to be amusing. Then enters Boylan and orders for himself a sloe gin and a bitter for his satellite.

Bloom was buying a twopenny packet of writing paper and envelopes for his letter to Martha when he saw the organiser of his wife's concert tour on an outside car cross Essex Bridge. ". . . He eyed and saw afar on Essex Bridge a gay hat riding on an outside car. It is. Third time. Coincidence.

"Jingling on supple rubbers it jaunted from the bridge to Ormond Quay. Follow. Risk it. Go quick. At four. Near now. Out."

Boylan's outside car pulls up before the Ormond Hotel. Bloom is observing it when he meets Richie Goulding. Together they go in to the Ormond for a meal and, unnoticed by Blazes Boylan, reach the dining-room. Bloom is agitated. If he wants to interfere in his wife's love affair he must hurry. The time of the rendezvous is four o'clock, and just as they enter the hotel the clock strikes four.

"The bag of Goulding, Colles, Ward led Bloom by ryebloom flowered tables. Aimless he chose with agitated aim, bald Pat attending, a table near the door. Be near. At four. Has he forgotten? Perhaps a trick. Not come: whet appetite. I couldn't do. Wait, wait. Pat, waiter, waited."

Boylan is evidently a conquering hero with women. It is his presence rather than Lenehan's pleadings that persuades Miss Douce to perform the trick called by Lenehan "*Sonnez la cloche.*" The trick consists in pinching her garter through her skirt and letting the taut elastic smack back on her thigh. Boylan appreciates it. He is well up in campanology. But this is a mere tinkle compared with the carillon that awaits him in Eccles Street. He empties his glass at a gulp and hurries off, with Lenehan expostulating in his wake. Bloom hears him go.

"Bloom heard a jing, a little sound. He's off. Light sob of breath. Bloom sighed on the silent, blue-hued flowers. Jingling. He's gone. Jingle. Hear."

Bob Cowley and Ben Dollard enter, flushed with their success in gaining for Cowley a respite from distraint. They heard friend Simon Dedalus at the piano and hail him as he comes through the saloon door. They will have a song to celebrate Cowley's temporary escape, and Simon shall sing it. Bloom, in the dining-room, is at the end of his liver and bacon when he hears Simon begin. Music lover Richie Goulding, disdained by his proud brother-in-law but visited by his nephew Stephen, first recognises "that glorious voice." They never speak when they pass each other by. Simon sneers at his in-law and at his in-law's family, but Richie Goulding is a loyal admirer of "Si Dedalus's voice." The description of Simon Dedalus's singing of the romance from *Martha,* as heard by Bloom and fused with his own experience, illuminated with his own comment, is among the most brilliant passages in *Ulysses.* It begins

"Braintipped, cheek touched with flame, they listened feeling that flow endearing flow over skin limbs human heart soul spine. Bloom signed to Pat, bald Pat is a waiter hard of hearing, to set ajar the door of the bar. The door of the bar. So. That will do. Pat, waiter, waited, waiting to hear, for he was hard of hear by the door.

" *'Sorrow from me seemed to depart.'*

"Through the hush of air a voice sang to them, low, not rain, not leaves in murmur, like no voice of strings of reeds or whatdoyoucallthem dulcimers, touching their still ears with words, still hearts of their each his remembered lives. Good, good to hear: sorrow from them each seemed to from both depart when first they heard. When first they saw, lost Richie, Poldy, mercy of beauty, heard from a person wouldn't expect it in the least, her first merciful lovesoft oftloved word.

"Love that is singing: love's old sweet song. Bloom unwound slowly the elastic band of his packet. Love's old sweet *sonnez la gold*. Bloom wound a skein round four fork-fingers, stretched it, relaxed, and wound it round his troubled double, fourfold, in octave, gyved them fast. . . ."

The surplus of his listening sensibility brings in thoughts of his wife and Blazes Boylan. "Last look at mirror always before she answers the door," and of the singer and his life. "Glorious tone he has still. . . . Wore out his wife: now sings. But hard to tell. Only the two themselves." Then of the coincidence that just to-day they should be singing "Martha."

"Martha. How strange! To-day." With "Charmed my Eye" come recollections of the first time he met Marion at Mat Dillon's in Terenure, and the whole ends in his tribute to the tenor voice already quoted. Music moves Bloom, but does not carry him away. He arms his nerves against its seductions in the same way that he protects his intelligence against the mass suggestions of religion. His ear "gives instant warning of each sound's repair, which soon is thence conveyed into the judgment chair." He despises the over-enthusiastic music fanatic of which Richie Goulding is a type, yet when Simon Dedalus has finished his song and the clamour of applause has died down, his own thought is the truest comment. To himself he says, "That man's voice was a lamentation." The ear is also an organ of balance.

Of all the second plane figures in *Ulysses* none is more delicately drawn than Simon Dedalus. He has had good positions in his day, and has owned property, but now he has fallen on evil days and his prospects of acquiring position or property must be decidedly thin. But it is an admirable trait, in a society which puts a premium on domestic sacrifice, that a man shall not allow his personal expansiveness to be swallowed up in misfortune. In his position many would have gone about whining and complaining and uselessly mortifying themselves. The death of his wife was a grievous blow, as we gather from his tears in Glasnevin cemetery and from his thoughts as he gazes into the open piano, but his elastic spirit, courage, and feeling for style of the Victorian gentleman keep him upright and cheerful in misfortune. One thinks of him as a martial type. He was antiparnellite until the hue-and-cry set in against the nationalist chief and then he turned and rallied to his support.

Bloom calls for pen, ink and pad and begins a letter to Martha. Thoughts of Eccles Street agitate him. The music has distracted him and he appears to be passably bored with his epistolary flirtation, but the logic which says "you have begun and you must go on," forces him to write. Richie Goulding is a sharp-eyed man and might guess what he is writing, so, to put his inquisitive table companion off the scent, he pretends to be answering an ad. for a town traveller in his *Freeman's*.

"Folly am I writing? Husbands don't. That's marriage does, their wives. Because I'm away from. Suppose. But how? She must. Keep young. If she found out. Card in my high grade ha. No, not tell all. Useless pain. If they don't see. Woman. Sauce for the gander."

He listens with one ear to Bob Cowley's improvisation and keeps one watchful eye on Richie Goulding. The letter is a thin and scrappy affair, and Bloom is conscious of this, so he fattens it out with two postscripts and a present, a postal order for 2s. 6d. Then he gets up to go while Cowley's tune wanders into the minuet from *Don Giovanni,* and Boylan knocks on the door of 7 Eccles Street. Bloom pays and is about to go when he hears Ben Dollard's "bass barreltone" begin to sing *The Croppy Boy,* by special request. Ben Dollard comes to "Last of my name and race." Bloom thinks:

"I too, last my race. Milly young student. Well, my fault perhaps. No son. Rudy. Too late now. Or if not? If not? If still?

"He bore no hate.

"Hate. Love. Those are names. Rudy. Soon I am old."

He enfilades the bar with his eye, and sees the barmaids and all the customers listening, sees also "popped corks, splashes of beerfroth, stacks of empties," and, no friend of sad endings, leaves before the sad end of the song.

"By rose, by satiny bosom, by the fondling hand, by slops, by empties, by popped corks, greeting in going, past eyes and maidenhair, bronze and faint gold in deep sea shadow, went Bloom, soft Bloom, I feel so lonely Bloom."

Pleasure in the glittering material of *The Sirens* might distract us from the serious action going on if we failed to hear the undertones of the music. *Ulysses* is never solemn, is often fantastically comic, is amoral and philosophically humane, but it is always serious. Joyce no more analyses his characters than he describes their surroundings, but we are to suppose that he intended them to be comprehended just as he wished the nature of the city of Dublin to be felt. Half of Bloom's day is over. Thrice he has seen Boylan—here in the Ormond for the last time—and Marion's appointment is at four. He sees Blazes Boylan leave, and knows quite well that the singing of *Love's Old Sweet Song* is less than half the business on the agenda. All his reflections go to show that prospect causes him a degree of suffering. Why, then, does he not interfere? It would be possible even now, without causing any violent disturbance, to return to his home in Eccles Street with an I-have-forgotten-something-most-important sort of air. On three occasions during the day he has thought of going home with a view to stopping the affair. In the *Telegraph* office he says to himself, "I could go home still: tram: something I forgot." And again in Grafton Street: "Useless to go back. Had to be. Tell me all." While in Daly's, seeing the outside car come over Essex Bridge, he thinks, "Follow. Risk it. Go quick. At four. Near now. Out." But he chose to let the matter take its course. Why? This is my own solution:

Bloom is a Jew, an Oriental, and the Oriental races are fatalistic in outlook. What has to be will be. What is written will come to pass. You may prevent a thing to-day, but what about to-morrow? He feels that it is as useless to fight against destiny in the shape of his wife's desires as it is to try to turn rivers from their courses or dam back the tides. But fatalism is not all. Fatalism is often the fighter's, the soldier's philosophy, but the soldier fights none the worse for knowing that on the appointed day the tide of battle will turn against him.

But Bloom makes no effort, no fight at all. Why? Because if he fought he would be denied his suffering. His Jewish masochism is deprived of its traditional outlet in religious observances. For him are no black fasts, no lamentations for the fall of Jerusalem, none of the griefs and penances of Israel, because he has left the faith of his fathers. But the racial pessimism, the will to suffer are there, and the only instrument through which he can suffer is his wife. The griefs and exaltations of the cuckolded husband are a substitute for the griefs and exaltations of Israel from which he is exiled. Therefore, negative as it may seem, there was will power behind Bloom's masterly inactivity on that bright June day.

Linked to the fatalism of the Oriental and organically connected with his Jewish and personal masochism is the homosexual wish to share his wife with other men. He is surrounded with acquaintances, yet he is a lonely man, condemned never to experience the warmth of male fellowship—incapable, perhaps, of accepting it were it offered him. That his wife is possessed by other males gives him a physical contact with them at second hand. It is an underground substitute for noisy back-slapping, arm-gripping comradeship. In *The Circe* episode he offers his wife in thought to "all strong-membered males." And why does he carry around with him constantly the photograph of his wife? It is not for his own private gaze. He knows quite well what she looks like. He carries it around so that he may show it on any convenient occasion to any favoured man as, later in the day, he shows it to Stephen. Her image is for him a bond of union with menfolk, as with the average man is the cigarette case and "What'll you have to drink?"

And Marion acquires new value for him through the fact that her flesh is desirable to other men. All amateurs love to share and show, and Bloom, the slavishly uxorious husband, amateur of his wife, desires to show and share her. He wishes, perhaps, to be first but not alone.

Then, as we have seen, Bloom is a non-authoritarian husband and father. His rule of conduct forbids him to say no to that which his wife desires. He is a fair-minded man who, claiming liberty for himself, cannot deny it to others. That is to say, the best of him does not and the rest of him dares not. Apart from all fair-mindedness, what his better half desires is for him also the wishful thing. Just as he prepares her breakfast, fetches her lotion, buys her erotic literature, so he claims indulgence from himself for her Spanish blood.

Lastly he desires a son, as all males, and particularly Jewish males, desire a son to bear their name and perpetuate their individuality. Marion is the only possible giver of that blessing. He is not old as men go—he is only thirty-eight—but the question of age is a sore point with him. "Made me feel young": "Keep young": "I am getting old": such thoughts are ever in his mind. If he should carry his flirtation with Martha that far, the son born would not be his and would not bear his name. He would live in a different place, be brought up under other influences, and for Bloom a son is not merely a confirmation of his virility. He wants to foster, protect, educate. Something happened to the relationship between him and Marion at the time of Rudy's death. The old intimacy waned and died, but he vaguely hopes that it may be re-established, and they are both of an age when a son may yet be born to them. If he complained about or fought against her other loves the breach might be widened, a complete separation might follow, and his hopes of offspring be for ever frustrated. And what are a few men more or less compared with the possible realisation of his family hopes and ambitions?

CHAPTER VIII

The one-eyed man may be king in the realm of the blind, but the two-eyed man is nothing but a nuisance in the kingdom of the one-eyed. The blind man is thankful for the seeing eye and guiding hand of another, but the one-eyed man needs no such assistance. He sees quite well, and has no thanks to spare for the man who tells him that the shape he thinks is as flat as cardboard is in reality round, or that there are such things as half-tones, values and nuances of colour. To him all shapes are flat, all darks black, all lights blinding white. They are perverted enemies of the truth who affirm the contrary.

The Sirens episode is swift-moving, bright-coloured, and for its effect depends on nuances of colour. The persons in it are drawn to a natural scale, whereas *The Cyclops* episode is built up of vast masses of contrasting colour, light and dark; the persons are over life-size and are drawn in the exaggerated outlines of grotesque comedy. The one provokes the ripple and the other the roar of laughter. Two-eyed Bloom ventures into the cavern of one-eyed nationalism. On the matter of the Dignam insurance he calls at Barney Kiernan's to look for Martin Cunningham, and finds there a few Irish patriots discussing the woes and virtues of their native land. He reasons with them but they think his humanity out of place, his moderation untimely. Besides, he is a Jew and has no country, so how should he know anything about it? Bloom generally avoids frontal attacks on obstacles, preferring to go round them like a river. He is not at all quarrelsome by nature, but here he is provoked into displaying vehemence in argument, even to the length of risking personal injury. Big Boy Polyphemus in the person of a giant Fenian assails him with rocks. Long-suffering Bloom addresses to his adversary winged words.

The unspoken thoughts of Bloom are often political. He has ideas, for example, as to how the city's tram service might be improved, and he is in favour of endowment at birth and other desirable reforms. But here he takes part actively in political debate. He is a rational humanitarian and believes in non-violent methods of realising his aims. Patience and reason are to him more effective weapons than bombs and machine-guns. It is a standpoint more Asiatic than European. It found expression in the beginnings of Christianity, and it persists in the Christianity of Tolstoy's followers. Gandhi holds to it, and the Quaker sect practises it. The theory is that if you resist what you regard as injustice and oppression with violence you will be forced to create the same apparatus of violence as the unjust oppressor; and the end will be, not that the oppressed man becomes a free man, but that he, in his turn, becomes an oppressor by virtue of his possessing the necessary instruments and the accompanying state of mind.

Stephen's attitude towards politics is a clear and consistent negative. As an artist he must keep his mind and body free for his artist's purposes. He has one life, so many days and hours, and has neither time nor energy to spare for the tyranny of parties and their policies. Generally speaking, *la patrie* asks only for our bodies in war time and for our money all the time, but Ireland demands of her sons a continual service of soul as well. This service he will not give. And there is something more in Stephen's attitude than the egoism of the artist. He was nine years old at the time of Parnell's downfall, and that event stamped itself ineffaceably on his growing consciousness. Sensitive and sceptical as he was, he would not be likely to forget it. Why should loyalty to any new party be less brittle than loyalty to the great parliamentary chief? Stephen says to Davin in *A Portrait of the Artist as a Young Man:* "No honourable and sincere man has given to you his life and his youth and his affections, from the days of Tone to those of Parnell, but you sold him to the enemy or failed him in need or reviled him and left him for another. And you invite me to be one of you. I'd see you damned first."

When the partisan asks Stephen, "Under which flag?" Stephen replies, "Neither." So does Bloom. But Bloom hoists a flag of his own, whereas Stephen refuses to serve or govern under any flag. Bloom does not deny his responsibility for the just government of the city. He is political and belongs to a party, but there is only one in it—himself. He throws the whole weight of his party into the scale on the side of reason and justice, but it weighs only eleven stone four. Stephen is anarchist, Bloom is Utopian. Utopia and Anarchy are old neighbours and near of kin, but they have never got on well together.

Sinn Fein existed in 1904, but at that time had no Labour ally to mix the slogans of Marx with those of Kossuth and Garibaldi. In the main Ireland is a country of peasants and small producers but the wage-worker, even in such a country, is too valuable an ally and too redoubtable an adversary to reject or antagonise. Connolly, the man who was to unite the forces of proletarian wage-workers with those of peasants and small producers in the service of the nationalist cause, was still in America. *The Harp* was not yet founded. The Citizen Army was not yet in being. There was as yet no distinctly Labour ally fighting under its own banner in the nationalist camp.

Joyce is more a Dubliner than an Irishman. His form of patriotism is that of a citizen of a free town in the middle ages. He has told me that he would rather be burgomaster of a city like Amsterdam than emperor of any empire; for a burgomaster is somebody among people he knows, while an emperor rules over unknowable people in unknown territories. His interest in Ireland is intense, from Howth Head to the far side of Phœnix Park, and from Glasnevin to Rathmines (conterminous, therefore, with the old Scandinavian kingdom of Dyfflinarsky), but begins to fade before it reaches Leitrim, and hardly exists at all at the Atlantic seaboard. In *Work in Progress* Ireland figures only as the estate of the Lord of Dublin and is populated with his quarrelsome and troublesome tenants.

Early in 1919, when the deeds of militant Sinn Fein were becoming world news, I was sitting with Joyce one evening in my workroom in the Usteristrasse. It was a quiet room overlooking the Sihl, and it had for furniture two quite comfortable chairs, a table, and a copious litter of newspaper files, English, Swiss and German. Thither we often went at that time to continue a conversation interrupted by *Polizeistunde* in the *Wirtschaft,* and to be stayed with a further flagon. We spoke of the happenings in Ireland. Joyce stated no positive, personal opinion on the solution to the conflict, but I put my own in this way:

"All this fighting with Ireland is absorbing too much English energy. History is leading us up the garden. We are being ruined by politics. Let us give economics a chance. The Irish want political autonomy. Why not give them what they want, give them at any rate what will satisfy them? Then, perhaps, when history is satisfied, the two islands will be able to realise their unity on an economic basis."

"Ireland is what she is," said Joyce, "and therefore I am what I am because of the relations that have existed between England and Ireland. Tell me why you think I ought to wish to change the conditions that gave Ireland and me a shape and a destiny?"

"But what about us?" I said with indignation. "Do you think that we English exist to further the spiritual development of the Irish people?"

Joyce's eyes flickered laughter behind their powerful lenses. He made no answer, and I took his silence to mean that he did think that that was one of our useful functions. Meeting Joyce a day or two later, he referred to our conversation in my room and laughed again, this time loudly.

"That talk of ours the other evening amuses me," he said. "You, an Englishman, trying to convince me, an Irishman, of the necessity of home rule for Ireland on the premises of the British Consulate, representing more or less the British Empire in Zürich."

We were strolling along the Bahnhofstrasse one evening after he had read to me a passage where the Fenian giant, representative of the most one-eyed nationalism, denounces the bloody and brutal Sassenach.

"I wonder," said Joyce suddenly, "what my own countrymen will think of my work?"

"I think they won't like it," I said. "The ardent party man is apt to believe that he who is not with him is against him. He understands opposition, but doesn't like criticism. Your countrymen are men of violent beliefs, and your book is the book of a sceptic."

"I know it is," said Joyce. "It is the work of a sceptic, but I don't want it to appear the work of a cynic. I don't want to hurt or offend those of my countrymen who are devoting their lives to a cause they feel to be necessary and just."

Sceptic, however, is a misleading term for a purely contemplative artist. Such an artist sees the world as standing still, not as advancing or retreating. Joyce may be musical in taste rather than pictorial, yet his view of life is that of a painter surveying a still scene rather than that of a musician following a development through time.

Compared with the two preceding episodes, *The Cyclops* episode is simple to follow. It is a straightforward tale told by one whose name is never mentioned, Noman. This unnamed one meets Joe Hynes, and together they adjourn to Barney Kiernan's in Little Britain Street, where they meet several others, and where a discussion takes place on what, to Englishmen, is known as the Irish question. But the easy colloquial flow of the narrative is interrupted at intervals with barriers of prose of a fabulous, legendary, or merely official and important order. This is the other side of the question. It is the subject of discussion seen suddenly through a telescope.

"Does this episode strike you as being futuristic?" said Joyce.

"Rather cubist than futurist," I said. "Every event is a many-sided object. You first state one view of it and then you draw it from another angle to another scale, and both aspects lie side by side in the same picture."

Mention of an uncollectable debt, for example, calls forth a copy of a hire purchase agreement between Moses Hertzog, "hereinafter to be called the vendor," and Michael Geraghty, "hereinafter to be called the purchaser." A case of mistaken identity (Alf Bergan thinks he saw the dead and buried Paddy Dignam walking down the street with Willy Murray) is rewritten in the complacent familiar-with-ghosts style of a spiritist séance report. The Myler-Keogh v. Percy Bennett fight is referred to and retold in the ding-dong style of the boxing reporter. The citizen swabs his mouth after spitting, and his handkerchief is described as if it were a rare specimen of early Irish illumination. The fall of the biscuit tin, thrown by the citizen at Bloom, is magnified to earthquake dimension. Bloom is driven away in Martin Cunningham's car, and the event is described as an ascent into heaven. And so on.

Through the narrative and commentary of the Nameless One, "I," a wonderful back view of Dublin and Dubliners is obtained. He knows no good of anybody, and the bad that he knows has been collected by way of keyholes, torn curtains, thin partitions, waste-paper baskets and scraps of gossip. To him all heroes are blockheads, all saints are rogues, and he looks at the gods only to see if their clay feet are cracking up nicely. He communes at times with a kindred soul, Pisser (Andrew) Burke. Should some habitually honest Dubliner perform for once a shady action, or a temporarily embarrassed gentleman slip furtively into a pawnshop, or a good husband one night stop to talk to a whore, or a brave man dodge into a doorway out of danger, and should the Nameless One himself not be present to witness their shame and discomfiture, then the ubiquitous Pisser Burke will be on duty at the worst angle, and "I" will add the piece to his scurvy repertoire at their next meeting. The observant Andrew does not appear in the flesh, but he is sufficiently represented in the narrative and commentary of his unnamed friend.

So vividly presented is the grotesque life of "I" that we are forced to like him in spite of his poisonousness. Himself a snarling Thersites, he liberates the Thersites in us. The detective story and the music-hall platesmasher do the same thing for our sleuths, mass murderers and crockery destroyers. Bloom, I take it, can be so rationally humane because the presence of "I" relieves him of all hatred, malice and uncharitableness. "I" is an aspect of Bloom's mind, for the moment given separate form and life. Like Bloom, the Nameless One can see two sides of a question, only for him both sides are equally rotten. He is two-eyed, but both eyes are evil eyes. In the rich collection of "characters" in English literature "I" is sure of his place on the line; and so is the Citizen, who shares with Bloom and the Nameless One the honours of the sitting.

The Citizen is an over lifesize Fenian nationalist. His vituperative eloquence reaches the colossal. For him the world is a simple and vivid place. There is one supremely good thing in it, Ireland, and one thing too vile for words (though he does his best)—England. The rest of it has for him only a vague existence. The French, a set of dancing masters, "never worth a roasted fart to Ireland," and the Germans, "sausageeating bastards," are brushed aside in a couple of phrases; as for the English, they have no re-deeming feature. Their religion is hypocrisy; their form of government is slavery; their art, music and literature were stolen from the Irish. In this connection he addresses to them the following benison: "Their syphilisation, you mean," says the Citizen. "To hell with them! The curse of a goodfornothing God light sideways on the bloody, thicklugged sons of whores' gets! No music and no art and no literature worthy of the name. Any civilisation they have they stole from us. Tonguetied sons of bastards' ghosts." Their deeds in Ireland are one long record of incessant crime. Patriots like Joe Hynes and John Wyse Nolan seem watery and weak by the side of this ferocious Fenian, although one surmises that Hynes and Nolan may have been "out" in the Easter rising, whereas the Citizen would certainly have been absent. For he is represented as something of a public-house windbag with a prodigious gift of the gab, hanging round and waiting for a patient listener who will put up the pints. How he gets his living we are not told, but "I," as usual, knows something to his discredit. He bought the holding of an evicted tenant, and the Molly Maguires are going to let daylight through him for this betrayal of the cause. Bloom knows that he hawked round a particularly ugly sister with a view, probably, to finding a good Fenian brother-in-law who might help to quench his thirst. By way of local colour he is always accompanied by a great wolfhound; but it doesn't belong to him. He borrows it from Mr. Giltrap.

The Nameless One is a collector of bad and doubtful debts and, while trying to get information about Michael Geraghty, who owes money to Moses Hertzog, he meets Joe Hynes. At Hynes's invitation he accompanies him to Barney Kiernan's saloon. This pub is still going strong in Little Britain Street, but its great days were from fifty to a hundred years ago. Yet still it stands as it was then, non-party market scales hanging from smoked rafters, cobwebs and all complete. Time was when Dan O'Connell and his contemporaries dropped in from the courthouse for a drink, and later on the Earl of Dudley, the popular Viceroy, was an occasional guest, but now, so the genial proprietor assures me, the art of and the taste for conversation (an art developed in the tavern through centuries to perfection) have been vanquished by the cinema, the football field and puritan licensing laws. Besides, the greater part of the business of the courthouse, whose frequenters formed the major part of its clientele, has been transferred to more commodious and accessible premises. Joe tells the Nameless One that he wants to give the hard word to the Citizen about a meeting of the cattle traders' association that had taken place the previous night at the City Arms and, sure enough, on arriving at Barney Kiernan's, they

see the Citizen with Giltrap's wolfhound, Garryowen, and
his pocket full of papers, working for the cause. Bob
Doran is huddled in a corner, drunk. Alf Bergan comes
in, laughing at Denis Breen whom he has just seen, still
on the warpath after the sender of the postcard, U.P. up,
but his laughter wakes Bob Doran. It is a few minutes
later that Bloom enters the house. He has for some time
been walking to and fro from the door of the pub to the
corner of Little Green Street, trying to catch Martin
Cunningham. On the third sight of him, walking up and
down, the Citizen hails him and tells him to come in.
The others are so interested in a few letters from pros-
pective hangmen, brought in for their delectation by Alf
Bergan, that Bloom's entry passes unnoticed.

Bloom's mood has changed. Taciturn and reserved as
he was in the Ormond Hotel, in Barney Kiernan's he is
nervous and talkative. No matter what the subject of conversation may be he can always amplify it with an instruc-
tive lecture. He refuses a drink from his colleague, Joe
Hynes, but accepts a cigar, and at once joins in the talk
on the effect of hanging on the male sexual organ. There
is no interior monologue to inform us of Bloom's thought
processes. The Bloom of *The Cyclops* episode is the Bloom
seen and heard by the nameless narrator.

" 'That can be explained by science,' says Bloom. 'It's
only a natural phenomenon, don't you see, because on
account of the . . .'

"And then he starts off with his jaw-breakers about phenomenon and science, and this phenomenon and the
other phenomenon. . . ."

The Citizen, Joe and Bloom go on from this one aspect
of capital punishment to the champions of Ireland who
suffered death for the cause (most of them, the brothers
Shears, Emmet, Tone, sentenced in the neighbouring

sessions-house by Lord Norbury) and "I" proceeds, aided by the observation and memory of his friend, Pisser Burke:

"And Bloom, of course, with his knockmedown cigar putting on swank with his lardy face. Phenomenon! The fat heap he married is a nice old phenomenon, with a back on her like a ball-alley. Time they were stopping up in the City Arms Pisser Burke told me there was an old one there with a cracked loodheramaun of a nephew, and Bloom trying to get the soft side of her doing the molly-coddle playing bezique to come in for a bit of the wam-pum in her will and not eating meat of a Friday because the old one was always thumping her craw and taking the lout out for a walk. At one time he led him the rounds of Dublin, and by the holy farmer he never cried crack till he brought him home as drunk as a boiled owl . . . Jesus, I had to laugh at Pisser Burke taking them off chew-ing the fat and Bloom with his *but don't you see?* and *but on the other hand . . ."*

Bloom's nerves betray him into a significant lapse of speech. Joe Hynes is standing another round of drinks and Bloom again declines. He must see Martin Cunning-ham. Dignam's insurance policy is mortgaged, but as he neglected to serve a notice of assignment on the company the mortgagee can't recover.

" 'Holly wars,' says Joe, laughing. 'That's a good one if old Shylock is landed. So the wife comes out top dog, what?'

" 'Well, that's a point,' says Bloom, 'for the wife's ad-mirers.'

" 'Whose admirers?' says Joe.

" 'The wife's advisers, I mean,' says Bloom.

"Then he starts all confused mucking it up about the mortgagor under the act. . . . He was bloody safe he wasn't run in himself under the act that time as a rogue and vagabond only he had a friend in court. Selling bazaar tickets, or what do you call it, Royal Hungarian privileged lottery. . . ."

Mention of the meeting of the cattle traders' association brings up the subject of the foot and mouth disease, and here again Bloom has plenty to say. "Because he was up one time in a knacker's yard walking about with his book and his pencil, here's my head and my heels are coming till Joe Cuffe gave him the order of the boot for giving lip to a grazier. Mister Knowall. Teach your grandmother how to milk ducks. . . ."

The conversation veering to the subject of Irish national sports and pastimes finds Bloom equally well informed.

". . . And of course Bloom had to have his say, that if a fellow had rower's heart violent exercise was bad. I declare to my antimacassar if you took up a straw from the bloody floor and if you said to Bloom: 'Look at, Bloom. Do you see that straw? That's a straw.' Declare to my aunt he'd talk about it for an hour so he would and talk steady."

From sport in general to the Keogh-Bennett fight is but a step. Bloom tries hard to turn their attention to lawn tennis and the circulation of the blood, but in vain. First comes the fight, and after the fight the projected concert tour, just what Bloom expected, and just what he wanted to avoid.

" 'Mrs. Bloom is the bright particular star, isn't she?' says Joe.

" 'My wife?' says Bloom. 'She's singing, yes. I think it will be a success, too. He's an excellent man to organise. Excellent.'

" 'Hoho, begob,' says I to myself, says I. 'That explains the milk in the cocoanut and the absence of hair on the animal's chest. . . . That's the bucko that'll organise her, take my tip. 'Twixt me and you, Caddereesh.' "

J. J. O'Molloy and Ned Lambert come in and after them John Wyse Nolan and Lenehan, the latter with a long face on account of the failure of his tip to win the Gold Cup. Looking around for something for nothing as usual he spies an open biscuit tin, but finds it empty. The Citizen tries to quarrel with Bloom, but his only success is to provoke that moderate man to the rejoinder: "Some people can see the mote in others' eyes but they can't see the beam in their own." The Citizen replies with another saw: "There's none so blind as the fellow that won't see." And with a great flow of patriotic eloquence predicts a day when the products of Irish industry shall be sought after the world over, and when, to protect her merchandise and her shores, Ireland shall have her own battleships upon the seas.

" 'And will again,' says he, 'when the first Irish battleship is seen breasting the waves with our own flag to the fore, none of your Henry Tudor harps, no, the oldest flag afloat, the flag of Desmond and Thomond, three crowns on a blue field, the three sons of Milesius.' "

They all condemn the cruel discipline and degrading flogging in the British navy, till the irrepressible Bloom interrupts:

" 'But,' says Bloom, 'isn't discipline the same everywhere? I mean wouldn't it be the same here if you put force against force?' "

A moment later the Citizen asks Bloom bluntly what *his* nation is.

" '. . . Ireland,' says Bloom. 'I was born here. Ireland. . . . And I belong to a race too,' says Bloom, 'that is hated and persecuted. Also now. This very moment. This very instant . . . But it's no use,' says he. 'Force, hatred, his-

tory, all that. That's not life for men and women, insult
and hatred. And everybody knows that it's the very opposite of that that is really life.'

" 'What?' says Alf.

" 'Love,' says Bloom. 'I mean the opposite of hatred. I
must go now,' says he to John Wyse, 'just round to the
court a moment to see if Martin is there. If he comes just
say I'll be back in a second. Just a moment.' "

While Bloom is away Lenehan suggests as a reason for
his hasty departure that he has a few bob on the Gold Cup
winner Throwaway, and has gone round to collect his
winnings from the bookmaker.

" 'That's where he's gone,' says Lenehan. 'I met Bantam
Lyons going to back that horse only I put him off it, and
he told me Bloom gave him the tip. Bet you what you like
he has a hundred shillings to five on. He's the only man
in Dublin has it. A dark horse.' "

"I" goes out into the yard to pumpship, and on his return hears John Wyse Nolan telling the others that it was
Bloom who revealed to Arthur Griffith the forms of organisation and methods of action of certain Hungarian patriots and that Griffith had adapted these to the use of
Sinn Fein. Martin Cunningham, entering with two
friends, is appealed to and confirms the statement. "I"
comments on it: " '. . . Gob, that puts the bloody kybosh
on it if old sloppyeyes is mucking up the show. Give us
a bloody chance. God save Ireland from the likes of that
bloody mouseabout.' " Further commentary on Bloom, his
character and his family, is in progress when that innocent
man reappears in a great hurry. This is too much for the
Citizen. Bloom has been the reasonable man among par-
tisans, a Jew among Gentiles and now, to crown it all, he
is, as they mistakenly think, the lucky punter who basely

avoids standing a round of drinks for the less fortunate brethren.

" 'Don't tell anyone,' says the Citizen, letting a bawl out of him. 'It's a secret.' "

Martin Cunningham sees trouble brewing, and hustles Bloom out of the pub into the waiting car. The Citizen shouts: "Three cheers for Israel!" and the excited Bloom stands up in the car talking and gesticulating.

" 'And,' says he:

" 'Mendelssohn was a Jew, and Karl Marx, and Mercadante and Spinoza. And the Saviour was a Jew and his Father was a Jew. Your God.'

" 'He had no Father,' says Martin. 'That'll do now. Drive ahead.'

" 'Whose God!' says the Citizen.

" 'Well, his uncle was a Jew,' says he. 'Your God was a Jew. Christ was a Jew like me.'

"Gob, the Citizen, made a plunge back into the shop.

" 'By Jesus,' says he, 'I'll brain that bloody Jewman for using the Holy name. By Jesus, I'll crucify him, so I will. Give us that biscuit box here.' "

He dives back into the pub, grabs the empty biscuit tin, sniffed at by Garryowen, approached in vain by the hungry Lenehan, rushes out into Little Britain Street, and hurls the missile at Bloom. But the car was already on the way and rounding the corner into Little Green Street, and the sun got in the Citizen's eye so that he missed, and the tin clattered harmlessly on the pavement.

"And the last we saw was the bloody car rounding the corner and old sheepsface on it gesticulating, and the bloody mongrel after it with his lugs back for all he was bloody well worth to tear him limb from limb. Hundred to five! Jesus! He took the value of it out of him, I promise you.

"When, lo, there came about them all a great brightness, and they beheld the chariot wherein He stood ascend to heaven. And they beheld Him in the chariot, clothed upon in the glory of the brightness, having raiment as of the sun, fair as the moon and terrible that for awe they durst not look upon Him. And there came a voice out of heaven, calling: *Elijah! Elijah!* And he answered with a main cry: *Abba! Adonai!* And they beheld Him, even Him, ben Bloom Elijah, amid clouds of angels ascend to the glory of the brightness at an angle of fortyfive degrees over Donohoe's in Little Green Street like a shot off a shovel."

This is the only episode, *Penelope* excepted, in which Bloom is seen entirely through other eyes. There is no comment of his own on himself or others. First he appears performing furtively a good deed, looking after the Dignam insurance for the grief-stricken widow and orphans. Then he is guest in the strangers' house. A child of light, he is entertained by the children of this world. He begins at the beginning by bringing the light of intelligence to bear on such simple questions as physical exercise, diseases of cattle and so on, but soon enters the dangerous ground of the conduct of life and the relation of living man to his past. Messengers from Mars and such-like people, who, having swallowed history, talk as if there were no past, are asking for the glory of martyrdom. The religious reformer is all very well while he sticks to form, but let him not go to the root of the matter and tell people how to think and live. Bloom, who has no son in whom to place his messianic hopes, must be son and messiah to himself. He asks for martyrdom and gets it. He appreciates it.

There is only one explanation of Bloom's change of mood and that is that the spirit bloweth whither it listeth;

yet his argumentative nervousness is evidently due to happenings in 7 Eccles Street. He shows this in his blunders in speech: "admirers" for "advisers," and in his desperate efforts to avoid the subject of Blazes Boylan, Marion and the concert tour. He is perfectly certain that by this time Boylan and Marion are past rehearsing *Love's Old Sweet Song*. In the Ormond Hotel his nerves were stilled and drugged with music, drink and food, and he was critical and taciturn. In Barney Kiernan's they are set on edge by political discussion. He becomes a man with a mission, reforming the world by the force of the spoken word. It is beautifully normal and logical that he shall seize the opportunity of making good on the large field of society what he has lost in the family bedroom, thus turning private woe into a source of public weal. The ideas he defends are his own. He always held humanity to be above races and creeds, but on many occasions he would have let the Irish nationalists talk their fill unopposed. His Irish fellow citizens will have none of him as Irishman or world-reformer, and so he goes one better. He affirms his Judaism and becomes prophet and messiah.

There is a strain of naïveté in Bloom. He seems not to know that oppressed nationalities have a peculiar and ferocious snobbery that for exclusiveness far outdoes the snobbery of schools and clubs. When he makes his perfectly reasonable claim as a Jew to be regarded as belonging to an oppressed people they look on him as a vile outsider, an impudent gate-crasher. He is in the position of the council schoolboy caught wearing a Harrow tie. And when he adds to that a recital of the cultural achievements of the Jews, one of which is the Christian religion, there is nothing for it but the ascent into heaven. On Irish soil there is no longer room for him. Yet Bloom furthered the cause of Irish nationalism. He informed Arthur Griffith of the Hungarian scheme of action on which Sinn Fein was founded although he must have done so in a scientific, not a combative spirit. All the others in Barney Kiernan's are proud, violent men, willing to kill and be killed for their cause. Not so Bloom. For him the human body, its well-being and continued existence, is the greatest good, the worthiest cause of all.

Hitherto for Bloom's past we have had to rely on Bloom's memory. In *The Cyclops* episode Bloom's recollections are extended and confirmed by the observation of Pisser Burke and the Nameless One. Bloom once hung round an elderly female with a view to being mentioned in her will. Cattle merchant Joe Cuffe gave him the sack because he cheeked a grazier customer. We learn, too, that Bloom was once in danger of being proceeded against on a charge of selling illegal lottery tickets.

All these things are no doubt part of Bloom's history, for neither Pisser Burke nor "I" invent facts. They are too artistic to ignore nature. They merely select, arrange and exaggerate. Joyce read to me on the day he wrote it the passage, already quoted, where "I" says: "I declare to my antimacassar if you took up a straw from the bloody floor and if you said to Bloom: *'Look at, Bloom. Do you see that straw? That's a straw.'* Declare to my aunt he'd talk about it for an hour, so he would, and talk steady."

"You see," said Joyce, " 'I' is really a great admirer of Bloom who, besides being a better man, is also more cunning, a better talker, and more fertile in expedients. If you reread *Troilus and Cressida* you will see that of all the heroes Thersites respects only Ulysses. Thersites admires Ulysses."

CHAPTER IX

From the time of my meeting with Joyce to the time of the completion of *The Cyclops* episode was a period packed with great events. The Allies gathered themselves together after the great Ludendorff offensive, took the offensive themselves on all fronts, and forced the Germans to sue for peace. The influenza pestilence was very severe in Switzerland, and in the middle of it came the general strike. Cavalry patrols and an unending procession of funeral hearses took the place of trams and trains for a week till the strike collapsed, as general strikes, passive and aimless as they are, must collapse. They state a problem but have no means of solving it. The soldiers who were called up from the peasant cantons to protect the town of Zürich suffered terribly in the epidemic. Khaki-clad, blue-clad British and French soldiers invalided out of Germany into Switzerland in exchange for badly wounded German and Austrian soldiers in French and English captivity went back to their homes. There was a hasty shutting-down of expensive wartime institutions, including the one in which I was employed, the Ministry of Information. Typists and secretaries hurried to Versailles. Nations began to beat their howitzers into typewriters for the forthcoming series of conferences. *Schiebers,* whispering business in the corners of cafés, vanished, and their places were taken by official representatives of international trade. Foreign merchandise began to trickle in.

"Who won this war?" said Joyce.

"We shall know," I said, "when the mass production goods come pouring in. The salesmen are the new shock troops."

The first we saw were tins of Japanese salmon at eight-pence a tin filling a shop window on the Limmat Quai. We built no general conclusion on this one fact, but we bought a tin apiece. It was not until March 1919 that the office to which I was attached, then fully liquidated, dispensed with my services.

Apart from its Föhn winds, dreaded by some, Zürich is a pleasant place to live in. It is big enough for solitude and small enough for intimacy. It can be seen as a whole and thought of as a whole. Friends are often, but not inevitably, met on the Bahnhofstrasse. The cafés, wineshops and restaurants are numerous, good and to suit all tastes. For the élite there are the Élite and the Baur au Lac; for the strong there are Spanish and Swiss wineshops and Swiss beerhouses; for the indifferent, the impecunious or the teetotallers there are the alkoholfreie restaurants of the Frauenverein, and for the lover of good wine there is, among others, the Pfauen restaurant-café. The Pfauen was Joyce's favourite and our general rendezvous. Across the courtyard at the back of it was the Pfauentheater, the smaller of the two municipal theatres of Zürich. The standard of dramatic art was very high there. I remember a wonderful performance of Heinrich von Kleist's *Der Zerbrochene Krug,* and I have often heard Joyce praise the Bluntschli of Bruno Wunschmann and the Thersites of Karstens.

The white wine at the Pfauen was excellent. I never saw Joyce drink red wine unless white was unobtainable, and then he did it with a bad grace. It is one of the few things on which he is rigidly doctrinaire. When I asked the reason for his preference he said:

"White wine is like electricity. Red wine looks and tastes like a liquified beefsteak."

A Fendant de Sion in carafe was the specialty of the house. It was supplied by Mr. Paul Wiederkehr, who was a pupil of Joyce and also the inventor of that very drinkable temperance beverage Bilzbrause, now no longer obtainable, I understand, for love or money. The colour of Fendant is a pale greenish amber, and its taste suggests an earth rich in copper ore.

"Er schmeckt nach Erz," said Paul Suter. ("It tastes like ore.")

And Joyce, staring thoughtfully and with malice behindthought, at the yellow-tinted contents of the carafe, said slowly:

"Erzherzogin." ("Archduchess.")

And Erzherzogin it was and remained. Under this guise, or by her Italian title more affected by the Triestine Dubliner, this imaginary *arciduchessa* has had many a brimming cup raised and lowered in her *Minnedienst*.

The waitress knew our simple wants, and supplied them without unnecessary questions and responses. First came the carafe of Archduchess, and then followed two Brissagos already aglow. Our table was in a curtained-off corner of the establishment, and was neighbour to the *Stammtisch* of a *Studentenkorps*. The wall above their table was decorated with their caps and other symbols of their mysteries. They drifted in at intervals, read correspondence and papers, smoked pipes, talked little, and drank beer. Joyce and I were, perhaps, the most punctual attenders at the Pfauen, but Mrs. Joyce and Mr. and Mrs. Sykes were often there, as were also Paul Suter and another Basler friend and colleague, Danni Hummel. August Suter's work and family kept him in Zollikon and prevented him from paying the *Stammtisch* more than an occasional visit. My friends Louis and Katherine Sargent turned up for a few séances on the occasion of their fortnight's stay in Zürich in 1919.

The sculptors and painters of our little society often went to the Spanish wineshops of Niederdorf, but it was rare that Joyce met us in these haunts. He found the sweet, syrupy and, probably, doctored Spanish wines un-drinkable. But one of August Suter's sculptor assistants discovered an excellent restaurant in the Augustinergasse, overshadowed by the pile of the Augustiner-Kirche where worship the Old-Catholics, seceders from the Roman Church in 1871 when the infallibility of the Pope was proclaimed a dogma. This restaurant, the Augustinerhof, was patronised by Zürich working men and a group of Czechs, all lured, no doubt, by the irresistible lure of a copious lunch at the modest price of one franc fifty. When I told Joyce about it he said:

"Good. I'm glad you told me. Some Greek friends of mine were asking me if I knew of a cheap restaurant. I'll tell them. You don't mind?"

I said I didn't, but I feared the worst. And in fact, the Czechs discussing business and the Zürich working men holding an inquest on each hand of cards never made half the noise of this table full of Greeks.

"Have they turned up yet?" asked Joyce. "What do you think of them?"

"Not much," I said. It was a coincidence, of course, but a line of *Hellas* occurred to me when I looked at them: "Kill. Burn. Let not a Greek escape."

"That's Kriegspsychose," said Joyce. "Seriously, they are very nice people, and they have been very useful to me."

"Aren't they strangely like Jews?" I said. "They look like Jews, and they all talk at once and nobody listens."

"Not so strangely," said Joyce. "Anyway, they are Greeks. And there's a lot to be said for the theory that the *Odyssey* is a Semitic poem."

The Augustinerhof was also the rendezvous of a society of deaf mutes. Joyce regarded them as symbols of ill-fortune. Paul Suter's nerves could never abide their inhuman efforts at human speech. For myself I considreed it a duty of human solidarity to suppress all nervous reactions in presence of the afflicted brethren.

Joyce believed that the best gate of entry to the spirit of ancient Greece was the modern Greek. He told me something about my new lunchmates. Nikola Santos was illiterate, but could recite many long passages of the *Odyssey* learned by ear. Pavlos Phokas bore the name of a Byzantine emperor, but was clerk in a Zürich commercial house. Antonio Chalas had written a book proving that the centre of gravity of the earth passed through Athens, and that therefore the great powers should guarantee the perpetual immunity of Greece. He sent a copy of this work to President Wilson, but whether his opus played any great part in subsequent international councils is not recorded. Joyce must have known a great number of the Zürich Greeks of those days. I met only one of them, Mr. Paulo Ruggiero, who was invaluable on Joyce's birthday night (a great event in the Joycean household) for the preparation of middle eastern exotic dishes. He was an amiable man, and as resourceful as he was amiable. His one great wish was to return to his native levantine land, but he is still, I believe, a bank employee in Athens on the Limmat. The name of Joyce's Jewish friends was legion, for the rule regarding Greeks applied with still greater force to the unchanging Jew, whose nationality is fortified with religion. They were of all classes and from all countries, and included rich merchants and manufacturers of Zürich and poor Galician immigrants.

"It was through the intervention of a Greek merchant prince of the great house of Ralli and of a Greek nobleman, Count Francesco de Sordina, the *Grand Seigneur* of Trieste and one of the greatest swordsmen in Europe in his time," said Joyce, "that I was enabled to leave Austria in war time on parole."

Believing that human nature is, in the main, subdued to what it works in, like the dyer's hand, I always regarded trade or caste as primary influences in forming character. Joyce, on the other hand, attached greater weight to race, nation, and to some real yet indefinite thing one might call type.

Joyce's method of composition always seemed to me to be that of a poet rather than that of a prose writer. The words he wrote were far advanced in his mind before they found shape on paper. He was constantly and indefatigably in pursuit of the solution to some problem of homeric correspondence or technical expression or trait of character in Bloom or another personage of *Ulysses;* or some physiological fact was necessary to give him the key to some part of his epic of the human body. Sculptor or painter, daylight worker, having laid aside the tools of his trade for the day, would relax, but Joyce's preoccupation with his book was never ending. He was always looking and listening for the necessary fact or word; and he was a great believer in his luck. What he needed would come to him. That which he collected would prove useful in its time and place. And as, in a sense, the theme of *Ulysses* is the whole of life, there was no end to the variety of material that went to its building. Of the time detail of 1904 there was none around him, but what he saw and heard in 1918 or 1919 would do just as well, for the shapes of life remain constant: only the dress and manners change. I have seen him collect in the space of a few hours the oddest assortment of material: a parody on the *House that Jack Built,* the name and action of a poison, the method of caning boys on training ships, the wobbly cessation of a tired unfinished sentence, the nervous trick of a convive turning his glass in inward-turning circles, a Swiss music-hall joke turning on a pun in Swiss dialect, a description of the Fitzsimmons shift.

In one of the richest pages of *Ulysses* Stephen, on the sea shore, communing with himself and tentatively building with words, calls for his tablets. These should have been library slips, acquired by the impecunious and ingenious poet from the library counter. On that occasion he had forgotten to provide himself with this convenient writing material, and was forced to use the fag-end of Mr. Deasy's letter. As far as concerns the need for tablets, the self-portrait was still like, only in Zürich Joyce was never without them. And they were not library slips, but little writing blocks specially made for the waistcoat pocket. At intervals, alone or in conversation, seated or walking, one of these tablets was produced, and a word or two scribbled on it at lightning speed as ear or memory served his turn. No one knew how all this material was given place in the completed pattern of his work, but from time to time in Joyce's flat one caught glimpses of a few of those big orange-coloured envelopes that are one of the glories of Switzerland, and these I always took to be storehouses of building material. The method of making a multitude of criss-cross notes in pencil was a strange one for a man whose sight was never good. A necessary adjunct to the method was a huge oblong magnifying glass. Early in 1919 Joyce had reason to fear an eye attack and, to stave it off, left Zürich, plagued with Föhn wind, and went to Locarno. I accompanied him.

"What an experience it is," said Joyce, "to go through the Gothard tunnel. On one side of the mountain everything is gloomy and depressing, and on the other side everything is bright and tonic."

One day in Locarno I had taken my painting material out to the Delta and, tired of prospecting for a motive, was lying on the grass, when Joyce appeared between the trees.

"Take a look at this, will you?" he said. "I can't make head or tail of it."

He handed me a leaf I recognised as having been torn from the familiar waistcoat pocket block.

"Can you read it?" he asked.

"I can't," said I. "There are about a dozen words written in all directions, up, down and across. I can't make out one complete word."

"Try with this," he said, handing me the magnifying glass. "A few letters will do if you can't read a whole word."

But the magnifying glass magnified also the pencil smudges and made the labyrinth of pencilled lines bigger but not clearer, so I had to give it up after sighting and reporting several foggy shapes of letters which, however, were sufficient to give him his bearings. By the way, when I first met Joyce he had undergone the first of his ten eye operations.

From time to time I have sought among painters a correspondence for Joyce and his writing, but the art of painting with oil paint has cultivated a human quality that can render no service in Joyce's workshop. Oil painting has, more than any other creative art, demanded temperament of its servants; and temperament I define as the involuntary co-operation of the body in the work of the mind. Every great master of oil painting—Rembrandt, Rubens, Delacroix—had this quality in great measure and under due control. No writer can use temperament as the painter can use it, but Joyce has no use for it at all. Sudden impulses and vehemences are to him a disturbance. They must wait their turn, which is discouraging for them. If there is a correspondence for Joyce's writing in the pictorial arts it is the mosaic artists of Rome and Ravenna who would supply it. No nervous impulses created for them or disturbed their handiwork. They built up with inexhaustible patience their figures of saints and angels out of tiny pieces of coloured stone.

The name Rembrandt has occasionally occurred to me as a correspondence. Not in temperament, colour, mood. In these respects no two artists were ever less alike. Joyce paints in a light key and his shadows are full of colour. But there are other similarities. Both are adepts at the self and family portrait, and both take ancient legends and present them in the dress and accent of their own day. Perhaps, too, just as Joyce may have seemed to us to be a collector of words for words' sake, Rembrandt seemed to his neighbours to be a great harbourer of junk for junk's sake in the shape of odds and ends picked up in the market-place. Until, behold, the useless antique helmet, the strange unwearable eastern gown, the odd-shaped sword reappeared, flooded with light, in a picture, clothing and adorning a brace of his neighbours, true-to-life portraits yet with all the significance of religious symbols. And in Joyce's case the word that fell from the lips of cardriver or convive would be noted on the waistcoat pocket block, receive its shape and setting and be heard again with a new intonation in the mouth of one of the personages of his invention—wandering Jew, troglodyte or bartender, but for sure a phantom portrait of one of his neighbours.

Every artist loves his material as well as the design to which it gives body—the painter his precious colour; the sculptor his stone, metal, wood; the stained glass artist his tinted hyaline; the poet words. But to Joyce words are more than a pleasurable material out of which agreeable patterns can be made, or thought and emotion communicated. They are quick with human history as pitchblende with radium, or coal with heat and flame. They have a will and life of their own and are not to be put like lead soldiers, but to be energised and persuaded like soldiers of flesh and blood. The commerce of life new mints them every day and gives them new values in the exchanges, and Joyce is ever listening for living speech from any human lips.

"What a lot of nonsense is talked about style," he said.

This was apropos of *The Oxen of the Sun*.

Mr. Deasy said to Stephen: "To learn one must be humble," and in the sense of listening and learning Joyce certainly has the virtue of humility. There is nothing snobbish in his devotion to his material.

A visitor to Joyce's apartment alluded to a picture on the wall as a photograph. In mentioning the fact to me, Joyce said:

"Now I couldn't see anything ridiculous in that. It isn't the usual word, but surely light-writing is a beautiful word to apply to a painted picture.

Seeing words as mysterious means of expression as well as an instrument of communication made Joyce sometimes a severe critic of his contemporaries. Not that he often praised or condemned or even mentioned their productions. I once alluded to one of his contemporaries as a great writer.

"Is he?" said Joyce. "What has he written?"

I began to describe a dramatic scene in a provincial hotel, when Joyce interrupted:

"Tell me something of it in his own words."

"Ah, the words. I can't remember the actual words of the book."

"But why can't you?" said Joyce. "When you remember a scene or a sonnet of Shakespeare you can tell me about it in the words that conveyed it to you. Why can't you do so in this case? Some one passage ought to stick."

"Do you think that is necessary?"

"I do. When you talk painting to Taylor, Sargent or Suter you don't talk about the object represented but about the painting. It is the material that conveys the image of jug, loaf of bread, or whatever it is, that interests you. And quite rightly, I should say, because that is where the beauty of the artist's thought and handiwork become one. If this writer is as good as you say he is, I can't understand why some of his prose hasn't stuck in your otherwise excellent memory."

Joyce's memory for the words of his own compositions and for those of all writers he admired was prodigious. He knew by heart whole pages of Flaubert and of Newman and De Quincey and of many others. Most human memories begin to fail at midnight, and lapse into the vague and *à peu près,* but not that of Joyce. It was while we were at Locarno that we returned once to our pension at about midnight, and sat for a while in Joyce's room. We had been talking about Milton's *Lycidas,* and I wanted to quote some lines of it that pleased me. My memory gave out, but Joyce said the whole poem from beginning to end, and followed it up with *L'Allegro.* I wonder if Macaulay could have done as much at midnight after a litre of Nostrano? Dante he knew as lover and scholar, and he was an ardent admirer of Verlaine. One evening in my studio in the Seefeldstrasse Paul Suter recited that poem of Verlaine which begins:

> *Les roses étaient toutes rouges*
> *Et les lierres étaient tout noirs.*
> *Chère, pour peu que tu te bouges,*
> *Renaissent tous mes désespoirs.*

Joyce asked him to repeat it.

"That," he said, "is perfection. No more beautiful poem has ever been made. And yet I wonder at what hour, a.m. or p.m., are roses quite red and ivy perfectly black?"

That same evening Joyce sang to us a passage from Palestrina's "Mass for Pope Marcellus," and after that a medieval introit. His tenor voice pleased my untrained ear. It made me think of stones lying at the bottom of a river. He had a piano in his flat, and often sang, but I never heard him sing better than that night in the studio without any accompanying instrument. He was in exceptional form, or it was on account of the structure, mainly wood, and entirely without hangings of any kind.

I was a better judge of his voice as an organ for speaking verse. His gramophone records of the end of *Anna Livia Plurabelle* are typical of voice and method. The lower pitch of his speaking voice is darkly metallic, and he slows down the tempo of the verse to the last reasonable degree to extract from each syllable its full essence of sound. Shelley's "When the lamp is shattered" is a poem I often heard him speak, and occasionally he would reinforce "O Love, who bewailest" with the gesture of an upheld, straight stretched hand. Mangan, the subject of one of his rare critical essays, was a favourite of his among Irish poets. We often heard him recite "Dark Rosaleen" and "O'Hussey's Ode to the MacGuire." A poem of Yeats', new to Joyce, appeared in *The Little Review,* "When the heart grows old." Joyce read it, and exclaimed:

"No living poet can write better than that."

"It sounds like the song of experience," I said.

We both agreed in admiring Coleridge, but when I expressed great admiration for the lyrical dramas of Shelley he objected:

"No doubt there is much beauty in 'Prometheus Unbound' and 'Hellas,' but I feel that it's all on the wrong track."

Joyce spoke Italian like a native. It was, and still is, the house language of his family. In German he was fluent, but I have heard him say of both German and Italian that they were not "persuasive" languages; and of French: "A poor instrument, perhaps, compared with Italian or English, but how wonderfully they use it!" One evening, however, when four of us were sitting in the Augustinerhof—Joyce, Hummel, Paul Suter and myself—Joyce asked Paul to repeat a poem in German, and Paul recited to us the verses of the ill-fated Hölderlin:

> *Wo bist du? trunken dämmert die Seele mir*
> *Von aller deiner Wonne; denn eben ist's,*
> *Das ich gesehn wie, müde seiner*
> *Fahrt, der entzückende Götterjüngling*
> *Die jungen Locken badet im Goldgewölk. . . .*

And on this occasion Joyce expressed the opinion that German was a rich, musical tongue. Joyce studied Irish under Pearse, but Pearse's lessons, he said, were marred by his prejudice against the English language and on this account he discontinued the Irish lessons and turned his attention to Norwegian which he has studied to this day. To him, in any case, Dublin is more a Scandinavian than a Celtic city.

The name, fate and work of Shakespeare shimmer, a recurrent colour motive, through the pages of *Ulysses*. He was a Ulyssean type, a wanderer from home, ever longing to return and at last returning. Joyce pictures him in the full maturity of his creative life, spurred on to creation by the certainty of change and death. "In Gerard's rosery of Fetter lane he walks, greyedauburn. One life is all. One body. Do. But do." If he were not a constant preoccupation with Joyce his shade would not have haunted Dublin on Bloomsday, 1904. Therefore it was a slight shock to me when I heard Joyce with an accent of conviction refuse him pre-eminence as a dramatist. The man himself with his human problem, the mystery of his destiny, the inventor of a throng of thoughts and forms, above all the peerless master of words: Yes. But as a dramatist he placed him far below Ibsen. It was shortly after I had met Joyce that we were sitting in the Astoria café one evening and talking of the play. Joyce asked me what as drama I found excellent in Shakespeare. I cited at random the despair of Othello: "I pray you in your letters . . ."

"Yes," said Joyce. "I see the pathos of the situation and the force of the words, but not the tragic conflict. When Rubek and Irene meet in *When We Dead Awaken,* the one spiritually dead, the other, into whom his genius had passed, fiercely alive yet without power to give form to the life within her, their most trivial word is more dramatic than all the magical verses of *Othello.*

Nevertheless, when the question, often put, "If on a desert island what one book?" was again raised, Joyce said:

"I should hesitate between Dante and Shakespeare but not for long. The Englishman is richer and would get my vote."

Of all the great nineteenth century masters of fiction

Joyce held Flaubert in highest esteem. When I mentioned Balzac, he said:

"I am inclined to think that Balzac's reputation rests on a lot of neat generalisations about life."

I asked him if he did not think Dostoevsky a supremely great writer.

"No," said Joyce, bluntly. "Rousseau, confessing to stealing silver spoons he had really stolen, is much more interesting than one of Dostoevsky's people confessing to an unreal murder."

"And what about Tolstoy?"

"He is different," Joyce said. "Tolstoy is a great writer. Think of the story of the rich man's devotion to his poor manservant—*Master and Man.* After Flaubert the best work in novel form has been done by Tolstoy, Jacobsen and D'Annunzio."

Of modern English fiction writers Joyce spoke little, and I suspected that that was what he thought, but I have heard him express admiration for the work of George Moore. Speaking of *Esther Waters,* he said:

"Strange that it should have been left to an Irishman to write the best novel of modern English life!"

Very often, however, he would break off his references to other writers with a hasty, "But, you know, I don't pretend to be a good critic." And this I took to be neither an attitude of modesty nor a fear of committing himself, but a plain statement of a necessary limitation; for the artist's admirations and denials are active forces in shaping and directing his own work. He cannot allow himself the luxury of catholicity.

While Joyce was planning and composing *The Cyclops* episode of his book he reread Swift. At the same time Thackeray's essay on Swift came into my hands. We were

walking down the Rämistrasse when, the Uetliberg before
us suggesting a giant, Joyce said:

"Swift treated the giant-dwarf theme a little too simply.
He just multiplies or divides by twelve, and forgets that
when you multiply or divide you create another organism.
There must be a relative difference of speed, resistance to
air pressure, and so on."

I mentioned Thackeray's opinion that Swift was an
Englishman, to which Joyce demurred, both on account
of Swift being born in Dublin and of much in his character that is essentially Irish.

"Thackeray writes also of Swift's secret grief," I said.

"Yes? What do you make of that?"

"I suppose," I said, "that the proud, sensitive man
needed love but that pride robbed him of the power of
self-surrender that love demands of man or woman."

"Maybe," said Joyce. "But that isn't enough. The reason must be not latent but manifest. Anyway, the man was
a strong and stingy sentimentalist. He meddled with and
muddled up two women's lives."

Joyce was a great admirer of Defoe. He possessed his
complete works, and had read every line of them. Of only
three other writers, he said, could he make this claim:
Flaubert, Ben Jonson and Ibsen. *Robinson Crusoe* he
called the English *Ulysses*. Joyce read to me once the *Prologue* to *The Canterbury Tales,* stopping often to repeat
the lines and retaste the elegant humour of each one.

"Of all English writers Chaucer is the clearest. He is as
precise and slick as a Frenchman."

Music was an art on which Joyce could talk with authority, and Zürich in the days when we were there was
a great town for the music lover. We were sitting in the
Astoria café one evening when the band, after playing a

fragment of Beethoven, began Mozart's Don Giovanni overture.

"Listen," said Joyce. "How full of grace and invention is Mozart after the muscle-bound Beethoven."

When the Mozart overture was finished Joyce said:

"Beethoven is generally regarded as greatest of all musicians. Is there any painter who would be given the same place among painters?"

I said I thought if any pre-eminence were accorded it would be to Michelangelo.

One evening, while Joyce was writing *The Sirens* episode, he went to hear Bach's *Matthäus Passion*. When I met him afterwards I asked him if he had enjoyed the music. He was silent for a moment, then said:

"I simply cannot understand how any man can mix the synoptic gospels with the gospel according to Saint John."

And I never knew whether he enjoyed Bach's music or not. He was a great admirer of Palestrina, and that not alone for Palestrina's musical achievements. It was as something of a hero that he regarded the great Italian.

"In writing the 'Mass for Pope Marcellus,' " said Joyce, "Palestrina did more than surpass himself as a musician. With that great effort, consciously made, he saved music for the Church."

I once asked Joyce what in all music he considered most beautiful.

"The flute solo in Gluck's *Orpheus*," he said. "It tells of the sick longing for earth of one in Elysian fields. I know of nothing more beautiful than that."

Of all instruments the human voice was Joyce's preference, and of all voices the tenor voice. He had heard de Reszke in Paris. That was a voice he said, that in quality reminded him of his father's voice. He had yet to hear the Franco-Irish Sullivan, for him the tenor in excelsis. He was not a great admirer of Wagner, with the exception of *die Meistersinger* (some famous passages were Bierhalle music) but, in any case, he could listen to opera for the singing alone. The music of the giants in *Rheingold* was perfectly expressive of creative unreproductive beings.

Joyce always disclaimed any knowledge of the plastic and pictorial arts, but he said he had more feeling for sculpture than for painting. He claimed to have been one of the first to recognise the genius of Mestrovic. My own objection to Mestrovic's work as Magic City sculpture he rebutted by showing me a photograph of one piece he particularly admired of the Mestrovic of 1910. It was a relief of a mother and child, and was certainly a work far superior to the exaggerated gestures I had in mind. He picked up a little statuette in Zürich, in plaster I think, representing a woman in modern dress, seated, with a cat on her shoulder. We told him we could see no merit in it.

"But why isn't it good?" said Joyce.

"Because it has no plastic expression at all," said Paul Suter. "You are reading literature into it."

Paul was right. But perhaps the sculptors and painters of the last few decades, in their reaction against anecdote and history, have developed an unnecessary purism in respect of the literature in their productions. They are not content with the purity of their plastic or pictorial vision but, like Emerson's Englishman when the subject of religion was broached, they begin to fidget uneasily when anyone sees a content in their work. Yet this might be a pleasing revelation. On one of the walls of Joyce's flat in the Universitätstrasse was pinned a photograph of a Greek statue of Penelope. It represented a woman, draped, seated, looking at her upheld forefinger. Paul Suter and I went to the flat one evening to plaster up a troublesome mousehole at the back of the stove with plaster brought from August's studio in Zollikon. Joyce swore that Z'ch was visited by an eighth plague of mice. I never noticed it. We stayed on for a glass of Fendant and a Brissago.

"What is she thinking about," said Joyce, pointing to the photograph of the sculptured Penelope.

"She is weighing up her wooers," I said, "trying to decide which one of them will make the most manageable husband."

"To me," said Paul, "she seems to be saying: 'I'll give him just one week more.' "

"My own idea," said Joyce, "is that she is trying to recollect what Ulysses looks like. You see, he has been away many years, and they had no photographs in those days."

When I showed him a photograph of Bourdelle's Penelope he looked on it with disfavour and said:

"That reminds me of modern commentators on Homer."

In spite of his bad sight and his professed lack of expert knowledge of painting, Joyce's flat is full of pictures. There are portraits of his greatgrandfather, James; and greatgrandmother Ann, born McCann; and of his grandfather James as man and boy; and grandmother Ellen, born O'Connell (through whom Joyce is related to Daniel O'Connell, the Liberator), all by Comerford of Cork. Then there are portraits of himself, Giorgio and his father painted by Tuohy, and two drawings of himself, one by Wyndham Lewis and one by Augustus John; a portrait of Lucia by Marie Laurencin, and one of his daughter-in-law by Marchand, portraits of Mrs. Joyce by Silvestri and myself and, among many other pictures, two studies of the Liffey by Jack Yeats and works by Umberto Veruda, Marie Monnier and Ivan Opfer. And besides all the original work there are the reproductions of the masters he admires, notably Vermeer.

Notwithstanding his professions to the contrary, Joyce is in reality a good judge of painting, and he looks, as all good critics do, for the personal qualities behind the material expression. That criticism which pretends to be standoffishly technical is always make-believe. We should be able to perceive at once the pure, serene and generous mind of Corot in the crystal clearness of his painting, and none of Picasso's ingenious disguises should hide from us the maudlin self-pity of the blue period which shines through them all. But Joyce's eyesight made his manner of looking at pictures strange and peculiar. I have seen him take pictures, when their size allowed him to do so, and look at them close up near a window like a myope reading small print. Perhaps (I never asked him) the facture of the painting, the pigment itself, is, in the language of Stephen, a signature there for him to read as it is for the painter. I wondered how he could ever see anything in a picture at that range until I remembered that, making allowance for difference of sight, I did the same thing myself. At the end of his examination he would always attribute to the painting the qualities it in fact had. Of my study for the portrait of Mrs. Joyce he wrote to me in 1919 (I was staying at the time with Louis and Katherine Sargent in Zermatt): "It seems to my barbarian eye a delicate and provocative object." But of the portrait of himself he urged me, "for the love of Manfield," to let people know that the rather outsize Jaeger houseboots were no criterion to the size of the enclosed feet. The difficulty about painting Joyce was to get him to sit at all. The moment arrived when he was suffering from eye trouble and was confined to a semi-darkened room. I accepted the light as I found it and the pose most natural to him. Joyce, when not standing or moving, prefers to lie down but will accept as a workable compromise a sprawl in an easy chair. Mrs. Joyce was an exceptionally good sitter. She sat to me in the studio lent to me by August Suter, came always to time, and posed steadfastly during the whole sitting.

It was in this studio that Joyce put to me one day Stephen's question to Lynch in their talk on aesthetics: "If a man hacking in fury at a block of wood make there an image of a cow, is that image a work of art?" I didn't know the right answer, but am inclined to think it should be "Yes." If a writer were a sleepwalker and in his sleep wrote a page of his book, that page, if worthy, would be allowed to stand part of the text. How it found its way there is a historical consideration. But it seemed to me, in any case, that works of art are so rarely produced in this manner that for all practical purposes (the only purposes I had ever considered) the question would hardly arise.

Joyce frequently alluded to the ceremony, history and dogma of the Catholic Church; and I supposed that this was because the Church, like the city of Dublin and the *Odyssey,* was a part of himself and his history. If the Protestant-Roman Catholic split in Christendom was mentioned he would usually observe that a coherent absurdity is preferable to an incoherent one. Quite right, philosophically, no doubt, but religions are also secular institutions, and from this angle their relative absurdity is less important than the question of the good or harm they do. He did not consider Jesus Christ a perfect man.

"He was a bachelor," said Joyce, "and never lived with a woman. Surely living with a woman is one of the most difficult things a man has to do, and he never did it."

Joyce talked rarely of perversity or crime. One saw in him none of that natural awareness of sexual perversity

characteristic of Proust, none of Dostoevsky's preoccupation with the nightmare of crime. Both these aspects of
life he saw from without, and in the main they were to
him comic. He regarded the English interest in crime in
the shape of the detective story as exceptionally ludicrous,
and considered the English (I don't know on what
grounds, for the French, too, have their Fantomas and
Grand Guignol) prone to thoughts of crime.

On one subject he was more uncommunicative than any
man I know: the subject of politics. He often spoke of
Parnell with great admiration, but it was the mystical
realist navigating the bark of his reputation through the
whirlpool of *The Times* commission that interested him
and not his political principles. An occasional vague reference to the pacific American anarchist, Tucker, was the
only indication I ever heard of a political outlook. His
view seemed to be that government is work for the specialist; and the artist, another specialist, had better leave it
alone. And then government is in the last resort the use
of force, whereas the artist's method is persuasion. True,
the artist, like the rest of the world, is also a citizen, and
laws are made for him to obey and taxes are levied for
him to pay. Actively or passively he is a member of the
social organisation. "Then let it be passively," would express roughly Joyce's attitude. In short, *il cultivait son
jardin*. Generally, if a political discussion arose he would
remain silent waiting a turn of the tide; but once in the
Augustinerhof I said to him:

"Some artists do take an active part in the life of the
State. They feel they want to do something for their kind,
and they look on the State as an instrument. They want
to leave the world better than they found it."

"Or perhaps more like themselves," said Joyce.

"Very likely," I said. "But don't you think they are justified?"

"If they think they are, certainly," said Joyce. "But it isn't my function. And don't you think that when it is a question of bettering and saving the world, the artist has a means nearer to hand than politics?"

"You mean the agency of beauty?"

Joyce nodded, and I saw that this was as much as he was capable of giving assent to.

There is nothing that more characterises a man than how he laughs and why he laughs, and nothing so difficult to hide or affect. The mask of melancholy or solemnity sits well on a man, but a mask of laughter would be an intolerable grimace, and useless, for it would deceive no one. Joyce's sense of humour was of a tonic and refreshing kind that delighted in strange words, puns, incongruities, odd situations, exaggerations and impish angles of vision. There was no sniggering defeatism in it; it was not a bitter, sardonic humour, nor did one ever feel that it was an armour for a vulnerable sensibility. All readers of Joyce's books must have been struck with his gift for mimicry in literature, but if he possesses this gift in the spoken word or in gesture he hides the light of it carefully under a bushel. Mimicry in three-dimensional space can often seem unkind, and Joyce's humour is for his own and his friends' pleasure. Slick verbal wit he never practised among his friends, nor was he an habitual maker of epigrams in the sense of Wilde or Whistler. He kept literature for his books. His humour was altogether unforced and boyish. In impish moods he is the magpie, gloating gravely with bright eyes over the efforts of clumsy humans to find the hidden orange-peel. During our stay in Locarno in the spring of 1919 I came back to lunch one day and found Joyce with a particularly gleeful expression on his face. I asked for a share in the joke.

"What do you call that village of yours?" said Joyce.

"You mean the village where I was born?" I said. "Crowhurst."

"I know," said Joyce. "But when a uniformed official came this morning to get our names and pedigrees for the visitors' tax I told him your birthplace was Crow's Thirst. It was that double litre of Nostrano of ours on the pension table that caught my eye and made me say it."

The following is a story he told Paul Suter and me one evening in the Pfauen:

"A German lady called to see me to-day. She is a writer and wanted me to give an opinion on her work, but she told me she had already shown it to the porter of the hotel where she stays. So I said to her: 'What did your hotel porter think of your work?' She said: 'He objected to a scene in my novel where my hero goes out into the forest, finds a locket of the girl he loves, picks it up and kisses it passionately.' 'But,' I said, 'that seems to me to be a very pleasing and touching incident. What did your hotel porter find wrong with it?' And then she tells me he said: 'It's all right for the hero to find the locket and to pick it up and kiss it, but before he kissed it you should have made him wipe the dirt off it with his coat sleeve.'"

"And what did you tell her?" said Paul and I together.

"I told her," said Joyce "(and I meant it too) to go back to that hotel porter and always to take his advice. 'That man,' I said, 'is a critical genius. There is nothing I can tell you that he can't tell you.'"

One evening in the Pfauen the conversation turned on types of feminine beauty, and I said that I had read somewhere of a king of some cannibal island or other who lined the women folk of the tribe, naked backs against a long horizontal pole. With his royal eye he enfiladed the exposed posteriors, and the possessor of that of greatest prominence he chose for his royal consort. Joyce listened till I had finished the description, then said without a ghost of a smile:

"I sincerely hope that when Bolshevism finally sweeps the world it will spare that enlightened potentate."

On festive occasions and with a suitable stimulus, be-ribboned and wearing a straw picture hat (Autolycus turned pedant and keeping school, Malvolio snapping up unconsidered trifles) Joyce would execute a fantastic dance. It was not a terpsichorean effort of the statuesque Isadora Duncan variety, but a thing of whirling arms, high-kicking legs, grotesque capers and coy grimaces that suggested somehow the ritual antics of a comic religion.

"You look like David," I said, "leaping and dancing before the ark."

As I have said, August Suter made six figures in stone for the Amtshäuser in Zürich. I stood for one of them, and even in the frozen music of stone the likeness persists. It always amused Joyce vastly to see this over-lifesize stone effigy resembling me gazing sternly down upon the free burgesses of Switzerland's commercial capital; and whenever a few of us on our way to the Usteristrasse passed under that gaze at a late hour, he would execute his comic ritual dance in honour of the stone guest, to whom would be poured out suitable libations. This tendency to invent dance figures he must have passed on to his daughter Lucia, who made the most promising beginnings in the art of dancing. She has since, however, abandoned the plastic rhythm of the dance for the more durable still movement of illumination as exemplified in her initial letters to Joyce's *Pomes Penyeach* and to the A.B.C. poem of Chaucer.

Both Joyce and myself experienced in our youth those vintage years of popular song associated with the names of Dan Leno, Harry Randall, Tom Costello, Gus Elen, Arthur Roberts and the other music-hall giants of that time. Then the dollar had not yet beat the pound, and people who lived in the Old Kent Road had not discovered that they had Old Kentucky Homes or Coal Black Mammies in Tennessee. What of that great epoch we knew we sang. Joyce could add "Blarney Castle," "Billy me luv me lad" and some "Come all yous," and I a shanty or two, so that our musical soirées were rich in genuine folksong.

The actual writing of *Ulysses* occupied Joyce about eight years. For half of that time all Europe was at war: and peace, when it came, was as disturbing as, though less destructive than, war. Several revolutions shook the world. Crowns and currencies fell. No permanence was in the air. A dozen times in that period Joyce changed his domicile. The Abbé Sieyés, asked what he did under the terror, replied: *"J'ai vecu."* Joyce, if asked what he did during the Great War, could reply: "I wrote *Ulysses*." He was of an extraordinary toughness of fibre and tenacity of purpose, but neither toughness nor tenacity would have helped him if he had not possessed the faculty of shutting out at will all noises in the street, if he had not been able not to be unduly distressed about what he could not alter. Every man with a self-imposed task in any field of creative effort knows the difficulties that beset him within and without. Van Gogh said that well might the symbol of Saint Luke, patron saint of painters, be an ox, for without the patience and strength of an ox no man could paint. The financial problem has to be faced and solved as well as may be. Hostility and indifference must be overcome, and allies found and cultivated. Doubts and fatigues arise. Sickness comes, or an infertile patch, when, with the best will in the world, the machine refuses to work. And all these things are not alone obstacles to be surmounted, but material to be turned to account. It was part of Joyce's code of action never to turn to journalism when in need. Requests for articles from his pen arrived occasionally in Zürich, but met with a refusal, one and all, although the money would have been acceptable. Joyce's distaste for the subject and his sense of expediency would account for the negative in the case of political articles, but requests for literary articles shared the same fate. He felt that journalism and *Ulysses* would not run well in double harness.

One saw little in Joyce of the normal impatiences of the average male. A retarded meal, a bus or a post missed, or any of the smaller annoyances of life, called forth no show of irritability. When faced with the hostility or ill-will of another human being his comment would purposely be toned down to the subnormal "tedious" and "tiresome," and his strongest term of abuse applied to such persons was the word "lout." The schooling of his reactions in fourteen years of Jesuit training accounted, I thought, for a good deal of this moderation, but there was more in it than a habit of self-discipline. It always seemed to me that he felt that giving way to irritability or anger might hinder his specialist's preoccupation with the detail of daily life as material for literature. A great collector of his neighbours' oaths (see the Citizen in *The Cyclops* episode, and Private Carr in *The Circe*), Joyce himself never or rarely swore by one god or nine. His favourite exclamation when annoyed was a crisply uttered, but in content harmless Italian, "Ma ché!" He has little feeling of attachment to animals. Flowers appeal to him but little. Only for trees among all organic forms has he a pronounced sympathy.

Joyce is a superstitious man. He accepts the popular superstitions with regard to colours and stones and numbers, and he sometimes, like the rest of us, invokes the aid of the tree god, but to all these he adds a few private superstitions of his own. One of these is the ascribing to the words he writes a singular force of prophecy. Here are two examples: Stephen, in *A Portrait of the Artist as a Young Man,* talking to McCann, uses the words: "Do you think you impress me when you flourish your wooden sword?" Several years later the original of McCann was out in a Sinn Fein rising and improvised a service of order, himself taking the street in company of a few comrades armed with blackthorn cudgels (a good substitute for wooden swords). They were arrested by a British officer, and McCann met his death before a firing party. The original of Davin, to whom Stephen says, "The next revolution you make with hurleysticks," became Lord Mayor of Limerick and was dragged from his bed and shot by Black and Tans. When Lynch deserts Stephen in *The Circe* episode, Stephen says: "Et laqueo se suspendit." Years afterwards the original of Lynch inherited a small fortune, went to London, spent it all and then threw himself into the Thames.

The multiplicity of technical devices in *Ulysses* is proof that Joyce subscribed to no limiting aesthetic creed, and proof also that he was willing to use any available instrument that might serve his purpose. It was hardly likely that, having denied all religious dogma, and having carefully avoided all political doctrine, he would submit to artistic limitations. There are hints of all practices in *Ulysses*—cubism, futurism, simultanism, dadaism and the rest—and this is the clearest proof that he was attached to none of the schools that followed them. At one time in Zürich I wanted to learn Italian and, as a reading exercise,

Joyce lent me Boccioni's book on futurism. I quoted to him one full-sounding phrase I had learned: "Noi futuristi italiani siamo senza passato." "E senza avvenire," said Joyce. Any other doctrine would have called forth the same comment. The sworn foe of sensibility in art is doctrine. When an artist believes in no creed he is the more likely to believe in himself, in what he sees, hears, experiences. Hence, I think, the stream of actual life that flows so strongly through the pages of *Ulysses*. Any partisan pledges would have cramped it in one way or another. Hence the insistence on the mystery of the body, which is the medium of experience. One brief life is here with its creative possibilities, and death is before us to make us humble and tolerant. Apropos of one contentious critic Joyce observed: "What a pity it is we don't take our coffins round with us like Chinese. It would give us a better sense of perspective."

Joyce displayed humour and tenacity enough in his dispute with the British Consulate General in Zürich, but an Englishman would probably have been more sceptical. I felt that, as an Irishman and an exile, he was surprised and disappointed that Englishmen failed to live up to the reputation invented for them by their friends. It was, perhaps, strange that I had heard nothing of the affair before meeting Joyce, seeing that I was an employee of the Consulate, but that was probably due to the fact that I worked in a consular sideshow called the *Handelsabteilung* situated about ten minutes' walk away from the Consulate proper. A day or two after our dinner at Taylor's pension on the Zürichberg, Taylor referred to the affair but without telling me the story of it. He said:

"No doubt Joyce has a grievance, but what he doesn't understand is that all these people are out for a quiet life."

Very likely Taylor was right, and his remark would apply to official institutions in all countries. It means that "we don't want no trouble" was an old departmental device before the gaffer of all gangsters made it his own.

The history of the trouble was told to me by Joyce one evening in the Astoria Café. Joyce arrived in Zürich with practically no resources at all. Three well-wishers in England, George Moore, Mr. W. B. Yeats and the late Sir Edmund Gosse, hearing of his plight, were influential in securing for him a gift of £100 from the Privy Purse. The gift was unconditional, but it came to Joyce's ears that at least one of the intermediaries thought he ought to do something for the Allied cause. This, in Joyce's case, could mean only one thing—write for it. But Joyce's preoccupation with *Ulysses,* his own distaste for politics and also his parole to the Austrian Government, forbade any such incursion into the field of war journalism. What to do that would show his acknowledgment and yet not harm his work or break his parole? Give plays in English, came the answer of a Zürich friend. With the assistance of Mr. Claude Sykes, who had acted in the company of Sir Herbert Beerbohm Tree, and who was an enthusiastic producer of plays of literary quality, and of Mrs. Sykes, known on the English stage as Miss Daisy Race, he founded the English Players,* for the purpose of giving plays in the English tongue in Swiss towns. That able actor, Mr. Tristan Rawson, aided powerfully in the enterprise, and Englishmen and Englishwomen living in Zürich were mobilised in its support around the solid nucleus of professional talent. In this way it came about that Mrs. Joyce played Maurya in Synge's *Riders to the*

---

* Not to be confused with the capable company of professional players who, under Messrs. Stirling and Reynolds, have fought for several years past a similar uphill battle against indifference, if not actual neglect.

Sea, and that after the Armistice I played Stingo in Goldsmith's *She Stoops to Conquer.*

Joyce's functions were numerous and important. He aided in the business arrangements, sang "off" or prompted as required, and had a general advisory voice in the proceedings. He did everything, in short, but act. He sang "off" in a performance of Browning's *In a Balcony,* and this was the occasion that inspired the poem beginning, "They mouth love's language," published in *Pomes Penyeach.* It was a reasonable expectation on the part of the English Players that their efforts would meet with consular approval, and receive official consular support as a valuable piece of British cultural propaganda, but the consulate, for some reason or other, refused its blessing. Nevertheless, when a performance of Wilde's *The Importance of Being Earnest* was given in the theatre of the Kaufmännische Verein a temporary employee of the British Consulate played the part of Algernon Moncrieff. I saw the performance. It was given before I became a consular employee, and it seemed to me a good one. The next day Joyce, in the exercise of part of his many functions, strolled round to the consulate to hand the actor the modest actor's fee which was his due, but the latter, on opening the pay envelope, became indignant and said, in effect:

"What the hell do you call this? Don't you know I spent much more than this in buying new trousers for the performance?"

"I am sorry," said Joyce, "if the fee contained in the envelope appears to you to be inadequate. But I shall be obliged if you will address any complaint on that score to Mr. Sykes, as I am only his agent in the matter and acting according to the instructions on his paysheet."

Evidently the atmosphere became quickly heated, for

Joyce told me that, in spite of all his politeness, at a certain point in the discussion the consular employee told him he would "wring his bloody neck and chuck him down the stairs" but for the fact that he had heard that he was ill. Joyce's closing remark on leaving the consulate was:

"That is not language that should be used in a government office."

That same day he addressed a letter to the Consul-General demanding an apology within twenty-four hours, or he would take legal proceedings for threatened assault.

"I think I was perfectly justified, don't you?" said Joyce.

Unformulated but active throughout the affair were the two different conceptions of consular powers and functions.

"I've seen it here," said Joyce, "and I've seen it elsewhere. These people look upon themselves as representatives of the King, and expect me to go to them cap in hand, but I look upon them as functionaries who are paid by my father in Dublin to look after my interests when I am abroad. I think mine is the sounder conception in law. What?"

No apology was forthcoming, so Joyce instituted legal proceedings at once. He appealed also from the consulate to the legation in Berne and, receiving no satisfaction from that quarter, he wrote to an Irish Member of Parliament and to the Prime Minister, the Right Hon. David Lloyd George, who replied, wishing the English Players every success. The letter from the Prime Minister was framed and displayed in a prominent position in the window of a tobacco shop right under the offices of the Consulate Generale.

"I always appeal to the highest instance," said Joyce. "Stephen appeals from Father Dolan to Father Conmee, the rector, and I now from the Consul-General to the Prime Minister."

As is usual in Switzerland, the parties were called before the conciliation court to see if litigation might be avoided. Here Joyce asked if he might speak to his adversary in English, and the *Friedens richter* gave him permission to do so. Joyce then produced the balance sheet of the English Players, turned to his opponent and invited him to examine the accounts and decide for himself whether or not the remuneration he received was in the circumstances of the company, a reasonable one. The young man wavered for a moment but then refused to examine the figures on the grounds that he had no guarantee that they were accurate. Meeting with such a rebuff there was nothing left for Joyce to do but to proceed with the case before a court of law.

After considerable delay the case came up for judgment. There were in fact three cases to be decided. (*a*) Joyce sued the consular employee for the price of three unpaid-for tickets of admission to a performance of *The Importance of Being Earnest;* (*b*) the consular employee counter-claimed for the price of clothes specially purchased for the performance. The garments fitted well, but his claim for £19 15s., alternatively £12, was surely allowing for the outlay on generous lines; (*c*) finally there was Joyce's action against the consular employee for threats of violence. The consulate made a bad start in claiming extra-territorial privilege. This is accorded always against the grain to an embassy. It was not at all likely that the privilege would be accorded to a consulate. Naturally the claim was refused.

Cases (*a*) and (*b*) were heard before the *Bezirksgericht* Zürich on the 15th October, 1918, Judge Billeter presiding. In case (*a*) Joyce's opponent was ordered to pay Dr.

James Joyce the sum of £1, plus interest at 5 per cent, from the 3rd, May 1918. Case (b) the counter claim against Dr. James Joyce for £19 15s., alternatively £12, was disallowed, the costs in both cases to be borne by Joyce's adversary who, in addition, was ordered to pay to Dr. James Joyce £2 10s. by way of damages. So far so good. But there was yet the third and, to Joyce, most important case. What law's delays intervened I don't know. When, however, the case should have been heard both Joyce's opponent and the only witness who could have testified to the truth of Joyce's allegations had already left. The case therefore fell to the ground, but the costs of the court had to be met, and Joyce was ordered to pay £4 16s. (120 Swiss francs). This he resolved not to do, and the court, after the usual delay, notified him that they would proceed by way of distraint. Furniture was none to be distrained upon, as the Joyce family occupied a furnished apartment, but the polite officer of the court came, nevertheless, to have a look round. The books? No, he could not take them. Books are the tools of the writer's trade. Typewriter? No, for in Joyce's special case (his eye trouble) a typewriter was considered a necessity.

"Then," said the official, "I am afraid, Herr Doktor, that I must ask you to show me what money you have on you."

Joyce produced his wallet. It contained a hundred francs, which he thought would be allowed him for the immediate needs of his family. He was wrong by forty per cent. The officer was obliged to trouble Herr Doktor for forty francs. There was nothing further to be done. News of Joyce's dispute with the British Consulate spread to America, and an admirer of his writings, one of the editors of the American review, *The Dial*, cabled ten thousand Swiss francs for the furtherance of Joyce's cause.

When the money arrived in the spring of 1919 Joyce had already severed his official connection with the English Players in order that the activities and success of that enterprise might not be prejudiced by association with himself. Nevertheless, he handed over the greater part of the money to the English Players. For that organisation it must be said that, in spite of official opposition, both passive and active, its members gave upwards of forty performances in most of the larger towns of Switzerland.

On the whole one may say that Joyce got distinctly the better of his contest with the consulate. And if the manifest objects over which the dispute was waged appear to be small, the principle involved in the dispute was of the highest importance. The relation of one citizen to another is never a trifling matter, nor is the relation of the simple citizen to a department entrusted with authority a trifle. It was, no doubt, at first a very disturbing affair to a writer with a task before him like the writing of *Ulysses,* but it would not have been Joyce if he had failed to see the humour of it or if, in the long run, he had failed to extract out of the incident material for his book. It inspired him also to compose an amusing parody on *Tipperary,* which begins:

Up to rheumy Zürich town came an Irishman one day,
And as the place was rather dull he thought he'd give a play
So that the German propagandists might be rightly riled,
But the bully British Philistine once more drove Oscar Wilde.

And which ends:

For the C.G.'s not literary and his handymen are rogues.
For the C.G.'s about as literary as an Irish kish of brogues.
We paid all expenses, as the good Swiss public knows,
But we'll be damned well damned before we pay for Private
C's trunk hose.

Another of Joyce's compositions in this genre, but in no way connected with the dispute, was *Mr. Dooley*. It expressed the point of view of the badgered yet optimistic individualist living through war, revolution and commercial depression. The final lines gives the spirit of the whole poem:

> *Who will release us from jingo Jesus*
> *Prays Mr. Dooleyooleyooley oo.*

CHAPTER X

Unlike *The Cyclops* episode, in which politics dominated and, appropriately, no woman appeared, *Nausikaa*
leaves the government of the city to whom it may concern
and deals with the way of a man with a maid, more particularly the way of a middle-ageing married man with a
maid. The social problem set by this relation of man and
woman of different ages is raised by implication. The
mystery of women's clothing and the lures of exhibition-
ism arise for consideration. The crime of Onan is suggested and the question arises whether in our present social
organisation the statute of limitations might not apply.
Aesthetically considered *Nausikaa* is more purely sensibility than any other episode in *Ulysses*. Sense organs, the
eye and the nose, are the presiding organs of the human
body: principally, however, the eye, for this is the painters' episode. The scene is on the seashore, the action begins at about eight o'clock, the light is a rich and magical
twilight.

Joyce is as little critical of the materials set before him
by society as is the landscape painter of the material set
before him by nature and man, but his works, nevertheless,
because of its candour and accuracy, a social document as
the painting of seventeenth century Dutch painters and of,
say, Canaletto, is a social document. *Nausikaa* shows us
(we knew it all along, of course) that those social forces
which, at a recent date, endowed the world with the institutions of private property and monogamic marriage

have not yet taught the wayward eye of man not to rove. The chemistry of his body and the imagination of his mind are older and newer than his laws and conventions. The eye of Mr. Bloom roves freely throughout the day and his desires are provoked by many women, yet, on the whole, the institution of marriage is triumphantly vindicated in his person. To his wife, who since a little past four o'clock that afternoon, has been studying her concert programme with the aid of her organiser, Blazes Boylan, his memories, desires and hopes constantly return. Leopold's wife is something more to him than his sexual complement. She is his destiny, like the weight of his body, the shape of his nose, his family, race and fortunes.

It has been a fine but, for Bloom, rather tiring day. He is dressed in black and is wearing a bowler hat, not an ideal garb for hot weather. He has walked a lot on the hot stones of Dublin streets, is very nervy about affairs at home, has recently been engaged in an exhausting argument, and now with a headache is down on the seashore for a breath of fresh air. We are to suppose that there is a gap of time between his hurried exit from Barney Kiernan's licensed premises and his appearance on Sandymount shore, which time has been occupied with a visit in the company of Martin Cunningham to the Dignam family at their home in Sandymount. This visit to the widow and orphans was no pleasure to Bloom and he does not pretend that it was. Three girls see him as he comes to rest on a rock not far from them. The girls are Cissy Caffrey, Edy Boardman and Gerty MacDowell, and they are there with baby Boardman and Tommy and Jacky Caffrey, twins, to have a "cosy chat beside the sparkling waves and discuss matters feminine." Of the three girls Gerty MacDowell is the star. She is described in the familiar novelette style of the period, and we must remember that

Poppy's Paper and *Florrie's Paper,* with their yarns about typists and factory hands who get off with the young governor in his sports Bentley, had not yet, in 1904, supplanted the *Bow Bells* and *Heartsease* novelettes, where the young governess makes the crowded ballroom floor gasp with her beauty, dressed in a simple white frock and wearing a single white rose. Carefully listening we can hear undertones of Gerty's own Sandymount outlook and dialect in the rich prose of the *Heartsease* library.

The waxen pallor of her face was almost spiritual in its ivorylike purity though her rosebud mouth was a genuine Cupid's bow. Greekly perfect. Her hands were of finely veined alabaster with tapering fingers and as white as lemon juice and queen of ointments could make them, thought it was not true that she used to wear kid gloves in bed or take a milk footbath either. . . . Why have women such eyes of witchery? Gerty's were of the bluest Irish blue, set off by lustrous lashes and dark, expressive brows. . . . But Gerty's crowning glory was her wealth of wonderful hair. It was dark brown with a natural wave in it. She had cut it that very morning on account of the new moon and it nestled about her pretty head in a profusion of luxuriant clusters, and pared her nails too. . . . Gerty was dressed simply but with the instinctive taste of a votary of Dame Fashion, for she felt there was just a might that he might be out. A neat blouse of electric blue, self-tinted by dolly dyes (because it was expected in the *Lady's Pictorial* that electric blue would be worn), with a smart vee opening down to the division and kerchief pocket (in which she always kept a piece of cottonwool scented with her favourite perfume, because the handkerchief spoiled the sit), and a navy three-quarter skirt cut to the stride showed off her slim graceful figure to perfection. She wore a coquettish little love of a hat of wideleaved nigger straw contrast trimmed with an under-brim of egg-blue chenille and at the side a butterfly bow to tone. . . ."

Gerty is granddaughter to Mr. Giltrap, whose wolf-hound, Garryowen, supplies local colour to the Citizen on his propagandist pubcrawls. The heart of the virgin leaps to the tinkle of the bicycle bell of the boy down the street (and Gerty MacDowell loves Reggie Wyllie, the boy with the bicycle bell) but it yearns for the handsome, unknown stranger of its dreams. And the heart of the handsome, dark stranger (known to us, unknown to Gerty, for it is Bloom) responds with desire for her youth, as nothing more fervently desires youth than the heart of middle-ageing man, conscious that its beats are numbered. The desires of both are favoured by the warmth and half darkness of the June evening.

Bloom's watch stopped at half-past four, significant hour, but when Cissy Caffrey asks him the time he knows it is after eight because the sun has set. From afar they hear the litany of Our Lady of Loreto, "Refuge of sinners, Comfortress of the afflicted," being sung in the church, Star of the Sea. The devotion in progress is the men's temperance retreat, rosary, sermon and benediction of the Most Blessed Sacrament. Gerty pictures to herself the scene in the church, "the stained glass windows lighted up, the candles, flowers and the blue banners of the Blessed Virgin's sodality." This is an aspect of Catholic Christian worship that seemed to Joyce peculiarly appropriate in an episode the main theme of which is sex appeal. In a letter to me from Trieste he wrote: "*Nausikaa* is written in a namby-pamby jammy marmalady drawersy (alto la!) style with effects of incense mariolatry, masturbation, stewed cockles, painters' palette, chitchat, circumlocutions, etc., etc." We may take it that Stephen is expressing Joyce's own mature view when, in expounding his Hamlet theory, he says: "Fatherhood in the sense of conscious begetting is unknown to man. It is a mystical estate, an apostolic succession, from only begetter to only begotten. On that mystery and not on the Madonna, which the cunning Italian intellect flung to the mob of Europe, the Church is founded and founded irremovably because founded, like the world, macro and microcosm, upon the void." It goes almost without saying that Gerty agrees thoroughly with the immediate social object of the mission because: "Had her father only avoided the clutches of the demon drink by taking the pledge or those powders the drink habit cured in *Pearson's Weekly,* she might now be rolling in her carriage, second to none. Over and over had she told herself that as she mused by the dying embers in a brown study without the lamp because she hated two lights or oftentimes gazing out of the window dreamily by the hour at the rain falling on the rusty bucket, thinking. But that vile decoction which has ruined so many hearths and homes had cast its shadow over her childhood days. . . ." And now Gerty has got the vote and unless she takes to porter or cocktails herself we shall see.

The dusk deepens and a bat flies through the air around them "with a tiny lost cry." At the Mirus bazaar in aid of funds for Mercer's Hospital a firework display begins, "And they all ran down the strand to see over the houses and the church, helter-skelter, Edy with the push-car with baby Boardman in it and Cissy holding Tommy and Jacky by the hand so they wouldn't fall running." The two girls call to Gerty to follow them, but Gerty prefers to remain where she is, sitting on a rock. She can see just as well from that point and she is glad they are going for it leaves her alone in the gathering darkness with the dark, handsome stranger, who, from his position, leaning against a nearby rock, is devouring her with his eyes. They are letting off Roman candles and Gerty leans back as far as possible to see the display, one uplifted knee clasped with both hands. One strange thing about the light of after sundown is that all white things look mysteriously and dominatingly white in a landscape in which half tones have begun to merge into a predominating dark. "And she saw a long Roman candle going up over the trees up, up, and, in the tense hush, they were all breathless with excitement as it went higher and higher, and she had to lean back more and more to look up after it, high, high, almost out of sight, and her face was suffused with a divine, an entrancing blush from straining back and he could see her other things, too, nainsook knickers, the fabric that caresses the skin, better than those other pettiwidth, the green, four and eleven. . . ."

The female form divine, undraped, is a sight for gods, artists, philosophers, physicians and suchlike. It is a majestic object, sometimes awe-inspiring, sometimes pitiful and, but rarely, and to some few, erotically provoking. It is made more alluring and approachable when its majestic beauties and stark realities are appropriately veiled. It is easy to believe the nudists when they claim that nudist colonies are haunts of austere purity. Erudite French writers have maintained that the garments so attractive to Bloom were of Greek origin—that the Greeks had a word for them—that after centuries of eclipse they came back again in the seventeenth century, that during the eighteenth century they again went out of sight and mind, only to reach the point of highest culture at about the time of Zola and Mr. Bloom. Modesty, it is said, was the cause of this development, modest forethought for possible falls from horses and, later on, from bicycles. Then it was also a precaution against masculine invasiveness. Climate also played a part and, in generations when a belief in microbes was prevalent, hygiene. But none of these solid historical reasons seems to explain satisfactorily how colour, form and fabric combined to provide the female sex with such a remarkable instrument of coquetterie.

Change in the concealings and revealings of coquettish allurements seems, as in all other matters, to be the only constant thing about it. That the female form must be veiled is on all sides, excepting nudist colonies, admitted, but not always with the same chiffon, for the imagination of man is lazy and that of the dress designer and tailor active. He is served with a constant novelty of provocation, if he demands it or not. The question whether the tempo of these changes of fashion is conditioned by the tempo of social transformation as a whole is one that the historian of costume must answer (Chapter: Figleaf to Mulberry leaf and beyond). But, so headlong has been the rate of change in the last quarter of a century that if Gerty MacDowell's undies, so attractive to Bloom, were displayed (*à titre de documentation historique*) in a Regent Street shop window they would provoke, but only to laughter. And the loudest and longest laugh would be that of Gerty MacDowell herself, passing the window with her streamlined, grown up daughter. Could Dan Leno now say, "Red or White, Madam?" without mystifying nine-tenths of his audience? The easiest film laugh available is got by showing a bedroom of that epoch, when the great white Queen Victoria ruled these islands, with a lady in it, draped in the voluminous undergarments of the period. The next easiest laugh is got by showing a ten years pre-war motor car. For all its pruderies of speech and manner the period of Bloom's youth and manhood was erotic to a tropical degree. Let anyone behold the ladies' underwear in artificial silk in all colours but the right one exhibited now-

NAUSIKAA

adays in shop windows everywhere and admit that they
are woefully unerotic. They are a visible sign that the
tide is now setting in the direction of candour, co-educa-
tion and companionate marriages with surgically clean,
scientific instruction in erotic and contraceptive mysteries,
classic treatises on which will, no doubt, soon be borne
home with the latest vitamin cookery book as school prizes.
But when the life force, if that most depressing divinity
happens to be in fashion at the time, finds that tabulated
knowledge, the good pal girl and the fifty-fifty boy lead
only to tweeds for everybody and general indifference,
then social and sexual taboos, ignorance, inhibitions,
white undies, black stockings, and furtiveness, will come
in again with all their tensions, as in the days of Gerty
MacDowell.

What is the usual result of mutual erotic attraction
between the middle-aged, married man and the young
virgin? There is a gap of time and experience, not to
mention social convenience, between the *grisonnant* and
the *grisette* not easily bridged except by some variation,
more or less involved, of the expeditious practice of
Bloom. The consideration of expediency dominates. One
gathers that children in the days of Judah were a form
of social riches and that Judah's son objected to increas-
ing his brother's store, just as he might have refused to
bear a hand with the ploughing and sowing in his brother's field. Onan was condemned not for a contraceptual
practice as such, but for a lack of tribal solidarity, of broth-
erly love. His excessive individualism was punished. It is
as if he had hoarded or wasted national property in time
of war or famine. The only thought in Bloom's subsequent
monologue that at all bears on this aspect of the question
is: "Glad to get away from other chap's wife. Eating off
his cold plate." But this is a purely aesthetic or hygienic

motive and has nothing to do with social and religious considerations.

Bloom is a married man, a father, and is twenty years the senior of Gerty, the maid. A solution to the problem of their mutual attraction that leaves nobody a penny the worse off cannot be considered entirely unsuccessful. Had Bloom spoken to Gerty, immediate disillusionment might have followed. What seemed so attractive at ten yards might, at arm's length, have left them indifferent, in which case mutual embarrassment would have put an end to the matter. But if at the first "Good evening" the attraction had increased, and an affair had started, Gerty would have written letters and started a rivalry with his wife just as, to Bloom's annoyance, Martha Clifford has begun to do. Bloom himself reflects: "Suppose I spoke to her. What about? Bad plan, however, if you don't know how to end a conversation. Ask them a question and they ask you another." And again: "Might have made a worse fool of myself. Instead of talking about nothing."

It is easy for a rich man, who has energy as well as money to burn to keep separate establishments for a variety of loves. But Bloom is a poor man. He has work to do and a family to keep. He is, besides, a prudent man and, although open to a variety of sexual excitations, is not a passionate man in the sense that he could ever allow the integrity of his life to be endangered by any one object. Whatever the charms of other women he accepts them as adjuncts to, not as rivals of, his wife. And Marion's fixed empire over his mind is not shaken by his knowledge that she is possessed by other men. In fact, thinking of Boylan's visit to Marion, he even calmly considers whether her lover ought not to pay for the privilege of her love: "Suppose he gave her money. Why not? All a prejudice. She's worth ten, fifteen, more, a pound. What?

I think so. All that for nothing." After the fall of the greeny, dewy stars of the Roman candle, and Bloom's expense of spirit, Gerty rises and follows her two friends away from the seashore, waving to them as she does so the piece of scented cotton wool she carries in her kerchief pocket. It is one of "love's little ruses." The signal is for them but the sweet scent is for her dark, stranger lover. Then the style of the episode changes from the marmalady circumlocutions of the novelette to the hacked phrases of Bloom's thoughts.

Nausikaa is the one pictorial episode in *Ulysses*. It is pre-eminently the episode of sensibility in both the emotional and physical sense. Sight is the sense most in evidence, but nose, ear and touch reinforce the true organ of vision. A picture of the seashore is built up in the novelettish narrative of the seductive Gerty, and that picture becomes rarer and denser in the tightly woven texture of Bloom's unspoken thoughts. It must be regarded as something of a wonder that the seen thing should play the great part it does play in the writing of a man whose sight was never strong. But the many things in *Ulysses* vividly seen are generally closeups. They are vehemently drawn, sometimes photographed as with a stereoscopic camera, but not painted. Space, air and a diminishing force of sight towards the periphery of the field of vision are lacking. If there is a parallel in the art of painting for Joyce's swift, instantaneous shots of life it is in the art of Matisse, or, when Joyce's vision is graphic rather than pictorial, the art of the draughtsman, Rodin, watching, ready pencil in hand, the model doing whatever it pleased in his studio. For example:

"An elderly man shot up near the spur of rock a blowing red face. He scrambled up by the stones, water glistening on his pate and on its garland of grey hair, water rilling over his chest and paunch and spilling jets out of his black, sagging loincloth."

"Broken hoops on the shore, at the land a maze of dark, cunning nets; farther away chalkscrawled back doors and on the higher beach a drying line with two crucified shirts."

"Kind air defined the coigns of houses in Kildare Street. No birds. Frail from the housetops two plumes of smoke ascended, pluming, and in a flaw of softness softly were blown."

"Do you see the tide flowing quickly in on all sides, sheeting the lows of sands quickly, shellcocoacoloured?"

The same for the human mannerism, a gesture caught quickly with the model on the move:

"Haines detached from his underlip some fibres of tobacco before he spoke."

"He took off his silk hat and, blowing out impatiently his bushy moustache, welshcombed his hair with raking fingers."

"He removed his large Henry Clay decisively and his large fierce eyes scowled intelligently over all their faces."

"His hands moulded ample curves of air. He shut his eyes tight in delight, his body shrinking, and blew a sweet chirp from his lips."

It may be because these things form part of the momentary life of the person or persons present that they seem to be instantaneously photographed or drawn with the object on the move. They are not presented as something outside, but as something inside, the acting personage. Some conversations ring so true that they might have been caught up from actual life by a sound-recording instrument. The mystery here is, how Joyce, through twenty years of exile, could preserve with such freshness the tones and mannerisms of his fellow citizens. Take, for example, the conversation—incredulous expostulation and confident affirmation—between Joe Hynes and Alf Bergan on the subject of Dignam appearing in the street with Willy Murray after his funeral. This is the same vividness and directness that drew upon Rodin the charge of lifting from nature by means of a plaster cast. And then there are Joyce's imitations with vowel and consonant of natural and mechanical sounds—those of the sea flowing over weed and rocks, those of the machines in the *Telegraph* office, those of the fireworks heard from Sandymount Beach.

Nausikaa is essentially pictorial, not because of any pictorial descriptions (there are very few), but because we are always made to feel conscious of the ambient of air around Bloom, Gerty and her friends. The surroundings of the persons, the beach, the town, the sky with clouds and fireworks, the sea and its crawling surf, Howth Head rising up out of the sea, everything, moving or stationary, affirms the idea of space. All the colour is enveloped in air. Here, too, is realised a landscape, foreshadowing, in conception though not in material, those mysterious dream glimpses of landscape in *Work in Progress,* where the earth comes to life and shares consciousness with its creatures. It occurs in a space of no thoughts while Bloom is still standing on the seashore.

"A lost long candle wandered up the sky from Mirus bazaar in search of funds for Mercer's hospital and broke, drooping, and shed a cluster of violet but one white stars. They floated, fell: they faded. The shepherd's hour: the hour of holding: hour of tryst. From house to house, giving his ever-welcome double knock, went the nine o'clock postman, the glowworm's lamp at his belt gleaming here and there through the laurel hedges. And among the five young trees a hoisted lintstock lit the lamp at Leahy's terrace. . . . Twittering the bat flew here. flew there.

Far out over the sands the coming surf crept, grey. Howth settled for slumber tired of long days, of yumyum rhododendrons (he was old) and felt gladly the night breeze lift, ruffle his fell of ferns. He lay but opened a red eye unsleeping, deep and slowly breathing, slumberous but awake. And far on Kish bank the anchored lightship twinkled, winked at Mr. Bloom."

Sound aids the illusions of space, the hiss and splutter of fireworks, the voices of the girls and children and of the worshippers in the Star of the Sea Church. Smell, too: for Gerty MacDowell's farewell to Bloom is waved with scented wadding across the space that divides them. And movement, in the shape of the receding figures of Gerty, her friends, the twins and the basinette, of the hither and thither fluttering bat, of the clouds and the oncreeping surf, intensifies the pictorial lyricism. It is a Whistler theme, painted with the greater elegance and liveliness of a Fragonard. It is a stern tale of Swift swiftly told by Sterne. Joyce always held that these two writers ought to change names.

Some of Bloom's thoughts may disconcert, but they will ring true enough for all who have not too well learned the art of forgetting. They are the thoughts of a man who chooses his deeds carefully from among them. Bloom's mood, when he is left alone, is one of attention, dispassionate observation, and finally, as he walks slowly citywards, of trancelike relaxation. Standing still for a moment he closes his eyes and his thought becomes a kaleidoscope of remembered sensations. Then he pulls himself together and goes on. It is too late to go to the performance of *Leah* as he had intended. He will call instead at the lying-in hospital for news of Mina Purefoy. The cuckoo clock in the study of Father Conroy and Canon O'Hanlon sings nine as he re-enters the streets of Dublin.

Begun in Zürich, *Nausikaa* was completed in Trieste. Following *Nausikaa* comes *The Oxen of the Sun,* which was not completed till just before Joyce left Trieste for Paris. It was rare that Joyce spoke of a part of his book on which he was not working, but one day in Zürich, as we were walking by the Limmat, he said to me:

"What do you make of the story of *The Oxen of the Sun?*"

"How make of it?" I said. "It's the story of a fabulous happening to me. That's all."

"Not to me," said Joyce. "The companions of Ulysses disobey the commands of Pallas. They slay and flay the oxen of the Sungod and all are drowned save the prudent and pious Ulysses. I interpret the killing of the sacred oxen as the crime against fecundity by sterilising the act of coition. And I think my interpretation is as sound as that of any other commentator on Homer."

From the fresh air and vast open spaces of the seashore we enter a den where medical students and others are foregathered for drink and talk. The young men are drinking Bass's No. 1, which is a most potent mead, and their loud, coarse talk drowns, except for instants, the cries of women in travail. For they are in the lying-in hospital in Holles Street, conducted by Dr. Andrew Horne. Bloom, on leaving Sandymount Shore, calls to enquire after the progress of Mrs. Purefoy, who has been three days in labour. While standing, hat in hand, talking to the nurse in the vestibule, he is hailed by the young house surgeon, Dixon, who attended him for a wasp sting some time before. He demurs at first to Dixon's invitation to join them, but only to keep the good opinion of the nurse, who finds all this merriment and insobriety unseemly, eventually, however, yields to the doctor's persuasion and joins the young drinkers of ale.

After the sweet air and subtle sounds of Sandymount Beach, the reek of beer and tobacco and the clamour of men's voices! After the physical space of the seashore, the spaceless labyrinth of the human conscience and the physical space of the womb! *The Oxen of the Sun* is, with the exception, perhaps, of *Ithaca,* more .symbolical than any episode in the book. The chaste, faithful nurse is the ovum. Bloom, the vital principle, is the spermatozoon. Stephen, the growing and expanding soul, is ,the embryo, and all are contained within the womb for which the maternity hospital of Dr. Horne is symbol.

All Bloom's companions are young, unmarried men. He is married and the father of two children. They, who are neither chaste nor parents, are the slayers of the sacred animals, for they enjoy the pleasures of love, but by all means at their disposal prevent its fruitfulness. By their luxury and indulgence possible souls and bodies are denied the entry into life and experience. Outwardly the young men are bright and happy lives. It is in the mind and conscience of Bloom and Stephen that their crime and conflict are acknowledged and resolved. Bloom hears, as his race heard in the past, the command to increase and multiply, and Stephen hears the same voice through the Holy Roman Catholic Apostolic Church. Their companions have sworn allegiance to the newer gods of Malthus and the eugenic societies. Bloom is conscious of many acts of disobedience against the command of his racial god, including one most recent, but the vision of his wife and two children come to his defence. He has to that extent obeyed the law and can absolve himself from guilt. Even while they are sitting in the students' room in front of their beer, bread and sardines, the voice of the god is heard outside—a noise in the street. It is the Thunder God, who, according to Vico, drove with his terrifying

THE OXEN OF THE SUN

voice and fierce lightnings shameless primitive people to hide their fornications in caves and to begin civilised life. Stephen is afraid of thunder. He no more believes in the skygod than in Christ's salvation, but he is afraid of them both. The others are too drunk to care. With plausible speech Bloom assures them all, and Stephen in particular, that they need not be afraid, for the noise and fire are to be explained by cause and effect. It is not a god who is speaking, but the blind forces of nature—not divinity, but phenomenon. He believes in no god—neither in his own tribal god nor in the deities of the stranger. Everything is explicable. If there is some phenomenon of which we cannot to-day explain the natural order we shall be able to explain it to-morrow.

Men drinking ale and women bearing children: there is reason in Joyce's bringing these two phases of life together under the same roof. Each sex is about its most specialised function. One is producing bodies and the other making societies. Sitting together before ale or wine, or whatever the country affords, was ever one of the most serious and useful activities of men. It was not alone through mead that societies came into being, but fermented drinks were among the greatest of civilising agencies as all religions and legends testify. So important were they that they were deemed to be of divine origin. There were Bacchus and the other corn and wine gods, whilst Christ turned water into wine. And there was Odin, too, for we read in the Edda, "Gere and Freke, sates the warfaring, father of hosts, everyday with Saerimnher, but Odin himself, the renowned in arms, lives upon wine alone." When vain dwarfs misused, and stupid giants locked away, poetic inspiration in the form of the Gold Mead the god himself became wanderer, labourer, inventor, worm, lover and eagle to win it back for the right use of gods and men. Where once woman, in a fatal alliance with the petrol engine, laid a violent hand on the winecup instead of a gentle restraining hand upon the arm that raised it, the evil spirits of hooch and anarchy raised their heads and dire waste and ruin were the result.

The style has changed with the mood and motive. The novelette style of Gerty MacDowell and the truncated sentences of Bloom's unspoken thoughts have given place to a parade of costume styles, resembling an historical pageant. After a short opening, suggestive of conception and birth, the episode is introduced with what Joyce called, in a letter to me, "a Sallustian-Tacitean prelude (the unfertilised ovum)." From that the action proceeds through nine parts, but without divisions, to the birth of Mrs. Purefoy's child. From alliterative, monosyllabic, early English the prose passes in chronological sequence through progressive styles of literary English and ends, as all the festive youth rush from Horne's house to Burke's pub, in the no style at all, slang of half-drunken human utterance—pidgin English, Nigger English, Cockney, Irish, Scots, Welsh, Bowery slang and broken doggerel—a torrent of living, and therefore, except to those present, half-incomprehensible speech.

Through these progressive changes of language the development of the embryo and faunal evolution in general are shown, and throughout the episode we are subtly and constantly reminded of the events of the day. A double thudding Anglo-Saxon motive continually recurs to give the feeling of trampling oxen. "Woman's woe with wonder pondering." "Ruth red him, love led on with will to wander, loth to leave." "In Horne's house rest should reign." "With will will we withstand, withsay."

The action begins with Bloom's arrival at the hospital door. "Some man that wayfaring was stood by house door at night's oncoming." "In ward wary the watcher hearing come than man mildhearted eft rising with swire ywimpled to him her gate wide undid." Bloom had seen stormclouds gathering and now the storm breaks as the nurse opens the door. "Christ's rood made she on breastbone and him drew that he would rathe infare under her thatch." Dixon crosses the hall and invites Bloom to join them in the manner of Mandeville. "And the traveller Leopold went into the castle for to rest him for a space being sore of limb after many marches environing in divers lands and sometimes venery." The persons to whom the able and plausible Dixon leads him are Stephen, Lynch, Madden, Lenehan, Crotthers and Punch Costello. Malachi Mulligan is expected and later on arrives with Bannon of Mullingar, who has started a flirtation with Millicent Bloom. Lynch one supposes an able young man, but in character he is embittered and envious. He is the eater of dried cowdung who listens to Stephen's aesthetic theories in *A Portrait of the Artist*. Madden is a medical student with frequent fits of piety. Crotthers is a Scot. Lenehan we know is tipster of the loser for the Ascot Gold Cup, and Punch Costello is a Rowlandson-like caricature of a coarse, drunken bully. One sees them all as they sit, stand and move. In the thick, smoky atmosphere they are like chocolate-coloured fish swimming in a cobalt aquarium.

Bloom is here shown as a staunch defender of womanhood. He is always susceptible to women's physical charms, but in this house of birth he is particularly sympathetic to their woes. His commonsense is proof against the mysteries of religions. The mysterious destiny, however, that lays upon one half of the human race the pain of childbirth is one before which he bows. When Lenehan pours him out a drink he takes it and drinks to his companions' health, but while all are drinking as much as they can he drinks as little as possible. And this is not entirely the defensive attitude of the prudent member. It is because he feels that too much drink and noise in a house of birth is inhuman and unseemly. Another reason for his abstemiousness is that he sees that Stephen is getting drunk. He feels drawn towards Stephen, whom he has seen already three times that day. His thoughts of his own dead son are given in *Morte d'Arthur* style. ". . . and now Sir Leopold that had of his body no manchild for an heir looked upon him his friend's son and was shut up in sorrow for his forepast happiness and as sad as he was that him failed a son of such gentle courage (for all accounted him of real parts) so grieved he also in no less measure for young Stephen for that he lived riotously with those wastrels and murdered his goods with whores."

Then follows a passage in the Elizabethan chronicle style—"About that present time young Stephen filled all cups" and so on through Milton, Taylor, Hooker, Browne —all conveying the contempt of death and birth felt by young men living on a full tide of life and for that moment in which they live. Thunder is heard without and Stephen is afraid, but Bloom, to comfort him, points out that it is nothing but an electrical phenomenon. Stephen is not comforted and his pain of conscience is described in the manner of Bunyan:

"Yes, Pious had told him of that land and Chaste had pointed him to the way but the reason was that in the way he fell in with a certain whore of an eyepleasing exterior whose name, she said, is Bird-in-the-Hand, and she beguiled him wrongways from the true path by her flatteries that she said to him as, Ho, you pretty man, turn aside hither and I will show you a brave place, and she lay at him so flatteringly that she had him in her grot which is named Two-in-the-Bush or, by some learned, Carnal Con-

cupiscence." Bird-in-the-Hand is greatly desired by all
present and, "for that foul plague Allpox and the monsters they cared not for them, for Preservative had given
them a stout shield of oxengut and, third, that they might
take no hurt neither from Offspring that was that wicked
devil by virtue of this same shield which was named Kill-
child."

Stephen mentions Mr. Deasy's letter on the foot and
mouth disease, and this leads to a discussion on the reformation and the founding of the Anglican Church in
the style of Swift. Mulligan appears with Alec Bannon,
both wetted by the storm. The agreeable and witty Buck
adds to the gaiety by unfolding a plan to set up a human
stud-farm on Lambay Island, himself to be principal sire.
The ribald conversation, in which Bloom takes no part,
proceeds in the manner of Steele, Addison and Sterne,
until Bloom's sober air of superiority is rebuked in the
crushing prose of Junius. Then Haines appears, in a blue
light out of the castle of Otranto, but only for a moment
to fix a meeting with Mulligan at Westland Row Station
at half-past eleven. Unwilling to take part in the wild talk
of the others, Bloom turns inwards to his own memories,
his schooldays, his first bowler hat, his first efforts as a
traveller in cheap jewellery, his parents' home at evening
time, then of his first love (it was Bridie Kelly in Hatch
Street) and finally of his present state without a son and
heir. So far the coyly familiar Lamb. Then De Quincey
supplies the colour, accent and cadences for his vision of
his wife and daughter seen as mare and filly foal. The
vision fades and in its place come innumerable might-
have-beens of his virility in the shape of a ghostly company of beasts:

"Elk and yak, the bulls of Bashan and of Babylon, mam-
moth and mastodon, they come trooping to the sunken

sea. *Lacus Mortis*. Ominous, revengeful, zodiacal hosts! They moan, passing upon the clouds, horned and capricorned, the trumpeted with the tusked, the lionmaned the giantantlered, snouter and crawler, rodent, ruminant and pachyderm, all their moving, moaning multitude, murderers of the sun."

The others are speaking of the Gold Cup and regretting the downfall of Bass's mare, Sceptre. Bloom's dream arises while he is gazing fixedly at the well-known triangular sign on a bottle of Bass's No. 1. The gallant mare and her owner's sign coalesce, and through this transformation the vision of his female household triumphs over the regrets of a past wasteful of its seed. The "equine portent grows again" and silences the grievous shrieks of murdered oxen. It fills the sky of his dreams and comes to rest over the house of Virgo. The hope of earthly continuity that in him springs anew centres in his daughter, Millicent, with whom in confused amorousness he associates Martha, his secret love. From the one he may beget children and on the other children of his race and line may be begotten. Lenehan wants to drown his sorrows in more Bass and makes to seize the bottle, but Mulligan, whose watchful eye has observed Bloom's reverie, restrains him. "Warily, Malachi whispered, preserve a druid silence. His soul is far away. It is as painful perhaps to be awakened from a vision as to be born."

The prose lifts to Pater and Ruskin, degenerates into the prose of vulgarised science, and in a clammy morsel, resembling Dickens, we are told that Mina Purefoy has borne a manchild. The provender of beer has given out. Closing time is approaching. Stephen shouts, "Burke's." All the drunk or half-drunk company rush for the door. Only Bloom and Dixon, the one for professional and the other for humane reasons, remain behind. The voice of

Carlyle blesses the newborn babe and the ageing but still productive parents. At Burke's, where Stephen stands all the drinks—three rounds—Alec Bannon recognises Bloom as the father of the little girl in the photoshop. "Photo's papli, by all that's gorgeous." Drunk as he is, Stephen is still resolved not to return to the tower of which he has given Mulligan the key. When they are eventually flung out of Burke's one of the party sees the announcement of Dr. A. J. Christ Dowie's mission on a hoarding opposite and the episode concludes in a vain of ultra-Protestant American righteousness and with the authentic voice of Dowie himself.

"Come on, you triple extract of infamy! Alexander J. Christ Dowie, that's yanked to glory most half this planet from Frisco Beach to Vladivostok. The Deity ain't no nickel dime bumshow. I put it to you that he's on the square and a corking fine business proposition. He's the grandest thing yet and don't you forget it. Shout salvation in king Jesus. You'll need to rise precious early, you sinner there if you want to diddle the Almighty God. Pflaaaap! Not half. He's got a cough-mixture with a punch in it for you, my friend, in his back-pocket. Just you try it on."

The bark of Ulysses Bloom's companions founders under the curse of the Sky God. Bloom is safe, but is as a seaman who takes his discharge from a ship and a week later reads that she has gone down with all hands. Should he thank providence for his escape? Pity his companions? Feel flattered by a special destiny? He doesn't know. I didn't know myself what to think when I read that the *Eleanor Thomas* had gone down with all hands on the St. Nicholas bank.

CHAPTER XI

Joyce's stay in Trieste in 1920 was not a happy one. The Habsburg Empire no longer existed and Trieste had changed hands. With all its faults the old dual monarchy was a political roof over the heads of many peoples and even a leaky roof is better than a continual moving job. "If only the war would come to an end," said everybody while the war was on, but when it ended everybody found how horrible peace could be. The world was full of housing, currency, unemployment, transport and frontier problems. The bills to be met appalled everybody and the shareout satisfied nobody. This was everywhere the case but there was in addition an administrative change-over in progress in Trieste. Apart from the climate of the Adriatic port, which I understand suited him admirably, Joyce worked under a greater handicap in Trieste than in Zürich. This, however, had no effect on his rate of production. Two episodes, *Nausikaa* and *The Oxen of the Sun,* were completed during Joyce's six months' stay in Trieste. In several letters Joyce invited me to visit him there, but I had made up my mind to return to England at the earliest opportunity, and to make both journeys seemed to me to be impracticable. Fortunately, August Suter was able to give me employment in his studio in Zollikon. This work, with the addition of an intensive effort in the selling of pictures, enabled me to earn enough money to cover the cost of my journey with something in hand for a start in London. August Suter thought that going back to London was a crazy project.

"If you won't go to Trieste," said Suter, "go to Rome. There's no sense in returning to England. It's mere sentimentality."

But the lure of the Caledonian Road was too strong. In August 1920 I left Zürich for England. By that time Joyce had already left Trieste for the more congenial atmosphere of Paris. All homecomings are disappointments. Mine was. I found myself hating post-war London and I communicated my sentiments to Joyce, who, in a letter of December 1920, made the following comment: "A point about Ulysses (Bloom). He romances about Ithaca (Oi want teh gow bek teh the Mawl Enn Rowd s'elp me!) and when he gets back it gives him the pip. I mention this because you in your absence from England seemed to have forgotten the human atmosphere and I the atmospheric conditions of these zones."

On my way to England I stayed a week in Paris, at a little hotel in Passy, near Joyce's flat in the rue de l'Assomption. Joyce spoke with enthusiasm of Paris.

"There is an atmosphere of spiritual effort here," he said. "No other city is quite like it. It is a racecourse tension. I wake early, often at five o'clock, and start writing at once."

Since the month of June he had been working on *The Circe* episode, the longest, the strangest and in many ways the strongest episode of *Ulysses*. It is steeped in the atmosphere and governed by the logic of hallucination, but its dominant theme is the fatherly love and care of Bloom for Stephen Dedalus. Throughout the day, at the breakfast table, in the mourners' coach, in Grafton Street, in the Ormond Hotel, in the maternity hospital, Bloom has been constantly haunted by thoughts of his son, Rudy, dead eleven days old. Now the fatherhood in him sees sonship in the person of Stephen. In the words of Stephen, uttered some ten hours earlier, "He was and felt himself the father of all his race." Through all the changing laws and forms of marriage motherhood was always a plain, indisputable physical fact and fatherhood always a social, a spiritual affirmation. Even under group marriage the mother knew her own offspring, but even under official monogamy that child, according to popular wit, is wise who knows its own father. A memory of the past may appear to be an ideal, and an ideal may turn out to be a race memory. English revolutions, forward steps in time, always appealed for their justification to a past lost in the mists of legend, and the French Revolution garbed itself as Brutus and Cassius, Harmodius and Aristogeiton. The race memories and the aspirations of man are one and indivisible. Utopian Bloom adopts Stephen into the matriarchate where the male, once admitted to the society of the female tribe, becomes father of all its children jointly with all other males. There are indications enough in his own nineteenth century marriage of this more primitive marriage state. From Marion's point of view their union is a group organisation with the added advantage that it has a single responsible breadwinner. Her family, in the person of Major Brian Cooper Tweedy, is ever present in Bloom's memory but it seems that Marion pays no heed at all to the poor old Hungarian Jew who died of aconite poisoning in the Queen's Hotel, Ennis, Co. Clare, except to remember that he ruined himself. Marion wishes she bore her mother's name instead of her father's. Milly, too, their daughter, as soon as she arrives at woman's estate, joins forces with her mother, leaving Bloom in the household in a minority of one. That doubt of individual fatherhood and affirmation of universal fatherhood are expressed in the fatherhood of God which, as Stephen avers, is the basis of the Christian religion. In a simple and human way, without pose of humanity or sublimation of his own loss, Bloom follows Stephen and Lynch to Nighttown. Under this designation the English reader has to figure to himself a part of north-east Dublin where Catholic tradition and police tolerance allowed whole streets of houses to be used openly as brothels, whores sitting on the doorsteps soliciting, as freely as if they were in Marseilles. Illicit love was allowed. What was not allowed was illicit drinking. "Shebeening" was pursued with all the rigours of the law. It is in this haunt of Dublin nightlife that Bloom's individual and social fatherhood resolve themselves into one when, as he mounts guard over the prostrate form of Stephen, the vision of his own begotten son, Rudy, passes before his eyes.

There was a scene of some sort on Westland Row Railway Station and Stephen was one of the principal actors in it. Perhaps Mulligan, who is shown as having a vein of snobbery in his nature, dodged away with Haines, deserting Stephen. The key to the tower may have played a part in the dispute, for it is a grievance with Stephen that although he paid the rent Mulligan demanded the key. With all his real grievances and constellated discontents it is possible that Stephen's schooled reactions broke down under the influence of absinthe. Whatever happened, the general dispersal of the maternity hospital company leaves Stephen with the envious and unreliable Lynch on the way to the cheap brothels of Nighttown. In the mix up on Westland Row Station Bloom loses sight of Stephen and gets into another train by mistake and so is obliged to follow at a distance the drunken youth, to whom he is the preordained and self-appointed father, to guard him, as well as may be, against the worst perils of the place.

There is nothing in the actual material of *The Circe* that should confuse or mislead the attentive reader as, for example, there may be in *The Sirens*. The words, even when distorted, evoke at once the intended image. What may confuse is the rapidity of the action, the constant metamorphosis of men and things, the changes of time and costume, and the phantasmagorical character of all the happenings. Sitting with Joyce one day in a little café in the rue de Grenelle our conversation was interrupted by the fierce pounding of an electric piano garnished with coloured lights.

"Look!" said Joyce. "That's Bella Cohen's pianola. What a fantastic effect! All the keys moving and nobody playing."

And on another occasion during my week's stay in Paris Joyce said:

"*The Circe* is a costume episode. Disguises. Bloom changes clothes half a dozen times. And of course it's an animal episode, full of animal allusions, animal mannerisms. The rhythm is the rhythm of locomotor ataxia."

It seemed to me that he found the Homeric correspondence more difficult in *The Circe* than in any other episode. Ulysses is helped in this adventure not by Pallas but by her male counterpart or inferior, Hermes, god of signposts, public ways and crossroads. Why on this occasion the male principle? Then, what was the herb moly, a plant with dark roots and milk-white blossom given to the hero by Hermes to protect him against the drugs and magic of Circe? What might it signify as a moral, a human attribute? And what means the changing into swine of the companions of Ulysses?

Animals have always been for man something more and

something less than he. He desired to be brave as a lion, cunning as a fox, patient as an ox, grandly soaring as an eagle, wise as a serpent and innocent as a dove, but he desired to be neither lion, fox, ox, eagle, serpent, nor dove. Each was a specialist in its limited kind. Primitive peoples admiring this perfection in limitation, took the names of animals for their clans, and the Boy Scouts of our own day assemble under animal signs. The religion of ancient Egypt is full of half man, half animal beings and of animals worshipped in their own natural forms. Odin became for some special purpose an eagle, a worm. Jove became a bull, a swan. The Holy Spirit appeared in the likeness of a dove and the spirit of scientific enquiry appeared to Adam and Eve in serpent guise. On the negative side sloth and greed are hoggish, ill-tempered bearish, vindictiveness feline, stupidity, obstinancy are donkeyish, lechery is goatish and the vain man is likened to a peacock. The essence of the animal into man metamorphosis seems to be that man becomes an animal when he loses his many-sided human wholeness. One of his functions gets out of hand and usurps the powers belonging to the governing authority of his virtuous republic. Beastliness is one-sidedness. A man may be like a lion, a bull, an eagle or a serpent, but not for long or make a habit of it without losing his integrity. And as the greater includes the less man may be comparable to any animal, but the animals, with two exceptions, cannot simulate humanity. The lion can be only leonine, the bull only bovine, and so on. The two exceptions are apes and dogs—the apes because of their strong family likeness and the dogs because man has trained the fierce hysteria of the dog to love and protect his person and his property as he loves and protects them himself. Stephen's fear of the dog arises, perhaps, out of the dog's political affiliations. The dog is an executive organ of an authoritarian state. The animal into man metamorphosis, as in Dr. Moreau's Island, belongs to post-Darwin imagination trained to regard man as a product of evolution from lower animal states. To suppose that, by means of surgery and a drastic drilling of reflexes, a million years of that evolution might be crowded into a fraction of a human lifetime is a reasonable fancy for the evolutionist but is altogether too fantastic, not to say impious, for a mind brought up to regard the species as for all time fixed by the single act of a creator.

If in the moral sense the animals are symbols of man's lapses into one-sidedness, on the physical side they have given their names and something of the essence of their beings to his diseases—his lapses from wholeness, health. From the wolf, the cat, the owl, the cow, the chicken, the crab, the horse, the sow, the elephant, the parrot we have lupus, cat asthma, glaucoma, vaccination, chicken pox, cancer, horse asthma, scrofula, elephantiasis and psittacosis. No doubt but that Joyce regarded the Circean metamorphosis in this double sense of a corruption of the mind into the one-sidedness of vice, and the downfall of the body into the unwholesomeness of disease.

"Moly" was a harder nut to crack. What was the herb that conferred upon Ulysses immunity from Circe's magic, and thus enabled him to be of service to his companions? What was the "Moly" that saved Bloom from a surrender of his humanity? As a physical symbol Bloom's potato prophylactic against rheumatism and plague, inherited from his mother, would serve, but the real saviour of Bloom was a spiritual "Moly," a state of mind. Joyce wrote to me in 1920: "Moly is the gift of Hermes, god of public ways, and is the invisible influence (prayer, chance, agility, *presence of mind,* power of recuperation which saves in case of accident. This would cover immunity from syphilis—swine love). . . . In this special case his plant may be said to have many leaves, indifference due to masturbation, pessimism congenital, a sense of the ridiculous, sudden fastidiousness in some detail, experience." All these play their part in *The Circe,* but it will be noticed that one of Bloom's trouser buttons gives way just as he is about to suffer complete degradation under the spell of *la Belle Cohen sans merci.* Thus chance supplies the moment through which he reconquers his virility and presence of mind. The accident tickles his sense of the ridiculous, wakes him out of his masochistic trance, quickens his fastidiousness and makes his experience available for service. But there is another aspect of "Moly." Ulysses stands to his men somewhat in the nature of a father and guardian as well as captain. It is while on his way through the wood to liberate them that he meets the god of signposts and public ways. It seems appropriate that the male divinity shall counsel him on this not family or personal, but comradely and quasi-social mission. What Hermes advises him is a violent he-man gesture, an affirmation of manhood: to rush upon the enchantress with drawn sword and compel her to release his men. And may not fatherhood itself by a stretch of the imagination be considered as "Moly," a plant with black root and milk-white blossom? In any case, Bloom's new-found fatherhood is plainly the influence that led him to the palace of Circe Bella Cohen in Tyrone Street. It is the dominating influence throughout his stay in that place and is a potent defence against the spells of Circe, suggestions of perverse love. Almost the first thing Bloom does on recovering his self-possession is to prevent Stephen being robbed of his money by the whores and the whoremistress.

Bloom follows Stephen to the kips as his guardian, but

immediately assumes the principal rôle. Stephen is drunk, Lynch more or less drunk (and drunken men, as the porter in *Macbeth* assure us, are poor lechers), but Bloom though tired is sober. The little that he has drunk has stimulated his imagination and, the night and the place aiding, his thoughts and fancies assume three-dimensional shapes before him and claim independent existence. The daydream, well known in life and fiction, dominates, but scents, shape, the population of Nighttown, his memories, the furniture and objects of the brothel and of his own home crowd in with whirlwind speed. The thoughts of all persons become as visible and as tangible as their bodies. These swift changes, sudden appearings and vanishings, might confuse us if we did not remember the golden rule: keep your eye on Bloom.

Before I met Joyce I had for years collected dreams (my own) but not as material for a future liberation of myself from my complexes. Freud's ingenious demonstration that Hamlet was issue of a mother complex shows how valuable these things can be. I kept the dream book as one might keep a diary. The dreams I dreamed seemed to me to be as well worth recording as the deeds and thoughts of the day. The best of daylight experience, anyway, should be preserved in the form of work of some sort and should speak for itself. Writing down dreams does not in the least help to a knowledge of what they mean, but it does, at least, lead to a feeling for what they are. When I first read *The Circe* episode of *Ulysses* I knew something about the substance of the dream and had, besides, cultivated a kind of memory needed for pursuing the elusive phantoms of sleep to their hiding places and hauling them out for inspection. How to convey in daylight language the significance of dream images, the potency of dream emotions, I never learned. Perhaps it cannot be done except with some such word material as Joyce uses in his unfinished *Work in Progress* now appearing serially in *Transition*.

For me the problem was not to interpret the meaning of a dream, but to determine its shape, colour and action, to re-create the whole image in my memory and to re-construct it as like as possible in words. We feel that we saw something in a dream, but what was our field of vision? How did it diminish to left, to right, up and down? Objects were there, colour, too, but what lay between the objects? What were the colour relations? The dreamer is on what seems to be a canal bank, his back to a fence. A man and a boy, grey, approach with a half-grown tiger, orange and black, on a lead. With terror the dreamer sees the man hand the lead to the boy, who has neither the strength nor the authority to hold the beast. The man meanwhile makes notes in a book, right and left star-gazing. Run the dreamer dare not, or the savage animal would bound in pursuit. The tiger is now near enough that its claws can be plainly seen, now at a distance, a patchwork of colour only. But what is where the canal should be? And what is to the left, to the right and behind man, boy, tiger? Then the dreamer sees the masts of two sailing ships, a brigantine and a full rigged ship, against houses and a dark sky. But what is in the foreground between him and the ships? He feels that the bright image is vignetted off into dark. And then the continuity of the action. Crowds of men pour out of warehouses across the quay to a ship moored alongside. They are receiving their pay on the ship's fo'c'sle deck. The dreamer digs his companion in the ribs and both push their way through the jostling, good-natured queue. "Payday to-day," he says, and then finds himself on a ship where cargo is being discharged with an unnecessary complication of skips, ropes, guys, derricks. But what happened between the payday queue and the ship being unloaded? Between canal bank, tiger and masts of ships against houses? What concerned me was the colour, shape, continuity and atmosphere of the dream. I remember talking to Joyce about all this one evening in the Urania wineshop. Joyce was absorbed, preoccupied. Perhaps our talk on that occasion sowed some of the seed that has since born fruit in *Work in Progress*.

In the dream proper all pictures and actions are seemingly unrelated. While we dream we know that it must be so, but on waking, even if we know what, we ask ourselves in wonder, how? why? where? Holding the head of a white-moustached old man in his hands the dreamer watches a person, to him unknown, trying to weigh a huge pumpkin on a scales jammed in the balance. On the same wooden box where stands the scales an old man tries to cut streaky bacon with a small nail scissors. The dreamer's corn comes off his left little toe and out of its roots issue bright bubbles that rise aloft and float gaily round the delicatessen shop—an unidentifiable room, but one that seems to the dreamer to be more familiar than the bedroom of his flat in which he has lived for years. Call it a wish fulfilment. That can be denied as well as proved. But whence the phantasy that combines so many incongruous elements and endows them with so much significance? It is not a prolongation of his most recent waking thoughts, for the dreamer might just as well be a man awaiting execution as one to whom good fortune has just come in unexpected measure. On the other hand, the wish fulfilment of the daydream is immediately and indisputably clear.

Any odd moment of the day is sufficient for this simplest of all wish fulfilments. The poor man acquires vast wealth, the weak man world power. On a white horse, clad in golden armour, he leads the countless hordes of his obedient followers. A town appears in the path of his relentless march. Its contours are strangely like the contours of the town where he failed to get work and where the people gave him counterfeit half-crowns. A murmur of despair rises from the doomed city. Its gates open and burgesses with halters round their necks appear. In awful silence his army stands waiting for the order to execute the city. But what happens? The white horse cavorts, but only to show the superb seat of him who never rode one. The submissive burgesses, who vaguely resemble the refusers of jobs and the givers of bad half-crowns, are freed. They return to their city with tears of gratitude in their eyes, bearing with them gifts of fabulous value, but indeterminate shape. The white wish-horse, beggar-ridden, fades, the phantom army is demobbed and the dreamer takes up his burden and carries on.

Bloom's waking trances are three. He walks through filthy streets, populated with shuffling, limping, distorted creatures. He meets his dead father and mother, who reproach him for his lack of thrift and for his Gentile practices. To his conscience speaks also Gerty MacDowell, who emerges from the murk with immodest smirking exhibitions. Following her appears his old flame, Josie Powell, now Mrs. Breen. He met her after crossing O'Connell Bridge on his way to lunch. He now repeats with her fantastically a flirtatious scene that happened in his bachelor days twenty years ago. Real figures and creatures of his imagination pass him—the gaffer on a building job where Bloom had once committed a nuisance, loiterers, a gigantic navvy and, in the flesh, Private Compton and Private Carr. He had bought a crubeen and a trotter at the entrance to Nighttown and these he now gives to a stray dog. Here the first of his three waking trances begins.

The watch appears and demands his name and address. Bloom gives a false name and disguises himself, but the watch recognises him as Henry Flower, the poste restante lover. A phantom Martha arises to accuse him. Bloom disowns her and affirms that he has a distinguished army record, also that he is an author-journalist. This is too much for the author of the *Tid-Bits* prize story, "Matcham's Masterstroke," who heatedly denounces Bloom as a plagiarist, a low cad not fit to be mentioned in mixed society. Mary Driscoll, one-time servant to the Bloom family, adds weight to the accusation. Bloom is in the dock facing a multitude of accusers. He is "dynamiter, forger, bigamist, bawd and cuckold and a public nuisance to the citizens of Dublin." The grand dame he saw early that morning while talking to M'Coy takes shape as three ladies of the highest standing in Dublin society, who accuse him of writing to them anonymous, obscene letters. Bloom is courageously defended by the consumptive lawyer, J. J. O'Molloy, who had given support to Bloom's political moderation in Barney Kiernan's saloon, but in spite of his defender's eloquence Bloom is sentenced to be hanged, and Barber Rumbold arises to perform the fell act. The retriever at his feet has become a beagle and now becomes the half-putrefied corpse of Paddy Dignam. The trance ends. Bloom is standing before Mrs. Cohen's door, listening to grave music within. It is Stephen at the piano, as Bloom divines. Zoe Higgins, a whore, guesses that he is associated with the two young men and invites him in.

Hamlet tells Ophelia that he has more offences at his beck and call than he has thoughts to put them in, imagination to give them shape, or time to act them in. For all the multitude of his acted and unacted offences Bloom has condemned himself. And to Rosenkrantz Hamlet says: "Oh, God, I could be bounded by a nutshell and count myself a king of infinite space." Bloom's rise to world power occurs between question and answer in the nutshell of his mind when Zoe asks him if he has a "swagger root" and he replies lewdly, "The mouth can be better engaged than with a cylinder of rank weed." Zoe says, "Go on. Make a stump speech out of it." And forthwith Bloom begins, as many world conquerors and emperors have begun, as a proletarian agitator. "The Catiline," says Nietzsche, "is the pre-existent Cæsar." Bloom's first speech is that of a progressive municipal reformer advocating his own favourite scheme for the betterment of the city's tramway service. He then denounces the capitalists, owners of all the labour-saving machinery, exploiters of the labour of those without property. "The poor man starves while they are grassing their royal mountain stags or shooting peasants and partridges in their purblind pomp of pelf and power." In a split second he becomes Lord Mayor of Dublin. Celtic and Jewish flags wave over all the notabilities of Dublin, of the State, Church and City, and civil and military officials together with representatives of all trades and professions come to do him honour. The Bishop of Down and Connor proclaims him "Emperor President and King Chairman, the most serene and potent and very puissant ruler of this realm." Michael, Archbishop of Armagh, anoints him. Amidst scenes of unbounded enthusiasm he founds the new Bloomusalem in Erin's green and pleasant land. The only dissentient voice is that of the man with the macintosh, thirteenth mourner at Dignam's funeral. Bloom hoists the standard of Zion, proclaims the paradisiacal era, prophesies and unfolds to the world his scheme for a Utopian state.

But the opposition grows. Father Farley denounces his irreligion, and Mrs. Riordan, Paddy Leonard and Lenehan join in the hue and cry. Theodore Purefoy denounces his

contraceptual practices, Alexander J. Dowie condemns
him as a monster of all the iniquities, and the mob howl
for his blood. On Bloom's behalf Doctors Mulligan,
Crotthers and Dixon testify to his physical disabilities, and
Bloom bears eight distinguished children. The Papal
Nuncio demonstrates his descent from Moses, but Bloom's
fall is imminent. He thinks of joining his father by way
of poison. He is publicly burned. Then Zoe's voice brings
him back to his earthly whereabouts. Daydreaming Bloom
had, for a few seconds, lost his time identity in the force
and pregnancy of his vision. Every detail in his daydream
was filed to an edge of knife-like hardness not to be found
in the images of life and dream. It is as logically characteristic of Bloom as any of his acts. He is a friend of humanity but powerless and therefore he achieves world power
for the purpose of realising his Utopian schemes. But the
pessimist in him overthrows his benevolent empire and
he himself perishes in its ruins. The daydream is the native element of the poor man, just as play is the element
of the rich and powerful. No man need dream if he has
the means to act his imaginative desires. Marie Antoinette
can play at being a shepherdess but the shepherdess has
neither material nor time to play at being Marie Antoinette except in the parks and palaces of her imagination.
In our own day the millionaire can play at being a poor
man, and he often does, but the poor man can only daydream his visions of millionaire bliss. "Talk away till
you're black in the face," says Zoe. Appropriate, seeing
that he has, in his imagination, just been burnt to a cin-
der. Zoe thinks it not good business to be standing on the
doorstep and invites Bloom to come inside. This he does,
reluctantly and with hesitation. "She leads him towards
the steps, drawing him by the odour of her armpits, the
vice of her painted eyes, the rustle of her slip in whose

sinuous folds lurks the lion reek of all the male brutes who have possessed her."

In the salon sit Stephen at the piano and Lynch on the hearthrug, cap back to front. Two other whores, Kitty and Florry, people the apartment. Stephen is improvising at the piano and between whiles talking aesthetic philosophy to the gallful and contemptuous Lynch.

"Whetstone," Stephen calls him. From information received Florry knows that the end of the world is coming. It comes. Elijah, in the form of A. J. Christ Dowie, appears, anxious, even at the eleventh hour, to save souls with harmonial philosophy uplift. The whores get as far as confessing their first sexual faults. Then another and more important personage enters the room. It is Bloom's self-critical other self which has taken on the form of his grandfather, Lipoti Virag. Like Santa Claus, he comes down the chimney flue. An evident parallel to this apparition of Bloom's long since dead relative is Hilarion in *La Tentation de Saint Antoine,* only the doubts of the believer, personified in the pupil of Flaubert's tortured saint, is, in Joyce's *The Circe,* a mocking old man, surveying, without illusion of sex, the physical defects of the singularly unattractive whores. And Bloom listens, not with the agony of the saint, but as if in an embarrassed dream, to the bright mockery of his forbear, who appears in the guise of a fabulous bird and meticulously catalogues the ravages of time, lust and laziness on the bodies of Zoe, Kitty and Florry. The taut brain of Lipoti Virag, coiled like a watch-spring in his birdskull, is unable to bear the strain. He becomes epileptic, inarticulate and departs, cursing. Footfalls are heard without, the door opens, and the whoremistress, Bella Cohen, appears. She has an air of authority, of one accustomed to being obeyed. Bloom feels that the dominant woman is his master. Weakly he prepares for surrender.

I had not long been settled in London when, in the late autumn of 1920, Joyce wrote to me and asked if, among other things, I could get him some comic papers of as bold a type as might be found on our puritan shores. I took it that he meant those journals, usually entitled something or other Bits, full of mild nudities out of which the male buyer is to get what kick he may. I bought all I could at a shop in Camden Town and looked them over to find the likeliest. One of them stood out above the rest. On the cover it had the harmless bathing girl and the still more harmless joke, nitwit nudities suggesting perfectly a suet pudding of the sort they call in Yorkshire "sad," but the correspondence columns revealed it as the official organ of English tight lacing and heel drill specialists. Every letter had the authentic saccharine pedantic accent of perversity. Naturally I hurried to Fleet Street to buy what back numbers were available. A cool Scot rummaged round the office and found me half a dozen. Just in time, for the heavy hand of the law descended on that periodical the following week. Forty pounds and publication stopped was the penalty.

As I have already said, Joyce was a great believer in his luck. He was confident that what he needed for his book would come to him somehow, and come it did from all quarters, as the following incident shows. During a lull in the composition of an earlier episode he went to Locarno for a change of air, and there made the acquaintance of a lady who owned two of the islands in the Lago Maggiore. Along the near mainland she was called Circe and many far-fetched stories went to make up her Circean legend. During our stay in Locarno, in the spring of 1919, he met her again by chance in front of the post office and she invited us to visit her on her enchanted isle. This was a cunningly devised jungle paradise, holding, among other wonders, a grove of superb eucalyptus trees. I asked permission to paint them, which permission was given together with an invitation to spend a whole day on the island. Behind the house the Lady of the Lake had set up a doll factory wherein a Japanese artist struggled vainly to produce a doll, not after his own image, but after the image of western child beauty suitably commercialised. The portrait of a very beautiful young woman, that of our hostess, hung in the salon, the walls of which were further hung with oil colour drawings depicting scenes from the *Odyssey*, and with a tapestry bearing the words καλος φίλος καὶ ἔχθρος καλος (good friend and good foe). The long table bore a mountainous litter of paper, string, casts, fruits, books, vessels, silk stockings, letters and other gear such as no bachelor's table in Europe might hope to equal. When we assembled on the terrace for tea, the Lady of the Lake regaled us with a liqueur distilled by herself, tasting like a cross between Kümmel and Cointreau. Before we left she entrusted to Joyce a packet of letters and a valise of books on the theme of erotic perversion, remarking that he might find the contents useful as documentation for his writing. She was afraid too that in the event of sudden death these might be found and give rise to misunderstandings. All this material was no doubt useful enough to Joyce when a month or two later he began the composition of *The Circe*.

With the appearance of the whoremistress, Bella Cohen, in the doorway of the room begins the third of Bloom's daydream hallucinations. All in him that is slave to woman rises to take charge of his whole being. Bella Cohen's fan recognises the slave and commands him instantly to tie up the mistress's shoelace. Bloom changes his sex. "With a piercing, epileptic cry she sinks on all fours, grunting, snuffling, rooting at his feet, then lies, shamming dead with eyes shut tight, trembling eyelids, bowed upon the ground in the attitude of most excellent master." Bella, who now wears the trousers as Bello, commands and Bloom, who wears the petticoats, obeys. Bello insults and Bloom protests with weak whimperings. All the sins of Bloom's past rise to complete his degradation. When Bloom mentions Eccles Street as confirmation of his virility, Bello reminds him that there is a man of brawn in possession there. Bloom thinks he sees Marion as a young girl again, but it is his daughter with her lover, a student in Mullingar. Out of her frame on the wall over his bed the nymph he cut out of *Photo Bits* comes down to greet him, "passing under interlacing yews." The yews are the yews by Poulaphouca waterfall, and they remind him of his youthful abuse of their shade—the nymph of his bedroom manners and language. The nymph appears "Eyeless, in nun's white habit, coif and huge, winged wimple, softly, with remote eyes." Here a button breaks, "Bip," from Bloom's trousers and restores to him his manhood. He attacks the nun as Ulysses attacked the enchantress, and the nun-nymph, "with a cry, flees from him unveiled, her plaster cast cracking, a cloud of stench escaping from the cracks." He shouts insults after her. "The figure of Bella Cohen stands before him." How long had he been staring at her? Overlong, perhaps, for she remarks, "You'll know me next time."

Bella Cohen raises the question of payment for the hospitality. Lynch has no money and Stephen, too drunk and tired to count, lays too much on the table. Observant Bloom rescues ten shillings of it that else had gone into the whores' stockings. Seeing that Stephen is quite incapable of looking after money, he takes charge of the

whole lot. Then what Bloom failed to hinder in 7 Eccles
Street he actively aids and abets in his imagination. His
complaisance becomes connivance. He becomes a flunkey
to Boylan, accepting from the conquering hero a tip of
sixpence to buy himself a gin and splash, and is allowed
to peep through the keyhole of the bedroom door at the
sport of Marion and Blazes. Zoe puts twopence in the pianola and all dance to the tune of *My Girl's a Yorkshire
Girl.* To Stephen, tottering, giddy and weak from hunger
and drink, comes a vision of his mother, bidding him re-
pent, pray and save his soul from hellfire. He hears her
prayers for his soul and in exasperation stands, takes
his ashplant in both hands and with Siegfried's cry,
"Nothung," strikes and smashes the chandelier. There is
a commotion. Bella wants ten shillings for the damage.
Bloom gives her one shilling, the real value of the shattered gas chimney. Stephen and Lynch make for the street
and Bloom follows.

"At the corner of Beaver Street beneath the scaffolding
Bloom panting stops on the fringe of the noisy quarrelling knot, a lot not knowing a jot what hi! hi! row and
wrangle round the whowhat brawlall together." It is
Private Compton and Private Carr with their girls. Pri-
vate Carr, drunk and quarrelsome, affirms that his girl has
been insulted by the drunk and argumentative Stephen.
Bloom elbows his way through the crowd and tries to get
Stephen away, or at any rate to make peace. But no appeal
of Bloom can turn away the motiveless wrath of Carr, and
Stephen is resolved to stand and argue till he drops.
Lynch, with the choice between standing by his friend
and returning to the brothel with Kitty, basely deserts
Stephen and goes off with the whore. Carr knocks down
Stephen. The watch appears, disperses the crowd and is
about to go through the formalities of taking names when

"Corny Kelleher, weepers round his hat, a death wreath in his hand, appears among the bystanders." The castle spy undertaker refuses to take Stephen in his car to Sandycove, but performs the welcome service of sending away the watch. He then drives off himself, leaving Bloom and Stephen alone. Bloom brushes shavings off Stephen's clothes and tries to wake him, calling, "Stephen," but for all answer Stephen repeats words of the poem by Yeats he used to sing to his mother, the "Fergus" of which is assumed by the non-poetical Bloom to be a reference to a beloved Miss Ferguson. With Stephen's hat and stick in hand Bloom mounts guard over Stephen's prostrate form, and repeats to himself the Freemason's oath of secrecy when, against a dark wall, the bright, fairy figure of a boy of eleven years glides past. It is Rudy, his own son. Bloom calls to him, "Rudy," but the unseeing ghost passes on. The hero has rescued his companions from the spells of Circe as whole men.

Originality in the arts usually resolves itself into observing and interpreting some aspect of nature that before was hidden under the laziness of convention. The greatest of all artistic revolutions was that of impressionist painting, which consisted, in the main, of observing that shadows were full of light and colour. Cubism, futurism and all their variations are just so much literature by the side of this. *The Circe* episode is generally regarded as the clou of *Ulysses,* at any rate as the most original and striking of all the eighteen episodes. What is the natural material out of which it is made? It would not move us at all if it were not nature, our own and that of all men. The observed fact is that hallucination is common human experience. The art consists in treating it as such. We all know it in the certified mental case, in the case of the sufferer from fever delirium, in the case of the overdrunk individual who lives in a world full of serpents and rodents, but not in our own sane lives where also it plays its part. Joyce shows it as being a common experience of sane men. It may be objected that Stephen is drunk. Bloom, however, is soberer than many judges, and it is mainly Bloom's inner world that is projected into three dimensional space.

Faces with unseeing eyes pass us in the streets, sit near us in trams and buses, smiles lighting their lips or scowls darkening their brows. They are the daydreamers, reliving some past happiness or shame, reconstructing to their greater advantage scenes of the past in which the advantage lay not with them, open-handedly spending imaginary sweepstake prizes, playing Don Giovanni or Don Quixote, crowning themselves with laurels, "stepping forward to applause earnestly" like Stephen, committing crimes of vengeance or cruelty, ruling worlds, being tried for their lives, being buried with pomp or shot at dawn, winning the Grand National, lying luxuriously with film stars and winning the love of princesses. Sometimes the subconscious mask of social discipline falls, and they laugh and talk audibly. Unlucky for them if in such a moment their dreams are those of Mahon or Rouse, for whose deeds, normally, the dream is an adequate substitute. A worker on the railway allotment near my house, a very sane and mild gentleman, holds long conversations with people, to me invisible, among the raspberry canes. None of his guests could see the ghosts of slaughtered Banquos at Macbeth's feast. The widow, the widower can see in chair or bed the body that has long since rotted in the ground, while we wonder at their tenacity in saying "he is," "she is" and in avoiding the fatal "was" and "has been." The passion of the cuckold for absolute proof is not all doubt. It is as much a device to oust painful imaginings with less fearful realities. Take a time of crisis such as that in which Bloom is living, a Jew, sonless and with memories of his dead son all the day rolling back upon him, cuckolded to his own knowledge, physically tired, surrounded with the sights and smells of the brothel, and nothing is more natural than that the thin partition between daydream and hallucination shall break down—that for the space of seconds his waking dream shall dominate his fatigued senses.

The Circe episode of Joyce's *Ulysses*, which has justly been compared with the Walpurgisnacht in Goethe's *Faust*, to Flaubert's *La Tentation de Saint Antoine* and to Strindberg's *Dream Play*, differs from all these in its essential naturalness. The whole fantasia is steeped in an atmosphere of familiar simplicity. The scene is not the Theban desert nor the wild spaces and abysses of the Brocken nor the shifting scene of a dream, but the common streets of a known named city and the banal parlour of a cheap brothel. The persons are not legendary nor are they representative types, but a handful of people of flesh and blood who might, we think, pass us on the street any day. Their conflicts are not the remote and tragic conflicts of a tortured believer at war with his unbelief nor of the spirit of man rebelling against the limitations of its destiny. No supernatural beings intervene. The decaying Dignam, Bloom's grandfather, Lipoti Virag, Stephen's mother exist as thoughts of Bloom and Stephen. The music of the spheres is the music of Bella Cohen's pianola. Time and space are shattered when the blow of an ashplant shatters a gas chimney. All the fights of history assemble around a common street fight which ends with a knock down blow. The "Bip" of a burst trouser button is the martial music that rallies Bloom's forces for a successful defence of his manhood. Bloom's adoption of Stephen, through which the father in him receives sublimated expression, is presented as the simple act of a man of good will who throws the shield of his experience between a rash youth and the perils of the world.

Bloom's pessimism dominates the first two of his day-dream hallucinations. He feels himself guilty of a number of petty iniquities of thought and deed. He puts himself on trial, disguises himself, penetrates his own disguises, twists and turns and pursues himself like a hound through his twistings and turnings, throws himself on the mercy of the court, rejects his plea for mercy and condemns himself to be hanged. His megalomaniac messiah illusions are father to his dream of world power. According to the tradition of his race Bloom should be king in his own home. He is not. A Darwinian rationalist and a radical social reformer, he sees that the world is out of joint, but most irrationally believes that he was born to set it right. To this end he makes himself emperor president and king chairman, but the mere whisper of his petty sins shakes the fabric of his empire. He condemns himself for his in-sufficiencies, abdicates, causes himself to be publicly burned, a heretic's death, but is content to destroy him-self. He bears the world no ill will and does not condemn or destroy it in his imagination. The third of his day-dreams is the most dangerous because it proceeds from a natural and habitual masochism. To dream of himself as a prisoner in the dock or as emperor on the throne is not for Bloom such a luxurious experience as to dream of himself in women's clothes, performing menial offices for the whores in a brothel under the command of a mighty whoremistress. This is the form that swinelove, the de-basement of the imagination in sexual surrender, takes in Bloom's case. Here it is the best of Bloom, the responsibil-ities of his social fatherhood, that the "Bip" of his lost trouser button calls to arms. The god of public ways was standing behind him with Olympian shears. Like his Homeric seagoing forbear, he rushes upon the enchantress with drawn sword and death-denouncing looks. After that he may be tormented by visions of the suitors' insolence and his wife's frailty in Ithaca Eccles Street but the spells of the enchantress are broken.

CHAPTER XII

The journey home is described in the language of tired men. Sentences yawn, stumble, become involved and wander into blind alleys. The clichés are as many and as well worn as the good corporation cobblestones on which they walk, and the shapes of them are as familiar as those of the classic doorways of dignified Eccles Street. Bloom has had a long and exhausting day but is in better shape than Stephen, who has eaten nothing since breakfast and has drunk heavily. If there are pages in *Ulysses* of a more dazzling virtuosity than those of *Eumaeus* there are certainly none with more insight or tenderness. The effect of the slow flowing stream of familiar words is comic, till we see emerging out of the dull coloured material a delicate and intimate picture of the relations of a fatherly man to a young man who is a wayward son. Bloom is pathetically eager to do all that he knows is advisable to be done for the young man's physical welfare. In the first place he must be persuaded to eat. Then, as he is now homeless, his quarrel with Mulligan having made it impossible for him to return to the tower, his shelter for the night must be considered. After that, something may, perhaps, be done for the furtherance of his worldly interests and artistic aims. With all this in mind, and talking like one o'clock a.m. to keep the thoughts of both from sinking unnecesarily deep, Bloom is timid and deferential to the point of servility towards his young companion's scholastic and artistic attainments. His deference is that wistful defer-

ence of a kind father to a self-willed son, of a man edu-
cated in the "university of life" to the man of academic
training, and of a denationalised Jew to a Christian Gentile.

Stephen, still drunk and still suffering from the effects
of Private Carr's right swing to the jaw, talks little, and
when he does is sententious and occasionally irritable and
rude. He is too weak to take a direction for himself and
so accepts that indicated by Bloom, but he does so without pleasure or graciousness. To all Bloom's fussy solicitude he is indifferent. While Bloom is busy with him, all
the thought of which he is capable is busy with himself.
Between them is a barrier of race and years, and Bloom, as
a Jew, is older than Stephen by more than the sixteen years
that on the calendar separate them. What he can do to sur-
mount that barrier Bloom does, but Stephen is too weak
and too preoccupied to try to meet him half way.

When Bloom helps Stephen to his feet after Carr's
knock-down blow Stephen's first thought is for a drink.
There are no pubs open and no fountain handy so Bloom
hits on the bright idea of visiting the cabman's shelter
near Butt Bridge. They walk slowly in that direction,
Bloom beguiling the way with a purling stream of talk,
all as sound as it is banal. From the dangers of Nighttown,
with its women and crooks, he goes on to the providential
appearance of Corney Kelleher, the unreliability of police
evidence and the indiscretion of entrusting the police with
arms. He evokes no response till he touches on the scene
on Westland Row station and the subsequent desertion of
Stephen by all his drinking companions with the exception of Lynch, to whom Stephen alludes grimly as
"Judas." Passing under Loop Line Bridge they see the
corporation watchman, Gumley, a friend of Simon Dedalus, minding the corporation stones asleep in his sentry

box, and then from out the darkness Stephen is hailed by Corley (Lenehan's mentor in the story, "The Two Gallants" in *Dubliners*). Corley is down and out, and touches Stephen for some money. Stephen gives him half a crown and then returns to Bloom, who had been standing discreetly out of earshot, and reports:

" 'He's down on his luck. He asked me to ask you to ask somebody named Boylan, a billsticker, to give him a job as a sandwichman.'

"At this intelligence, in which he seemingly evinced little interest, Mr. Bloom gazed abstractedly for the space of half a second or so in the direction of a bucket dredger, rejoicing in the far-famed name of Eblana. . . ."

There is no escaping Boylan for Bloom that day. In word, flesh or spoor he is ever present. The cabman's shelter is kept by one Fitzharris, reputed to be the famous Skin-the-Goat who drove the Phœnix Park murderers to and from the scene of their crime. Standing out among the general run of jarvies, stevedores and stay-out-late citizens is "a redbearded bibulous individual, a portion of whose hair was greyish, a sailor, probably. . . ." This worthy, overhearing a part of the conversation of Bloom and Stephen, interrupts, claiming to know Stephen's father. From this moment until their departure the redbearded man pours out a constant stream of tall stories to the admiration and bewilderment of all present. He is W. B. Murphy, A.B., of Carrigaloe, and he took his discharge that morning from the three-masted schooner, *Rosevean*, the same that Stephen saw from Sandymount shore gliding into Dublin river with her sails brailed up to her crosstrees. He is a mighty drinker and a splendid liar, and he takes his place worthily alongside the Nameless One and the Citizen in Joyce's gallery of comic-grotesque inventions. But he is a being of a more phantasmal order than are the nameless debt collector and the unnamed vocal patriot. These people live somewhere. We can see "I" with Pisser Burke at a street corner, swapping stories and filing barbed points to them, and we can see the Citizen reading the morning papers and stoking himself up with indignation for his day's work in the pubs of Dublin. But where did this man of the tribe of Vanderdecken come from? And where does he go after he leaves the cabman's shelter? Nobody believes that he has a home and a wife in Carrigaloe and a sixteen-year-old son, Danny. Even his lice seem unsubstantial, like the moving picture of Antonio on his broad chest. The rum he gurgles was sold to him by Caliban, who set up a distillery on the strength of a recipe he found in a drowned sailor's pocket. If he stood on the scales the pointing needle would not waver. Because he sailed on the *Rosevean*, that three-masted schooner herself becomes transparent. She is by Noland out of Bridgewater by Moonshine and she sails straight out of Lloyd's register into the records of Myth.

When I mentioned this character to Joyce he said to me:

"That's a portrait of you."

"What! Me? How's that? I understand the lice and the bottles. But the lies! All Englishmen are brought up on sticking to facts and understating them."

Joyce's only comment was a tight-lipped, eye-glittering laugh.

Bloom preserves an open mind on all the tall stories the sailor tells them, but they set him considering his own way of life, which he finds very stick-in-the-mud and lacking in enterprise. He swiftly plans a boat trip to London with which he might combine a concert tour for Marion through the south coast watering places. At the sight of a half-witted prostitute caught through the open door

Bloom hides behind a newspaper. He recognises her as
the woman who knows his wife by sight and who once
"begged the chance of his washing." When she is out of
view he glibly denounces the system that allows such people, probably diseased, to prey on the male community.
He is all for hygiene and medical supervision. The talk in
the shelter veers to the subject of Ireland, and Fitzharris
lets himself go in the Citizen vein. Bloom takes no part in
the discussion but tells Stephen briefly of his encounter
with the super-patriot in Barney Kiernan's saloon and asks
directly for Stephen's approval of his attitude. "He turned
a long you are wrong gaze on Stephen of timorous dark
pride at the soft impeachment, with a glance also of en-
treaty for he seemed to glean in a kind of way that it
wasn't all exactly. . . ." Stephen's mumbled reply gives
him neither enlightenment nor confirmation. His plea for
tolerance in religion and politics leads to the unfolding
of his Utopian plan of £300 per annum for everybody who
works, but this generous scheme finds no favour with Stephen, who asks to be counted out if there's any work in it.
A mention of the rich beauty and passionate nature of
southern women gives Bloom the chance to produce his
wallet photograph of Marion. Her physical excellences
are one of Bloom's pet hobbies. He lays the crumpled
image of Marion's abundant charms before Stephen, talking all the time, fussily, volubly, hopefully, like a small
picture collector showing his treasures to a Sir Joseph
Duveen, or a wireless fan tuning in his self-constructed
set for the benefit of a Marchese Marconi. Stephen pro-
nounces the likeness to be that of a handsome woman, and
Bloom is satisfied, but only the promptings of good taste
prevent his leaving it on the table for a conspicuously long
period so that his young friend can get a really good eye-
ful of it. When the other clients start talking about Par-

nell, Bloom is reminded of a personal encounter with the great man. Some of Parnell's faithful friends were smashing up an O'Brienite newspaper in retaliation for the scurrilities that had appeared in it, and both Parnell and Bloom were present in the crowd. Parnell's hat was knocked off and it was Mr. Bloom who picked up and returned to Ireland's uncrowned king his fallen headgear. Parnell rewarded him with a polite, "Thank you, sir."

There is something feminine in Bloom's distress about Stephen's starving condition. He preaches solid food to him like a mother. But there is another problem no less important than food: Where shall his young friend sleep? After some inner misgivings, Bloom solves it by taking the heroic course of inviting Stephen to come to Eccles Street for a cup of cocoa and a shakedown. This is his second act of courage on Stephen's behalf since closing time at Burke's. Many a married man would prefer to face the fists of Private Carr rather than face the endless whys and hows and whats of an indignant wife. Here for the first time we hear *en sourdine* the breath of affirmation on which Penelope ends. In passive mood, ready to say "yes" to anything because it is easier than saying "no," Stephen consents.

There is no moment in *Ulysses* that better exemplifies that indefinite repugnance to Bloom's physical presence, felt by so many throughout the day, than that in which Bloom offers his arm to the weak and still unsteady Stephen: "Accordingly he passed his left arm in Stephen's right and led him on accordingly.

" 'Yes,' Stephen said uncertainly, because he thought he felt a strange kind of flesh of a different man approach him, sinewless and wobbly and all that."

Stephen had quarrelled with at least one friend that evening and others had left him in the lurch. No doubt, even drunk, he felt resentful towards them; and yet he would have experienced no unpleasant shock at contact with their bodies. Mulligan's arm was supple and muscular, an athlete's arm like that of Cranly, and there was nothing repellent in the contact of Lynch's tough, strong body. We must suppose that part of Stephen's physical recoil was due to their difference of race. The Jew sometimes hates the Gentile, and the Gentile occasionally hates the Jew but, religious and political differences apart, there exists also a physical chemical repulsion, and this is felt only by the Gentile for the Jewish man, and is experienced by neither kind of menfolk for Gentile or Jewish women, nor, it seems, by the Jew man for his Gentile opposite number, nor by Gentile or Jewish women for the males of the other race. This physical incompatibility must explain in some measure the curious isolation of Bloom among the men of Dublin. Bloom is pathetically eager to proclaim himself a hundred per cent Irishman, and none of the men of Dublin believes him to be an elder of Zion or any other sort of conspirator; and further, he does not irritate them with any Jewish exclusiveness in the matter of eating, drinking, fasting, praying or marrying. Irishwomen, Josie Powell and Gerty MacDowell, for example, are very favourably inclined towards Bloom. He is not a proud, a self-pitying or in any way self-isolating sort of man.

On the walk to Eccles Street Stephen is so far recovered that he can talk music and sing snatches of seventeenth century songs. The conversation is far less one-sided than it was, but they talk past each other and establish no real contact. Bloom, hearing the quality of Stephen's voice, immediately busies himself with plans for Marion-Stephen concerts, lessons in Italian for Marion, general mental improvement all round and paying literature thrown in.

To all Bloom's reasonable and worldly-wise counsels and plan-making Stephen pays not the slightest heed, but he contributes to the discussion when the subject is one that does not at all concern himself.

"The slaughter of the suitors," said Joyce to me as he was nearing the end of his book, "always seemed to me unUlyssean." But early in 1921 he wrote to me that he had solved the slaughter problem.

I was glad to hear that; for if we take the end of the *Odyssey* literally the vengeance of Ulysses and his son does seem to take a savage and senseless form. If, as Stephen says, Act 5 of *Hamlet* is "a bloodboltered shambles," what is Book 22 of the *Odyssey?* "Nine lives are taken off for his father's one." Well, what about the fifty lives of the *Odyssey* taken off for no life at all? For there is no crime imputed to the suitors except that of eating a great deal of their hostess's food and drinking a lot of her wine, and behaving generally in a boisterous and untidy way. Slaughter is the right word. It never resembles a fight, for should a suitor get hold of a weapon, Pallas steps in and most unfairly mars his usage of it. And Telemachus performing the office of Rumbold, the demon barber, on the consenting servant girls after they have swabbed up the bloody mess of blood and entrails, seems to one very unGreek mind to be a sickeningly sadistic young prig. I knew that Joyce was a great hater of bloodshed. All intelligent men are. They have more effective weapons than arrows or howitzers or whatever the armourer of the day provides. On so many occasions has he prefaced an observation to me with: "You know, Budgen, I am not a bloodyminded man," that it became a kind of refrain.

One knew, of course, that it did not lie in Bloom's character to play the he-man in any way with violence of deed or word, nor would an emotional scene of any kind be native to him.

Joyce wrote to me in the February of 1921: "I am writing *Ithaca* in the form of a mathematical catechism. All events are resolved into their cosmic physical, psychical, etc., equivalents, e.g., Bloom jumping down the area, drawing water from the tap, the micturation in the garden, the cone of incense, lighted candle and statue, so that not only will the reader know everything and know it in the baldest coldest way but Bloom and Stephen thereby become heavenly bodies, wanderers like the stars at which they gaze."

So cold is the manner and the form so condensed that unless the vast amount of information contained in *Ithaca* is diluted with many times its weight of words it is unassimilable. It is the coldest episode in an unemotional book. Everything is conveyed in the same tone and tempo as if of equal importance. It is for the reader to assign the human values. How Bloom lets himself down into the area of 7 Eccles Street, lights the fire, draws water, counts up his money, undresses, and how he defeats the suitors is told in the same colourless even manner. The skeleton of each fact is stripped of its emotional covering. One fact stands by the other like the skeletons of man and woman, ape and tiger in an anatomical museum at twilight, all their differences of contour made secondary by their sameness of material, function and mechanism. Our senses that are wont to convey to us differentiations of outward seeming in the shape of clothes, flesh, fur, feathers, etc., are left deceived and unsatisfied. These questions and answers look like the noncommittal jars standing in rows on the chemist's shelves. Distilled water and deadly poison stare at us with the same transparent, icy stare. The same toneless, unhuman voice invites us to contemplate tragic and comic happenings and happenings of no importance. The comic of *Ithaca* is the terrible comic of masks, the comic of the comedian who always keeps a straight face. Something of the same sort is observable in the archaic sculpture of Greece where the unwounded victor and the dying warrior plucking the fatal barb from his side smile the same glassy smile.

Joyce once told me that *Ithaca* was his favourite episode. "It is the ugly duckling of the book," he said.

We are not brought suddenly into the presence of the bold, proud men who wasted the substance of Ulysses. Bloom, who has forgotten his street door key, must first answer the question: to knock or not to knock? A light in the bedroom is evidence that Molly is in bed, so he answers it in the negative. He enters the house by way of the area and the unfastened kitchen door, and then lets his guest in through the front door. Then he makes for Stephen a cup of Epps' Cocoa. What a lapse of time is revealed by this once so familiar name! Now it means nothing to the reader made grateful and comforted at bedtime with Ovaltine. The two men sit drinking their cocoa and talking on various subjects such as the Irish and Hebrew languages, ritual murder, their previous meetings and common acquaintances. They find that they have met on two previous occasions, once when Stephen was five and again when he was ten. Another point of contact between them is the elderly and infirm widow, Mrs. Riordan, the aunt Dante, Minerva of Stephen's childhood, and Bloom's fellow guest while he was staying at the City Arms Hotel. Stephen is in better humour than he was in the cabman's shelter and takes a lively part in the conversation. In Bloom's kitchen they get along excellently together. They make their voices heard across the gulf of time, race and temperament that separates them. Bloom tries to persuade his young friend to pass the night under his roof, but Stephen resolutely declines. They are like two ships bound for different ports that come within hail and disappear into the night.

They pause for a moment in the garden to gaze at the sky full of stars and to micturate, for, let the mind suffer and enjoy as it may, the moisture of the body, in the words of Phineas Fletcher, "Runs down to the Urine lake, his banks thrice daily filling."

Stephen must become and Bloom must be. As they shake hands at parting a sad thought of handshakes with friends now dead crosses Bloom's mind and he is assailed by a momentary pang of loneliness. We are not told where Stephen sleeps. Then Bloom enters the living room with the security of habit, but in his absence Molly has rearranged the furniture in one of those impulses of domestic revolution to which all women, not least mother Europe, are from time to time subject. He bumps his head on the wardrobe that during his absence has wandered from one side of the room to the other. Candlestick uplifted, he surveys the scene. With as little emotion as a Home Office pathologist on the scene of a crime, he takes note of the contents of the room, observing here and there evidences of Blazes Boylan's recent visit. On the music rest of the piano is "the music in the key of G natural for voice and piano of *Love's Old Sweet Song*" open at the last page, testifying to the studies of Blazes and Marion. Two chairs, one soiled, facing each other bear silent witness to the good feeling and comprehension existing between cantatrice and impresario. Bloom's reflections roam over a vast field as he sits in the silent room; space, the stars, the events of the day, the state of his fortunes, the home of his dreams, how to get rich, the perfect advertisement, where was Moses when the candle went out?

Appropriately it is in the bedroom that Bloom meets and disposes of the suitors. From this base he reviews and takes the salute of the host of his wife's admirers. He finishes undressing and enters the bed, head to his wife's feet.

"What did his limbs, when gradually extended, encounter?

"New clean bedlinen, additional odours, the presence of a human form, female, hers, the imprint of a human form, male, not his, some crumbs, some flakes of potted meat, recooked, which he removed.

"If he had smiled why would he have smiled?

"To reflect that each one who enters imagines himself to be the first to enter whereas he is always the last term of a preceding series even if the first term of a succeeding one, each imagining himself to be first, last, only and alone, whereas he is neither first nor last nor only nor alone in a series originating in and repeated to infinity."

Bloom considers the whole series of Marion's lovers and especially the latest addition thereto and recent occupant of his bed, Blazes Boylan. His subsequent reflections are affected by the antagonistic sentiments of envy, jealousy, abnegation and equanimity. There follows a rational explanation of the origin of these sentiments and of the order in which they are experienced.

"Why more abnegation than jealousy, less envy than equanimity?

"From outrage (matrimony) to outrage (adultery) there arose nought but outrage (copulation) yet the matrimonial violator of the matrimonially violated had not been outraged by the adulterous violator of the adulterously violated."

His ultimate reflections are those of the purely rational man whose emotional reactions are quickly stilled in thought. Tiredly he envisages some forms of husbandly

self-assertion but abandons them as either immoral or useless or inexpedient. In the vast scheme of things with
which he identifies himself the adultery of his wife becomes an unimportant event. He considers the nature and
desires of the human body and its functional necessities
and mechanisms . . . "the futility of triumph or protest
or vindication: the inanity of extolled virtue: the lethargy
of nescient matter: the apathy of the stars."

It is in the unsmiled smile of his equanimity that the
bowstring of the lord of 7 Eccles Street most loudly
twangs. It slaughters the suitors of Marion as effectively
as did the divinely aided Ulysses those of Penelope. With
bloodless thought Bloom banishes his rivals to nonentity,
and it must be admitted that he does his work just as
sweepingly well as the more bloody-minded archer king
of *Ithaca*. His triumph is, in a sense, all too complete; for
he condemns to vast spaces of time—hurls into eternity in
short—not only the adulterous violators but the adulterously violated, and himself too, the matrimonial violator.
The temporal institution of monogamic marriage also
goes by the board; for in that region whereto were ex-
pedited suitors, wife and husband there is neither marrying nor giving in marriage. What then remains after this
holocaust? Only himself with his desires—not as husband
or householder but as Leopold Bloom, an Einziger with
no Eigentum, the man of no property, and Marion by his
side, not as his wife but as a symbol of all fleshly womanhood, wherever or whenever existing. He gravely salutes
that womanhood in the shape of that flesh in which, for
him, it most truly resides. Byron wished that all the
women of the world had one rosy mouth to kiss, and
Bloom's salute is bestowed, I take it, in that sense though
not in that place. If we saw a hint of defeatist resignation
or masked bitterness in Bloom's unsmiling, smileful tran-

quillity, we should imagine a morrow on which the mask might fall, the reality take the place of the appearance. We are given no such hint. Bloom's victory is to all appearances complete. The derangement of the bed wakes Marion, who begins a truly wifely catechism, to which Bloom with perfect presence of mind replies, giving an account of his day's activities, largely true, but with such adaptations and omissions as shall make it domestically acceptable. The conversation becomes increasingly more laconic till it fades altogether, and then, but not before ordering two eggs for his to-morrow's breakfast, to variations on the name and adventures of Sinbad the sailor, the tired hero drops off to sleep.

But Marion remains awake and it is she who has the last word. Some strangenesses of manner on the part of Leopold have to be explained; some lapses in his narrative have to be filled in with guess work; and then, guessing and explaining, her mind runs through all the world that is hers. In eight unpunctuated sentences of about five thousand words each she paints a portrait of herself not known to Leopold, and a portrait of a Poldy not known to him or his friends, and a picture of the world, the values of which would be disputed by every other person in the book. There is none of the coldness of an abstraction in Molly Bloom, but she is more symbolical than any other person in Ulysses. What she symbolises is evident: it is the teeming earth with her countless brood of created things. Marion's monologue snakes its way through the last forty pages of *Ulysses* like a river winding through a plain, finding its true course by the compelling logic of its own fluidity and weight. Joyce wrote to me at the time he was composing *Penelope:* "Her monologue turns slowly, evenly, though with variations, capriciously, but surely like the huge earthball itself round and round spin-ning. Its four cardinal points are the female breasts, arse, womb and sex expressed by the words *because, bottom* (in all senses bottom button, bottom of the glass, bottom of the sea, bottom of his heart) *woman, yes."* It is clearly in her symbolical character as fruitful mother earth that Molly speaks, through the medium of her body, for what individual, socially limited woman, if she were capable of entertaining such thoughts, would not be secretive enough to suppress them? Her very isolation (she is alone on the stage while all the rest sleep) gives her the scale and proportion of a giantess. Her obscenities of thought lack no verisimilitude. They are of woman; but no obscenity is womanly. The province of social woman is the erotic: the obscene is to her a kind of brawling in church. Molly Bloom is the creation of a man; and Joyce is, perhaps, as one-sidedly masculine as D. H. Lawrence was one-sidedly feminine. Molly betrays her womanhood when she says she can find nothing interesting in the work of Master François Rabelais. She prefers *The Sweets of Sin* and the novels of Monsieur Paul de Kock. But on the other hand, her unspoken thoughts concerning her amours, remote and recent, are at least as precise and candid as those of her sleeping partner. As is quite natural, the prowess of Boylan occupies the foreground of her memory; but she has more romantic attachment to her first lover, Mulvey, a naval lieutenant, and to the gentlemanly soldier, Gardner, who lost his life in the Boer War, and even to the foppish tenor, Bartell d'Arcy. In the end her thoughts revert to Leopold. It is the memory of his proposal to her, in which thoughts of all her other lovers and recollections of her girlhood in Gibraltar mingle, that carries her into sleep.

". . . when I put the rose in my hair like the Andalusian girls used or shall I wear a red yes and how he kissed me under the Moorish wall and I thought well as well him as another and then I asked him with my eyes to ask again yes and then he asked me would I yes to say yes my mountain flower and first I put my arms around him yes and drew him down to me so he could feel my breasts all perfume yes and his heart was going like mad and yes I said yes I will Yes."

Both Bloom and Marion have this in common that they bring out of inconstancy tributes to fidelity. Bloom's eye roves throughout the world of women but always with the image of Marion as a standard with which to test their comparative excellencies, and Marion's measure of value for all males is Leopold. Joyce wrote to me of Molly Bloom's nonstop monologue: "It is the indispensable countersign to Bloom's passport to eternity." But what a passport officer! And what a countersign! The first use she makes of her consular authority is to retouch his photograph and alter his signature; and her distinguishing marks fill up pages. "Aggravating." "Fussy." "Gets in the way." "Sly boots but I can see through him." "Poser." "Muddler." Marion's visa on Leopold's passport will bring trouble on him in all the countries and mandated territories of eternity. To his wife, Bloom, the toilinured trier in many trades, is just an aggravating person who potters around the house instead of getting a good job in a bank. When he got the sack from Joe Cuffe's he sent Marion to try to persuade Joe to reinstate him. The Utopian socialist friend of the human race, Bloom, is a foolish man who wastes his time with a lot of good-or-nothing companions instead of looking after his family. She knows Leopold must be wrong about Arthur Griffiths being a political genius because Griffiths' trousers are such a bad fit. Bloom the rationalist philosopher, doubter in the existence of God, is to her a misguided, crotchety oddity who obstinately refuses to see what is right under his nose. The prudent man, so careful of his deportment away from home, is known to Molly as an incurable sniffer after women who can't be trusted alone in the house with a servant under fifty. For all his modest airs he is a megalomaniac. If they asked him could he ride the favourite in the Grand National he would say yes. And he is a blunderer who continually puts her in awkward situations, as when he took her out for a row in rough weather or sympathised flirtatiously with a pert and disobliging sales lady. The only things she can find to say in his favour are that he is thoughtful for elderly ladies, polite to waiters, doesn't drink and knows a lot about people's insides. Her judgment of Poldy may be summed up as, "a poor thing but my own."

Some characters in fiction ask us to measure and weigh them with moral weights and measures. Marion defies us to do so. If she lived in our world we should criticise her morals, and good mothers would warn their sons to have nothing to do with her, but she is out of reach of our yardstick and scales. She dwells in a region where there are no incertitudes to torture the mind and no Agenbite of Inwit to lacerate the soul, where there are no regrets, no reproaches, no conscience and consequently no sin. Perhaps she is so superwomanly because a man created her out of feminine elements only. Nature is rarely so exclusive. Her thoughts jostle one another like the citizens of an egalitarian republic. From her bodily functions and those of her lovers her attention flits impartially to to-morrow's dinner or where does all the dust come from, from the misdeeds of the skivvy of a year ago to the monkeys on the rock of Gibraltar, the contents of her linen cupboard or the lives of seamen and engine-drivers. And she is preoccupied with what men want her to be as the angler is preoccupied with the question of bait for fish. There can be but few women in literature that do not look sickly in their virtues or vices alongside Molly Bloom. She has neither vice nor virtue. She is neither mysterious vamp nor sentimental angel. In Joyce's own words in a letter to me she is, "sane full amoral fertilisable untrustworthy engaging limited prudent indifferent Weib. 'Ich bin das Fleisch das stets bejaht!' "

CHAPTER XIII

When *Ulysses* was first published, what struck most people was its size and after that its obscenity. Quite well known words, much used in speech, were set down in print. Functions of the human body, not often alluded to in works of fiction, were mentioned by their familiar names. Unspoken and unacted thoughts, multitudes of which pass through the minds of all of us, were called forth from their hiding place behind the social mask and given a hearing or, as in the case of Bloom's hallucinations in Bella Cohen's brothel, were given an objective fulfilment. If there were any who believed that *Ulysses* might prove to be an erotic book—a kind of *Sweets of Sin* only bulkier—they must have been quickly undeceived when they breathed the first breath of its cool air. Those whom the common obscenities of life could not surprise or shock were held fascinated by the multitude of technical devices employed with so much skill and, so needful is a convenient label, set Joyce down as a master of technique pure and simple. Yet others, who felt that they were face to face with a view of the world both novel and personal, dug for the underlying philosophy of the book, its evaluation of the world in terms of human experience; and these were forced, if they pushed their search for philosophic content to extremes, as they sometimes did, to regard the characters in the book as abstractions. They valued the characters not for what they are but for what they mean, thus stultifying their view of Joyce's book by conceiving it as a complicated allegorical picture. My own view was and is that the characters are, in the first place, living, breathing human beings. The life of the book comes first and the philosophy afterwards. Obscenity is a question of manners and conventions for ever changing. Virtuosity, if it stood alone, would soon become demoded, and philosophy too, but living character stays through whatever material it is presented.

In particular *Ulysses* depends on the plasticity and life of Bloom. Is he a whole man seen wholly, as it was intended that he should be? To me he is a man, organic, complete, individual and limited by his individuality, a living person created in the scale and proportion of nature and society. All men must be the same or they would not be able to communicate with one another and they must all be different or they would have nothing to communicate. Bloom is the same as all men and therefore communicable, and he is different from them all and therefore memorable. As little as any of the great characters of fiction is he a human average. He is a Jew, but not any Jew, and he is a man but not everyman. Everyman would be everybody, and everybody is a monstrosity. Noman is nobody, and nobody is a wraith. If we interpret Bloom as a symbol we must first accept him as a man. Hamlet may be regarded as the sacrificed king-god or the latest incarnation of the mother complex, but he must first interest us as the tragic prince. And Bloom in this sense is to be looked on first as a Jew born in Dublin, married, father of a family, occupying a modest position in the commercial life of the city, a man of singular tastes and rare thoughts, and with a unique though not spectacular destiny—something that was always possible, was, but can never happen again. After that he may be Wandering Jew, Messiah, Antichrist, Science or anything else.

Other persons in the book appear occasionally to be more pregnantly characterised than Bloom. The Citizen, for example, the Nameless One, but that is because they are graphically, not three dimensionally conceived and presented. They are caught and transfixed in some vital gesture as the draughtsman catches and transfixes his subject. What is more vivid than a drawing by Daumier or Rowlandson? The violent gesture, the grimace, are foreign to the medium in which Bloom was conceived. We must go round him, see him in all lights and from all angles; never forget the other side of him; and always feel the plane that leads into depth. His personality must grow on us rather than strike us. That we see inside Bloom is inevitable, for a man is not only flesh and blood but a living soul, personality if you like, whose habitation is that solid body. If we could not see behind the outer husk of him he would be no more than a papier mâché figure such as we see in a carnival procession. As a creature of his environment he reflects constantly the light, shade and colour of that environment, place and time. That present essence which is Bloom and that social ambient in which he lives mingle in him together with the past out of which he came. The action of the day is never suspended to enable us to enter Bloom's thoughts. While the barque of his body is gliding through the limited spaces of Dublin his mind is roaming freely through its own larger world. Part of it sits watchfully at the helm of his body; another part of it looks idly at sea, sky and far horizons; yet another part of it dwells continually on home and wife; there is a listener ready for all divine messages and there is a tale-teller constantly repeating the story of the past. It may seem strange, but it is certainly true, that we can live sixteen years in intimate contact with people and know less about them than we know about Bloom in sixteen hours. If any ingenious writer liked to change the mode of narration adopted by Joyce in *Ulysses* and turn his book into a Bloom saga in many volumes with an eventual omnibus, the material for that exercise is to hand in the seven hundred and thirty-two pages enclosed in the well-known blue and white covers.

It might begin in Szombathely, Hungary, with Leopold's father, a man approaching middle age. Hungarian local colour, economic conditions, decision to emigrate. The long journey to London. Conditions of transport in Europe in the late fifties. He arrives in London at about the time of the second Derby-Disraeli administration. A short stay in London and then on to Dublin where he has heard that good business is to be done. Picture him, a dark haired, swarthy complexioned Jew, hanging on to the weather rail as the ship dips her nose into the sea, Howth Head visible on the weather bow. Compatriots, bearded and pious, welcome him on the firm soil of Ireland. Two events of the greatest importance happen in 1865: after a visit to the offices of the Society for Promoting Christianity among the Jews he is converted to the Christian faith and he marries Ellen Higgins. Leopold is born in 1866 and is baptised in the Protestant church of Saint Nicholas Without, Coombe. Leopold's infancy and early schooldays. He becomes aware that he is different from the other boys. He makes acquaintance with racial antagonism expressed in the horseplay, occasionally good-humoured but often not, of Gentile schoolboys. He asks his father what they mean when they sing, "I had a bit of pork" and other ditties for his benefit. Patiently he tries to understand what the "difference" is. Three Irish boys baptise Leopold under the parish pump in the village of Swords. What his parents said when he returned with his collar and coat drenched with pump water. His equanimity, coupled with a fine feat of micturation, wins for him a certain measure of prestige among his schoolfellows. In his way he is a courageous boy, never sullen or rancorous, and he does his best to enter into the games and pursuits of the other boys. There is that incident with the harriers. Considering his milieu he is precociously intellectual. In his fourteenth year he is a freethinker. He divulges his disbelief in the Protestant church to his friend, Percy Apjohn. Two years later Leopold expresses to Daniel Magrane and Francis Wade, to the consternation of both of them, his agreement with the theories of Charles Darwin, expounded in his works, *The Descent of Man* and *The Origin of Species*. His father needs his services in the business, and at the age of sixteen he starts travelling in cheap jewellery. The social question claims his attention. At first he is an enthusiastic supporter of the Radical politics of the eighteen eighties and a follower of Michael Davitt, Parnell, and Gladstone. Later his humanitarianism and passion for social justice take the form of a vague and quite personal Utopianism. His first erotic encounter with a woman was with Bridie Kelly, "on a drizzling night in Hatch Street, hard by the bonded stores there," but the heavy tread of the watch interrupts the proceedings. On the 27th of June, 1886, at the Queen's Hotel, Ennis, Bloom's father dies of aconite poisoning. The sad pilgrimage of Leopold to his father's funeral. He meets Marion at a social evening at Matt Dillon's home in Terenure. "Singing. *Waiting* she sang. I turned her music. . . . Why did she me? Fate." Their great day was one on Howth Head together among the ferns and rhododendrons. Marion says "Yes." Bloom is baptised into the Roman Catholic Church with a view to his matrimony in 1888. Millicent is born in June of the following year. Bloom works for Joe Cuffe, cattle salesman, for Thom, auctioneer, for Wisdom Hely. Some domestic trouble there must have been every time he came home with the news his job had come to an end. At intervals he peddled lottery tickets, at that time illegal (he escaped criminal proceedings at one time only through the intervention of a friend at court), or bought and sold cast off clothes. He visits Mrs. Dandrade at her hotel on business and is astonished at the *sans gêne* with which she displays her intimate underwear. He appreciates her black silk garments of all descriptions. Bob Cowley and Ben Dollard come rushing to the Blooms one evening for a dress suit for Ben Dollard, who is due to sing at a concert and has no wedding garment. In the Bloom collection of left off garments in their Holles Street house is only one dress suit that Big Ben can get on and that is miles too small. This skin tight dress suit is for years one of the standing jokes of the Bloom household. "Molly did laugh when he went out. Threw herself back across the bed, screaming, kicking. . . . Oh, the women in the front row." While they are staying at the City Arms Hotel, Bloom dances attendance on an elderly widow, Mrs. Riordan. She did not remember him in her will. ". . . that old faggot Mrs. Riordan that he thought he had a great leg of and she never left us a farthing all for masses for herself and her soul. . . ." Rudolph is born and dies at the age of eleven days. This was the beginning of an estrangement between Marion and Leopold. Bloom's rivals in Marion's affections. His friends and their fortunes. The second Boer War must have found Bloom a convinced anti-imperialist, a pro-Boer but not a rabid one, one rather who could see also the Uitlander's point of view. He was sorry to see his friend, Percy Apjohn, join the army and leave for South Africa, but it grieved him still more to hear that that brave and serious man had fallen in action on the Modder

River. Marion was never perturbed by Leopold's pre-marital flirtation with Josie Powell, and his post-marital interferences with the servant girls were annoying and destructive to domestic authority but not otherwise dangerous. Marion and Blazes Boylan, Milly Bloom and Alec Bannon, provide material for the continuation of the Bloom saga in the political and social atmosphere of early twentieth century Dublin. This is but an indication of the vast amount of material available for turning the breadth of the one-day treatment of Bloom's history into the depth of fifty years. The past of Bloom is summed up in *Ulysses* in the day on which we see him. It could as well be extended into the thirty-eight years of his life, but we should be none the wiser.

Bloom is a Jew but he is no stage Jew. The stage figures representing races and nationalities must be put away from the foreground of our minds before we can see the realities. Who has ever seen in real life the English John Bull or the blue-eyed Michel of Germany or the Cohens and the Kellys? These are just bundles of community mannerisms. Bloom is a product of many years of patient and independent observation and is one of the least stagey characters in fiction. The English imagination is still haunted by the tragically one-sided figure of Shylock, but Shylock was a product of the ghetto of the middle ages. Inasmuch as he is a Jew, Bloom is the product of three hundred years of social and political emancipation. Shylock was a member of an outcast community (he was probably less oppressed than the poor peasant of his day) and we see him fighting back with all the weapons his racial solidarity and personal rancour find available. The Jew of our day, in England at any rate, has nothing to fight as a Jew. He can be a cabinet minister, viceroy of India, editor of a newspaper, director of a banking house, art critic or any other person of authority, and nobody cares what or why or when he worships. It occurs to Bloom that he might have been a Protestant minister, Catholic priest or revivalist missionary. No such thought could have occurred to Shylock.

But for all his social and political freedom Bloom is something of an exile in Dublin. Why? He has no religion. He is perhaps the most non-religious character in fiction. Having left the old gods of his race he has been unable to accept those of the stranger, so that he lacks all the resorts of tribal fellowship and defence. That he has become a Christian only makes his Jewish isolation the more complete. Whether on account of his race or his personality, he is not fully accepted into the intimacy of any group. In general he is neither liked nor disliked. He is respected but not desired, accepted but held at arm's length. Nothing brings people nearer to one another than community in fearing, loving and hating, and Bloom has a scale of values different from that of his fellow Dubliners. He feels and thinks differently. Lenehan says of him that he is a bit of an artist, John Wyse Nolan acknowledges his generosity, finding that "there is much virtue in this Jew," and Davy Byrne and Nosey Flynn testify to his prudence and good will, but nobody comes quite near him. It is as if a transparent film cut him off from his surroundings. He can see and be seen, but he can never be touched, and that despite all the apparent amiabilities of intercourse. He sits together with three acquaintances in the funeral carriage, but the others thwart his funny stories and hear in shocked silence his common sense humane views on death. Stephen's irreligion would shock them less than Bloom's agnostic indifference. Joe Hynes forgets his forename, never knew it, perhaps, but he remembers those of all the other mourners. Nobody says, "Come along, Leopold," when they pay a visit to Parnell's grave, and when, an hour later, some gentlemen of the press make a move in the direction of Mooney's it occurs to none of them to say, "Come and have a drink, Leopold." In fact, nobody in Dublin, with the exception of his wife, uses his forename. Even his colleague, Joe Hynes, evidently a decent sort of chap (he did Bloom the honour of borrowing three shillings off him, and he stands him a cigar), agrees with the others in Barney Kiernan's in their condemnation of Bloom. "He's a bloody dark horse himself," says Joe. The drunken students in the maternity hospital listen to him with attention and some respect but rather as a curious outsider than as one of themselves. Only in one scene does he completely dominate the situation and that, curiously enough, is when he is on an errand of fatherly protection bent and is opposed by a masterful woman of his own race. It is as if he were a hundred years older than his fellow Dubliners. His prudence and secretiveness are to them a reproach. His simple inborn pessimism has a depressing effect on a generation eager in pursuit of tonics. Nobody wants to slap him on the back or take hold of his arm. He has another consistency of flesh and a different family odour. Even in his home he is an unknown man. He breakfasts alone and sleeps at the opposite end of the bed from Molly. Their daughter has begun to form an alliance with her mother against him. The Poldy of whom Marion thinks with pleasure is becoming a memory of her past but is not a present fact.

But one feels that the isolation in which Bloom lives is not an unhappy one. He wills it, much as he wills his domestic betrayal in that he makes no effort to prevent it. If he showed signs of self-pity we should the better understand it, but there is no self-pity in his mind, no rancour and no bitterness. There is no rage or jealousy in the schoolboyish confusion he experiences at the sight of his rival, Blazes Boylan. That affair occupies him, but not to the exclusion of the world that he sees and knows. In fact, we may say that envy, hatred, malice and uncharitableness are absent from the mind of Bloom as are rancour and self-pity. His sexual life seems to be less free from blemish. It is not that he admires the back view of the next door servant girl, or that he yields to the glamour of the expensively clad rich woman, or that his senses are stimulated by the sight of silk petticoats in a shop window, or even that he reacts in the most masculine way possible at the moment to the provocation of Gerty MacDowell. But we cannot forget that (in thought at least) he offers his wife to other males and writes obscene letters to highly placed Dublin dames, that in his imagination he becomes a flagellant, and that (perhaps in fact) he persuades girls to use foul words. Let us, however, be honest and admit that we do not think that entertaining a guilty thought is equivalent to performing a guilty action whatever the Scriptures may say to the contrary, and let us be on our guard against allowing our jealousy to throw a wrath-provoking picture of an insulted virgin on the screen of our imagination. Then we can set it down that to complete his humanity Mr. Bloom has something of a little devil about him somewhere.

As an all round man he couldn't very well be a man of one job only. How he lost his job at Hely's or at Thom's we do not know, but it was busybody interference in the affairs of a grazier that cost him his job at Joe Cuffe's. One rather dreads the day when he will feel impelled to show Myles Crawford and Councillor Nannetti how to run the *Freeman's*. He is already beginning to do so. Here again we feel that if he is not a great success at holding down jobs it is because he doesn't want to stay too long in one place. Unlike the average of his race he is not a good business man. The occupation that suits him best is that of commercial traveller. It allows him time and scope for his dilettantisms and dreams. We are told that he represents the scientific spirit and Stephen the artistic, yet of the two Bloom is, perhaps, more the dreamer. Which is as it should be, for the artist, being under the necessity of doing something, may not dream all the time, but the man of science may do so if he chooses. This is no truer to-day than it was in 1904 but is rather more evident, for our scientists become daily more poetic and our poets hourly more scientific. It is very worthy of being noted that astronomy is the science that most attracts Bloom; and that, I take it, is because its real vagueness and its air of precision provoke his imagination and because the vast times and spaces with which it deals flatter his pessimism by making him feel small. And in spite of his unperturbed, complacent air, is there a character in literature more pessimistic than Bloom? He seems to have an innate knowledge of the second law of thermodynamics. His universe is running down.

It seems to me self-evident that there is more merit in the goodness and humanity of the godless unbeliever than in the righteousness of the godfearing. The one is following his own good instincts and the other is obeying the crack of the whip or is hoping for an eternal reward. Belief in any case is a positive force. Take away from it one object and it will attach itself to another. Bloom's disbelief in the existence of God and individual immortality is no hindrance to his appearing the most reasonable and humane of all the Dubliners in *Ulysses*. And this is quite logical, because his power of belief is concentrated, without any theological distraction, on the existence of his own person and of the social world in which he lives. Marx says somewhere that "Christianity is the sublime thought of Judaism, and Judaism is the common application of Christianity." In the sense in which this is probably meant, Bloom, the Jewish Agnostic, is more Christian than his religious contemporaries. Not because of his many little acts of kindness (Martin Cunningham or Simon Dedalus would be quite capable of doing as much) but because he is incapable of hating or knowingly harming anybody.

Bloom's politics are as little spectacular as are his good deeds, and yet I fear that they are of the kind that in the days that are with us and near us lead to the dungeon and the firing squad. To the conservative they are revolutionary; to the revolutionary they are Menshevik, social reformist; to the ardent nationalist they are pacifist, defeatist; to the fascist they are anarchist. And, for all his prudence, there is in Bloom a strain of impulsive simplicity, as there certainly was in Ulysses, that would probably lead him to speak up just when he ought for his own good to lie low. He did it in Barney Kiernan's saloon and might do it again in still more dangerous circumstances. The Jesuit trained Stephen would be more politic. Where his silence and indifference seem suspicious to the suspicious he would know how to secure himself protection through others. Bloom differs from Marx and Disraeli (both, by the way, baptised Jews like himself) in that he has no knowledge of or belief in historical development like the one, or sense of popular government and popular pageantry like the other. The content of Bloom's Utopia is the content of all Utopias worth while—the general good and unity of the whole human race. The form of it is that of a middle class daydream—endowment at birth, three hundred pounds a year for all who work, improvement in the public services, complete freedom of expression under the shelter of constituted authority mildly and justly exercised, and peace, of course, perpetual and universal with disarmament and general good will. He has no system, no party, no press and no platform, in short, no means whatever for carrying his ideas into effect, for he is too fastidious in his choice of means, too prudent to entrust the realisation of them to armed force whether from above or below.

Nietzsche wrote a book in which he advocated the transvaluation of all values. That book left me with only the vaguest ideas as to what the new values might be or how they would look if they received a final shape in individual action and social organisation. What was to be our attitude towards our neighbours and ourselves? Being in the dark myself, I watched others who tried to put Nietzschean values into practice, and their actions resembled so much those of bright young people that it was only fair to conclude that they knew no more about it than I. There is no transvaluation of values in *Ulysses*, but there is in it a revaluation of some human values that, whether the reader agrees with it or not, has the merit of being as clear as a representation of life can make it.

The human body is neither neglected as being a low material affair nor is it glorified as if its health and shapeliness were the chief thing in life. In fact, it is as if the dangerous diarchy of body and mind were altogether denied. Liver, lungs, heart, blood, sex, the senses and their organs are shown to be as much of the mind as thought is of the body. Generally throughout the book, and particularly in the person of Leopold Bloom, the much despised "bourgeois" virtues of honesty, kindliness, prudent generosity and the rest are reaffirmed and even exalted, but other accepted values are by implication written down. There is no anti-religion (or anti- anything) in the book, yet the most irreligious man in it is also the best and most human. A marriage is shown with its own form of constancy in which sexual possessiveness plays but a small part. The eternal triangle in that ménage is given a new isosceles twist. It is true that Bloom and his rival, Blazes Boylan, are presented in different materials. Bloom is modelled in the round while Blazes Boylan is drawn in a manner that verges on caricature. Yet the outcome of Marion Bloom's marital infidelity is that the husband cocu takes on a passive, heroic aspect, the wife is represented as so much a creature of instinct and appetite that she stands well out of reach of all reproach, and her lover appears as a somewhat comic super in a play which is essentially hers. The acts of Marion and her lover are viewed as purely mechanical exercises and therefore as something fundamentally comic.

There is no more virtue in the womanhood of *Ulysses* than there is in the earth under our feet. The greatness of woman lies in her absolute necessity, in the impossibility of imagining the world without her. As Joyce represents her she is too vast for any pedestal to bear her weight. The only note of awed respect for woman that creeps into the boisterous discussion on sex in the maternity hospital is when her austere function as childbearer is considered, and it is Bloom who sounds that note. The worship of motherhood and mother love is definitely deflated, and in the words of Stephen and the acts of Bloom fatherhood is given a new significance. But Bloom is not of the breed of Père Goriot. We can be greatly touched by the woes of Père Goriot, and yet think that his love and sufferings are motherly, father though he be. It would not be unnatural for a widower to act the mother. As is usual with Joyce, the simplest incidents are used to convey the deepest things. There are no tears of recognition, no rescues from shark-infested seas. Bloom cannot even save Stephen from a punch on the jaw. All that he does is to hover round him for three or four hours, look after his money, bore him with banal advice, serve him with Epps' Cocoa, and invite him to stay the night on an improvised bed. When they take leave of each other we feel certain that they will never meet again. And yet in a measure that no spectacular action could have achieved, we are led from the things done, felt and said to the contemplation of a mystery. It is not what is done; it is the revelation of what lies behind. What is revealed is the element of fatherhood in all social devotion.

Bloom is almost as lonely in literature as he is in Dublin, but if there is a kinship it is not with the tragic and uncontained Bouvard et Pécuchet. He is distant from them by the whole space of his scepticism and pessimism. He is cocu, but neither imaginaire like the Moor of Venice, nor like the comic lunatic of the *Cocu Magnifique*. He has neither the authority and the passion of the one, nor the insane doubt of the other. Seeing that in the actions he performs and in the thoughts he thinks there is no malice, no envy, no revenge, no hatred, I place him, notwithstanding his prudence, his flirtations, frillies for Raoul and all the rest, in the company of the pure of heart, as near as a father and a husband and a lover may be to Uncle Toby.

CHAPTER XIV

"WORK IN PROGRESS"

I left Paris shortly after the publication of *Ulysses* and did not return again until some fragments of *Work in Progress*—possibly half a dozen—had been published. One appeared in *The Transatlantic Review*, another in *Le Navire d'Argent*, another in *The Criterion* and then began the serial publication in *Transition*. I read them all and had the advantage and limitation of reading them alone, Joyce being in Paris and I in London. Not that I was not helped by the informative articles that appeared from time to time in *Transition*.

> *Denn bei den alten lieben Toten*
> *Braucht man Erklaerung, will man Noten.*
> *Die Neuen glaubt man blank zu verstehen;*
> *Doch ohne Dolmetsch wird's auch nicht gehen.*

But however complex the material, whatever the philosophic basis, two elements leap to the eye of every reader: Dublin (together with its awkward but necessary attachment, Ireland) and Joyce himself. For Joyce, like a true exile, is fast moored to his native earth with the cable of his memory. He becomes the more at one with his city in that it lives in him not he in it. It is an experience universal and personal like a dream. No gossip column writer will ever be able to say of him that he is in the Tyrol or Timbuctoo looking for local colour for his next book, for whatever the colour and legend of London, Paris, Trieste, Zürich, Rome, they must be baptised in the Liffey and acclimatised in Dublin before they become available for his art. This localism is, perhaps, a bigger difficulty for the reader of *Work in Progress* or *Ulysses* than the universality of the theme or the density of the verbal substance. The reader has his own local patriotisms and he knows little, unless he is a Dubliner, of the intimate legend of the town of the Ford of Hurdles, so that his jealousies are apt to form a defensive alliance with his ignorance. We are all *Weltkinder* these days and rather fancy ourselves when we find we can worry out a pun or two in any European dialect we happen to know, and in philosophy we are all willing to be instructed, but when our local allegiances are challenged we are like Naaman the Syrian who sought God's saving grace in the mouth of his prophet but jibbed violently at washing in the prophet's mouldy little river. Something in us echoes his proud cry: "Are not Abana and Pharphar, rivers of Damascus, better than all the waters of Israel?" But we quickly accept the Liffey as she tripples and dances through the pages of Joyce's book. She runs downhill, anyway, just like our own Thames, Amazon or village brook. And Dublin, too, we accept, for we know that Joyce's city rises, like all cities and villages, at an angle of ninety degrees to the neighbouring flood, and is lit by the same sun, moon, gas and electricity. If we are sufficiently curious or studious we can quite easily know its history. The really great difficulty arises when we know all about Clontarf and Connolly. We are then brought up all standing against Wetherup and there the history book fails us. How are we to know what such and such a car driver thought about the Duke of Clarence's collars?

The great thing, however, is to plunge in boldly and read as does every successful reader of a foreign language, and never mind a foreign word or two, for the infinitely

greater part is English. And if it is English with a difference let us not forget that English is spoken every day with
many differences. Attic dwellers who (to the annoyance
of the people underneath, who object to that mumbling
noise going on after midnight) have cultivated the habit
of reading aloud, stand the best chance. Myself an old
mansardist, I had this advantage and further there came
to my mind a few words Joyce let fall in Zürich. It was
about some writer, I forget which, but one as renowned
for the depth of his thought as for the richness of his language:

"You find him difficult to understand because his
thought is deep and strange," said Joyce. "If there is any
difficulty in reading what I write it is because of the material I use. In my case the thought is always simple."

When I am asked (I have been asked), "Do you understand all this new book of Joyce's?" I reply promptly,
"No, I don't." But I have read what has appeared and
have experienced many things. Some things are clear to
me and others not. Most of us might say the same of
Goethe's *Faust* or Shakespeare's sonnets. And therefore I
write as one who has visited a foreign country not yet on
Baedeker's list—not as an authoritative guide but as a
traveller with sufficient sensibility, sufficient power of
observation to record an impression that may encourage
the adventurous to risk a more extended visit to the same
shores. Anyway, a work of art is given us not in the first
place to be understood but to be enjoyed, and *Work in
Progress* can be enjoyed by all who are equipped with
some patience, some sensibility. And does not all art demand of us these qualities, whatever its material? "Signatures of all things I am here to read," says Stephen Dedalus as he sets foot on Sandymount shore. Let us suppose
that he has read them and will make them intelligible to

us. We cannot expect that it shall be clearer than a nursery rhyme, more intelligible than a dream. We are warned of our difficulties at the outset:

"For that is what papyr is meed of, made of, hides and hints and misses in prints. Till we finally (though not yet endlike) meet with the acquaintance of Mister Typus, Mistress Tope and all the little typtopies. Fillstup. So you need hardly spell me how every word will be bound over to carry three score and ten toptypsical readings throughout the book of Doublends Jined till Daleth, who oped it closeth thereof the dor."

The signatures are the present evidence of past life. To Stephen on the seashore they were sand-imprisoned stout bottles, pieces of wreckage. But we carry around with us in the unvisited yet still populous recesses of our minds signatures of a past infinitely more remote. From the dawn of life to the moment in which we live all experience is written in the structure and function of our bodies—all is preserved in the depths of our memories. This is the unknown country into which we are led when we begin to read *Work in Progress*.

It is as if we were suddenly from normal daylight taken and plunged into a dark world, but there is light in the darkness when our eyes become accustomed to the scene. "It darkles, all this our funnominal world," but it is not dark. Shapes of trees appear before us, bushes, familiar grasses and thistles, the dark contours of a hill, the expanse of a plain, a shimmering river, a cloud on high. Lightning flashes and a rainbow shines and fades. There is a city of living people with houses and churches all standing, and a city of the dead with its barrows, howes and menhirs and the one seems to be as alive as the other. There are shadowy shapes of giants, angels on high and below, a house warmly lit, and children playing before it.

But we must be careful, for there is a suspicious resemblance. The angels we saw may be playing at children or the children we see may have been pretending to be angels. Stones and treestumps look uncouthly human. Colour there is as in Aladdin's cave. The things and beings illumine themselves from within. Big man father works and waits and busy mother keeps house, cooking and scouring. But nobody keeps one size or age for long. Character is the one thing constant about the beings here. We hear voices above, below and all round—voices of big people, of children at lessons and play, obstinate mumbling of old men, stony and wooden accents of wood and stone, loud voices disputing across the river, a trial with cross examination, special pleading and jury's verdict, confidential conversations, nursery rhymes, comic songs, airs from operas, strange animals—Roamaloose and Rehmoose—nightbirds, thunder at intervals, the splash of fish in the river.

There is no fixed horizon from which we can rightly determine the size of the place. We hear a shape against a background of dark which might be a black curtain or no space, and then we hear placenames and catch a glimpse of a waterlogged plain just where we least expected it, and we know that all space is there. A house looks small from without but inside there is no end to it. The time is the beginning of things, or now, or any time in between, or all at once. But no one knows the time of day. It may be "ten O'Connel" and then again "nobody appeared to have the same time of beard, some saying by their Oorlog it was Sygstryggs to nine, more holding with the Ryan wacht it was Dane to pfife." If we stay long enough in a darkened room we begin to see like cats and owls. Pieces of furniture arch their backs and threaten us, a coat on a chair regards us with grisly intentions till we recognise them for what they are.

The air is not a nipping and an eager air. It is heavy with sleep. "And low stole o'er the stillness the heartbeats of sleep." "What was thaas? Fog was whaas? Too mult sleepth. Let sleepth." The voices we hear are the unfleshly voices of ghosts. The giants that stalk abroad are the weightless phantoms of a dream. But what is happening? Something important is going on, but we must listen intently to the noiseless eloquence in "Dinmurk" to find out what it is. Everything is happening and all at the same time. There are racial wanderings, tribal wars, "oystrygods gaggin fishygods!" and there is a building and rebuilding of cities. The conflict of good and evil, begun when Michael hurled Lucifer out of heaven, is continued through the ages according to the fixed pattern of the original event, and the children re-enact it in their dreams of lessons and play.

"Even so in dreams, perhaps, under some secret conflict of the midnight sleeper, lighted up to the consciousness at the time, but darkened to the memory as soon as all is finished, each several child of our mysterious race completes for himself the aboriginal fall."—DE QUINCEY.

Thus, although the names of places are those of Dublin city and suburbs (a Dublin tram and 'bus guide will give a complete list) the legend is universal. The persons are few, yet in a sense they are all who have ever existed or could exist.

Two brothers in their cradles, at their play and lessons, earning their daily bread, making love, are all *die feindlichen Brüder* that have ever been. They are Michael and Lucifer, Cain and Abel, the Urizen and Luvah of Blake's mythology, Wellington and Napoleon, Jacob and Esau, Brutus and Cassius, and they might as well be Jack Mastereton and Jasper Constantinopolos of the serial story synopsis, or Tommy and Jackey Caffrey quarrelling about a ball on Sandymount shore, or the cop and gangster opposite numbers on the films.

In *Work in Progress* these fatal opposites are named Shem and Shaun. Shem is Shem the Penman. He is a poor "acheseyeld from Ailing" and he writes. Shaun is Shaun the Post. He wends his way to "Armorica" and makes tons of money. Rivals, they occupy opposite banks of mother river. As babies they sleep on opposite sides in their cots in the paternal house of big man Earwicker. As children they play opposite each other before the door of the house. They continue their antagonism as grown men and quite naturally Shaun, who comes in direct line of descent from a skygod, is well in with the celestial powers, while the heterodox Shem of opposite stemming just wriggles and twists and repents his way through the world as best he may. It is never quite clear how big they are.

We look at them in their cradle and they grow up to any age before our eyes. "They are to come of twinning age so soon as they may be born." But it all seems right when we remember that we are looking at being not doing, that all that is done is only that which is. Here is Shaun, at first in his cradle: "Our bright bull babe Frank Kevin is on heartsleeveside. Do not you waken him. He is happily to sleep with his lifted in blessing like the blissed angel he looks so like and his mou is semiope as though he were blowdelling on a bugigle. By gorgeous, that boy will blare some knight when he will take his dane's pledges and quit our ingletears to wend him to Armorica."

He is the "fine frank fairhaired fellow of the fairy-tales" and a great eater . . . "while his knives of hearts made havoc he had recruited his strength by meals of spadefuls of mounded food constituting his threepartite meals—*plus* a collation, his breakfast of first, a bless us O blood and thirsthy orange next the half of a pint of becon with newled googs, and a segment of riceplummy padding, met of sunder suigar and some cold forsaken steak from the batblack night o'erflown then came along merendally his dinner of a half a pound of round steak very rare, Blong's best from Portarlington's Butchery with a side of ricey-peasy and Corkshire alla mellonge and bacon with a pair of chops and thrown in from the silver grid by the pro-prietoress of the roastery who lives on the hill and gau-lusch gravy and pumpernickel to wolp up and a gorger's bulby onion. . . ." And this is only the half of his meal. But it is all consumed, "While the loaves are aflowering and the nachtingale jugs."

Shaun is very dressy and wears his food: ". . . a star-spangled zephyr with a decidedly surpliced crinklydoodle front with his motto for dear life embrothered over it in peas rice and yeggyolk, R. for royal. M for Mail, R.M.D. hard cash on the nail and the most successfully carried gigot turnups now you ever, breaking over the ankle and hugging the shoeheel. . . ." What wonder then that he eats his clothes? " 'You may, ought and welcome,' Shaun replied, taking at the same time as his hunger got the bit-ter of him a hearty bite out of the honeycomb of his Braham and Melosedible hat. . . ."

When people eat their clothes and wear their food it isn't surprising to see the food itself get up and take a hand in the game.

"Lady Jane Shortbred will walk in for supper with her marchpane switch on, her necklace of almonds and her peach Sundae dress with bracelets of honey and her cochineal hose with the caramel dancings, the briskly best from Bootiestown, and her suckingstaff of ivorymint. You mustn't miss it or you'll be sorry. Charmeuses chloes, glycering juwells, lydialight fans and puffumed cynarettes. And the Prince Lemonade has been graciously pleased. His six chocolate pages will run bugling before him and Cococream toddle after with his sticksword in a pink cushion."

It seems natural that a man of Shaun's appetite should be a great favourite with the girls and a great lad among the boys. He impresses the girls who gather round him by giving them neatly cut chops of good advice. . . . "Moral if you can't point a lily get to henna out of here. Put your swell foot foremost on foulhardy pneumonia shertwaists, irreconcilible with true fiminin risirvition and ribbons of lace limenicks disgrace. Sure what is it all only holes tied together, the merest and transparent washing-tones to make Languid Lola's lingery longer? Whalebones and busks may hurt you but never lay bare your breast secret to joy Jonas in the Dolphin's Barncar." But he is overbearingly orotund when as the Mookse he browbeats the Gripes and he is "sair sullemn and wise chairmanlooking" when, as the Ondt, he views the improvident antics of the Grace-hoper behind the wateringcan. He wanders through wide open spaces delivering his letters—it is a kind of Noman's land or Tom Tiddler's ground—and he sleeps there on beds of poppies, dreaming of the girl he left behind him. As a G.P.O. employee he is singularly lucky. I never had the opportunity of sleeping while I was on night duty at St. Martin's le Grand and Mount Pleasant. He is a go-getter, eloquent, musical, orthodox, combative—something of a pugilist or a weight lifter.

Shem is a contortionist as supple as resourceful as Shaun is forceful and muscular. Already in the cradle his pen-man's future is present. He lies on "codliverside" and "has been crying in his sleep" . . . "You will know him by

name in the capers but you cannot see whose heel he
sheepfolds in his wrought hand because I have not told it
to you. He will be quite within the pale when he vows
him so tosset to be of the sir Blake tribes bleak. Are you
not somewhat bulgar with your bowels? What ever do you
mean with bleak? With pale blake I write inkhorn." As
playboy Glugg he is "the bold bad black boy of the story-
books." As Jerry he sits with brother Kevin, and solves
with him a problem in Euclid physically, geographically
and historically. But there is a full length portrait of Shem
(*Transition* No. 7) done with tremendous vitality, and
through this we know him best. Out of the fast moving
stream of words, shapes and colours emerge that remind
us of Stephen Dedalus, but Shem's portrait is bound by
no naturalistic considerations of time or scale. It is a gi-
gantesque caricature, irresistibly comic. It begins with his
looks. "Shem's bodily getup, it seems, included an adze of
a skull, an eighth of a larkseye, the whoel of a nose, one
numb arm up a sleeve, fortytwo hairs off his uncrown,
eighteen to his mock lip, a trio of barbels from his mega-
geg chin, the wrong shoulder higher than the right, all
ears, an artificial tongue with a natural curl, not a foot to
stand on, a handfull of thumbs, a blind stomach, a deaf
heart, a loose liver, two fifths of two buttocks, one glad
stone avoirdupoider for him, a manroot of all evil, a
salmonkelt's thin skin, eelsblood in his cold toes a bladder
Tristended. . . ." And then he propounds a riddle to his
playmates: "When is a man not a man?" He alone knew
the solution: "When he's a sham." There follows in a
score of pages a record of the low shamness of Shem. His
taste in food is low, for he prefers tinned salmon and
tinned pineapple out of "Ananias' cans" to the real article,
and instead of drinking good, honest beer as a man should,
he "sobbed himself wheywhiningly sick on some sort of a

rhubarbaros maundarin yellagreen funkleblue windigut diodying applejack squeezed from sour grapefruice," and pretends when drunk that he could live forever on the smell of lemonpeel. When any wellwishers tried to persuade him to abandon his evil courses and pull himself together, "he would pull a vacant landlubber's face, root with earwaker's pensile in the outer of his lauscher and then, lisping, the prattlepate parnella, to kill time, and swatting his deadbest to think what under the canopies of God would any decent son of a shedog who had bin to an university think, begin to tell all the intelligentsia admitted to that conclamazzione . . . the whole lifelong story of his entirely low existence. . . ."

While all the world was busy killing or getting killed for the greatest of principles Shem "corked himself up tight in his inkbattle house, badly the worse for boosegas, there to stay for the life, where, as there was not a moment to be lost, after he had boxed around with his fortepiano till he was whole bach and blues, he collapsed carefully under a bedtick from Switzer's, his face enveloped into a dead warrior's telemac, with a whotwaterwottle at his feet to stoke his energy of waiting, moaning feebly that his pawdry's purgatory was more than a nigger bloke could bear, hemiparalysed by all the shemozzle (Daily Maily, fullup lace! Holy Maly, Mothelup joss!) his cheeks and trousers changing colour every time a gat croaked." Shem's dwelling is described and its interior decoration and furniture inventoried: "The house O'Shea or O'Shame, Quivapieno, known as the Haunted Inkbottle no number Brimstone Walk, Asia in Ireland, as it was infested with the raps, with his penname Shut sepia-scraped on the doorplate and a blind of black sailcloth over its wan phwinshogue, in which he groped through life at the expense of the taxpayers, dejected into day and night with jesuit bark and bitter bite by full and forty Queasianos, every day in everyone's way more exceeding in violent abuse of self and others, was the worst, it is hoped, even in our western playboyish world for pure mouse-farm filth. . . ."

Ink and paper being denied him by a conspiracy of publishers, he "made synthetic ink and sensitive paper for his own end out of his own wit's waste" and "wrote over every square inch of the only foolscap available, his own body . . . but with each word that would not pass away the squidself which he had squirtscreened from the crystalline world waned chagreengold and doriangrayer in its dudhud." In the end he is denounced by his other self and himself agrees that the denunciation is just. The gay, bright voice of Anna Livia, babbling the cheerful song she has always sung, comforts and revives him.

Sister Iseult is all the fascinating *ingénues* that ever lived from the girls that were met in the land of Nod to the latest platinum blonde out of Hollywood. She dreams of passionate meetings with the beloved in the park near the river and of wondrous wedding mornings: "It will all take bloss as oranged at St. Audiens rosan chocolate chapelry with my diamants blickfeast after at minne owned hos and Father blesius Mindelsinn will be beminding hand." When she talks it is as if we heard the voice of a more impulsive Gerty MacDowell through a thin partition. A visitor, tiptoeing into her bedroom and beholding her maidenhood asleep, divines her inmost dream: "Would one but to do apart a lilybit her virginelles and, so, to breath, so, therebetween, behold she had instant with her handmade as to graps the myth inmid the air. Mother of moth! I will to show herword in flesh. Approach not for ghost sake! It is dormition!" She is a cloud, lovely and changeable, born of mountain and river. She glows with colour, then darkens, wilts and melts into tears. "She is fading out like Journee's clothes so you can't see her now. Still we know how Day the Dyer works in dims and deeps and dusks and darks. And among the shades that Eve's now wearing she'll meet anew fiancy tryst and trow."

She is the true leapyear daughter of February filldyke. Born on the 29th, she is always a quarter of the age of her twenty-eight companions. But elderly though they are while she is still young the sister playmates flutter around her with rainbow colours. They are all gone on Shaun, but they are very rude to Shem.

The big grownup man, H. C. E. (Here Comes Everybody) is the most named person in the book. He is forefather Adam, "the cause of all our grievances, the whirl the flash and the trouble," bearing up as cheerfully as possible under the blessings of love and work. He is also Noah, builder of the ark what time "a main chanced to burst and misflooded his fortunes" and he is a Viking who conquered and stayed and built a city and bought and sold and prospered "outreachesly." Sometimes he is manmountain Mr. Whiteoath, but more humanly often he is lord of a city and landlord of an inn where he does "big grossman's bigness." Joyce's hero has many names. It would take some time to count them all. But what practice is more popular than the giving of nicknames? Every boy at school is given one or more. Odin had a name for every function. He was Farmod, Valfather, Ganglere, Bolverk and many besides according as he protected seamen, gathered the slain, wandered in search of wisdom or laboured in Suptung's fields. We called the spirit of evil Satan in the village Sunday school and in church they called him also Beelzebub and Lucifer. When on Sunday afternoons we looked at the pictures in *Pilgrim's Progress* we saw him as fierce javelin-throwing Apollyon, straddling across the path of Christian. For the purposes of village conversation he was the devil and old Nick, but when we played at the back of the house we co-opted him into the game as old Gooseberry.

But an offence has been committed against the park by-laws and H. C. E. is accused. What the offence was is not quite clear, but we gather that somebody has to be held "ultimendly respunchable for the hubbub caused in Edenborough." . . . That Viking, as might be expected, keeps a straight bat against his accusers (his stammer seems to be put on with a view to gaining time), only his defence is so complete that most mixed juries would convict on the spot. It is (a) a complete alibi—he wasn't there at the time; (b) in the alternative the day was hot, he couldn't help it, and the fault was a venial one; (c) if he committed the offence complained of, it was so long ago that it ought to be covered by the statute of limitations. He reinforces his defence with an eloquent description of all the services he has rendered as builder, defender and lawgiver of the city.

". . . I am bubub brought up under a camel act of dynasties long out of print, the first of Shitric Shilkanbeard but I am known throughout the world wherever my good Allenglisches Angleslachsen is spoken by Sall and Will from Augustanus to Ergastulus, as this is, protested by Saints and sinners eyeeye alike as a cleanliving man and, as a matter of fact by my halfwife, I think how our public at large appreciates it most highly from me that I am as cleanliving as could be and that my game was a fair average since I perpetually kept my ouija ouija wicket up." For lady listeners-in he broadcasts a special appeal to the heart: "Old Whitehowth is speaking again. Pity poor Whiteoath! Dear gone mummeries, goby. Tell the woyld I have lived true thousand hells. Pity please, lady, for poor O. W. in this profoundest snobbing I have caught. Nine dirty years mine age, hairs white mummery failing deaf as Adder. I askt you dear lady, to judge on my tree by our fruits."

He reminds the world that he made law and order, built schools and hospitals, and the land became thereupon fit for merchants to live in. . . . "Hattentats have mindered, thuggeries are rere as glovers meeting, lepars lack, iegnerants show beneath suspicion like the bitterharfs of esculapuloids. All is waldly bonums. Aeros, we luft to you! Firebugs, good blazes! Lubbers, keep your poudies drier! Seamen, we bless your ship and wives! Seven ills havd I habt; seaventy seavens are your prospect. The chort of Nicholas Within was my guide and I raised a dom on the bog of Michan. By fineounce I grew and by grossscruple I grew outreachesly. To Milud old money, to Madame fresh advances. Dutch florriners moved against us and I met them Bartholemew; milreys onfell and I arose Daniel in Leonden. Who can tell their tale whom I filled ad liptum on the plain of Soulsbury? The more secretly bui built, the more openly plastered. I have reared my hut in the night and at morn I was encompassed of mushroofs. I considered the lilies on the veldt and unto Balkis did I disclose mine glory. This mayde my taughters, and these man my son, from the villa of the ostmanorum to thostan's recte Thomars Sraid they are my villeins, with chartularies I have talledged them."

For his wife, Anna Livia, the big man built bridges, embankments and lighthouses, and decorated her banks with churches . . . "and did raft her Riverworthily and did leftlead her overland the pace whimpering by Kevin's port and Hurdlesford and Gardener's mall to Ringsend ferry and there on wavebrink by mace of masthigh, did I

uplift my magicianer's puntpole and I bade those polly-
fizzyboisterous seas to retire with hemselves from us . . .
and I hung up at Yule my pigmy suns helphelped of Kettil
Flashnose, for the supperhour of my frigid one, coulumba
mea, frimosa mia, through all Livania's volted ampire
from anods to cathods and from the topazolites of Mourne
by Arklow's sapphire seamanslure and Waterford's hook
and crook lights to the polders of Hy Kinsella . . . and
thirdly for ewigs I did reform and restore for my smuggy
piggiesknees her paddypalace on the crossknoll and added
thereunto a shallow laver to put out her hellfire and
posied windows for her oriel house and she sass her nach,
chillybombom and forty bonnets, upon the altarstane, may
all have mossyhonours!"

The final boast of Hump the Cheapener, Esq., brings
loud applause from all the nursing mothers and other
thirsty souls in the world who have found (who hasn't?)
that Guinness is good for them . . . "and I planted for
my own hot lass a vineyard and I fenced it about with
huge Chesterfield elms and Kentish hops against lickbud
month and gleanermonth: and (hush! hush!) I brewed for
my alpine plurabelle (speakeasy!) my brandold Dublin
lindub, the free, the froh, the frothy freshener, puss puss
pussyfoot, to split the spleen of her maw."

Anna Livia is his "alefru," the river of his valley, his
lifepartner, mother Eve. She brightens his life, as he light-
ens hers. She is a happygolucky elderly lady, forever
changing and always the same. Her life story is told from
start to finish by two washerwomen who, when their tale
is ended, turn into elm and stone on her banks. We always
know her by the gay canter of the words. "Linking one
and knocking the next, tapting a flank and tipting a jutty
and palling in and pietaring out and clyding by on her
eastway." Or, as remembered by one of her sons:

". . . with a beck, with a spring, all her rillringlets shaking, rocks drops in her tachie, tramtickets in her hair, all waived to a point and then all inuendation, little old-fashioned mummy, little wonderful mummy ducking under bridges, bellhopping the weirs, dodging by a bit of bog, rapidshooting round the bends, by Tallaght's green hills, and the pools of the phooka and a place they call it Blessington and slipping sly by Sallynoggin, as happy as the day is wet, babbling, bubbling, chattering to herself, deloothering the fields on their elbows leaning with the sloothering side of her, giddgaddy, grannyma, gossipaceus Anna Livia. . . ."

Like most of her sex she spends her youth in playing and flirting, and her riper years in childbearing and cleaning, fetching and carrying. She seems, however, to be not at all implicated in "this municipal sin business" which causes her lord so much anxiety.

Then we meet from time to time and always unexpectedly four old men who appear suddenly, seemingly from nowhere. But appear is not quite the word. We hear rather than see them. Their old voices boom out of the darkness like the voices we hear endlessly repeating the same things in our ear before we go to sleep. They bring back memories of the visiting uncles and grandfathers we heard at the time when we were sent early to bed, voices that droned us to sleep and waked us an hour later. These nightmarish old men are accompanied always by an aged donkey. They are the Big Four with the Big Noise. Their function seems to be to keep tradition, search for precedent, to cross-examine, hold inquests and to censor. Whoever they are—four provinces of Ireland, the four evangelists, the fourbottle men, the four winds, the four seasons, analists, institutions—they are not what would be generally called nice old men. Their talk is principally of drink, "Pass the push for Craw's sake," or of "the good old days not worth remembering." And they are a lecherous lot in a senile way. Bedridden and "dolled up in their blankets" they hold the nurse's hand and count up the mother of pearl buttons on her glove. Feeling impelled always to imagine a shape at the back of a voice I lent these somewhat terrifying beings what I thought were appropriate bodies but I found that I had first borrowed the forms from William Blake. They forced me to conjure up a vision of human forms similar to those of the inhumanly ancient men in Blake's drawings. But with this difference. Blake's old men are majestic and venerable beings whereas the four old men in Joyce's book, whether they sit on their hams under their "sycomores," playing on banjos, or grope their way through skyey fields in search of the sleeping Shaun, are always greedy, censorious and malicious.

Another group personality is the twelve whose presence is always announced by long words ending in 'ation: "There was a koros of drouthdropping surfacemen, boomslanging and plugchewing, fruiteyeing and flowerfeeding, in contemplation of the fluctuation and the undification of her filimentation. . . ." Again they are a jury empanelled, evidently in the difficult case of Rex V. Earwicker . . . "whereas by reverendum they found him guilty of their and those imputations of fornicopulation with two of his albowcrural correlations . . . summing him up to be done, be what will of excess his exaltation, still we think with Sully there can be no right extinuation for contravention of common and statute legislation, for which the fit remedy resides for Mr. Sully in corporal amputation so three months for Gubbs Jeroboam, the frothwhiskered pest of the park. . . ." They are also "a band of twelve mercenaries, the Sullivani," and later or earlier, as the case may be, they are "a bundle of a dozen representative locomotive civics inn quest of outings," all sitting snug with their conversations in the big man's inn, just to show there is no ill feeling. They seem to be intelligent and rightminded citizens and in spite of their oath as jurymen not at all censorious.

As an offset to these honest citizens are two (or is it three?) soldiers who happened to be there or thereabouts when the breach of the park regulations took place. They hail from within sound of Bow Bells, and this is their hazy account of the matter: "Hiss! Which we had only our hazelight to see with in our point of view me and my auxy, Jimmy d'Arcy, hadn't we, Jimmy—who to be seen with? Kiss! No kidding which he stood us first a couple of Mountjoys and nutty woodbines with his cadbully's choculars in the snug at the Cambridge arms of Teddy Ales while we was laying was he stepmarm or a wouldower, which he said a taking off his Whitby hat and wishing his long life's strength to our allhallowed king. . . . Touching our Phœnix Rangers' nuisance, the daintylines, and those pest of parkies, twitch, thistle and charlock, were they for giving up their fogging trespasses by order which we foregathered he must be raw in cane sugar, the party, no, Jimmy MacCawthelock? Who trespass against me? Briss! That's him wiv his wig on, achewing of his maple gum, that's our grainpopaw Mister Beardall, an accompliced burgomaster, which he told us privates out of his own scented mouf he used to was afore this wineact come, what say, our Jimmy the chapelgoer?—Who fears all masters! Hi, Jocko Nowlong, my own sweet boosy love, which he puts his feeler to me behind the beggars bush does Freda, don't you be an emugee. We must spy a half a hind on honeysuckler now his old face's hardalone wiv his defences down during his wappin stillstand, says my Fred,

and Jamessime here which, pip it, she simply must, she
says, she'll do a retroussy from her point of view (Way you
fly! like a frush!) to keep her flouncies off the grass while
paying the wetmenots a music-hall visit and pair her
fiefighs fore him after his corkiness, lay up two bottles of
joy with a shandy had by Fred and a *fino oloroso* which
he was warming to, my right, Jimmy, my old brown
freer?" These privates are the only direct witnesses against
H. C. E. but their testimony is of no value because, (*a*)
they couldn't see properly, partly on account of the bushes
and partly on account of the "hazelight"; (*b*) they have
been drinking heavily; (*c*) they are friends of the accused
who, in his privileged position as burgomaster and landlord of a pub, has been standing them drinks and smokes.
To put it bluntly, they have been got at by H. C. E. However, the thing got round, for one of these privates, or
some similar person, blabbed the whole story "alcoher-
ently" while talking in his drunken sleep in a dosshouse,
and it came to the ears of Hosty, a down and out poet who
was prowling dejectedly around, "devising ways and manners of means, of somehow or other getting a hold of some
chap's parabellum in the hope of taking a tuppence
sociable and lighting upon a dive somewhere off the
Dullkey and Bleakrooky tramaline where he could go and
blow the sibicidal napper off himself in peace and qui-
etude." And Hosty worked the material up into a ballad.

Completing the household of Earwicker are his aboriginal man-of-all-work and maid-of-all-work, Joe and Dinah or
Knut and Kate or whatever they may be called. Not in the
city, but not far from its walls, strange shapes of wood and
stone arise to tell us the story of the place. Such are Mutt
and Jute who "swop hats and excheck a few strong verbs
weak oach eather yapyazzard abast the blooty creeks" in
the manner of slapstick musichall comedians until they

fade into the landscape at the coming of "the giant
Forficules with Amni the fay." Of the same family are the
two garrulous washerwomen who gossip the tale of Anna
Livia from the unknown nook where she was born to the
city she drudges for, and thence to the sea into which she
flows. Night falls and the two gossips are rooted in the
earth as elm and stone again.

Rathfarnham, Finglas, Howth Head and Lucan: the
stage is small, yet big enough. Roman history can be
enacted in the courtyard of an inn. As will be seen from
its frequent mention, Chapelizod, a little village just outside Dublin, is the centre of the action. This is the microcosm in which the macrocosm of Joyce's universe finds a
shape and a home. Phœnix Park lies behind it, the Liffey
runs through it, the villages of Lucan, Fox and Geese,
Island Bridge are its near neighbours. It is a small place.
If a motor-coach full of tourists drove through it the man
with the megaphone would just have time to turn and tell
the people that Alfred Harmsworth was born there, and
the village would be left behind. Its name proclaims its
association with the legend of Yseult. Sheridan Lefanu has
celebrated Chapelizod in his delightful novel, *The House
by the Churchyard*. Of its "stalworth elm" he writes:
"Thou hast a story to tell, thou slighted and solitary sage,
if only the winds would steal it musically forth." In *Work
in Progress* it tells the story of the river. And of the Liffey
the romantic Devereaux says to his beloved: "Look at the
river—is not it feminine? It's sad and it's merry, musical,
sparkling and oh, so deep! Always changing, yet still the
same. 'Twill show you the trees, or the clouds, or yourself,
or the stars."

Anna Livia there is truly "but a judy quean not up to
your elb." It should be possible for an Olympic pole-
jumper, with the permission of Mr. Platts, the manager of

the distillery, to take off from the distillery grounds on the north side, overleap the Liffey and land on the south bank, dryfoot, in Mr. Malone's garden. So much for width, but as for length a Dublin friend assures me that a good walker could start from Grattan Bridge early morning, walk across the chord of her arc to her source and return to his starting place on the same day. An atmosphere, sweet and glad, hangs over the river at Chapelizod. In slow mood or swift there is nothing terrible in her as sometimes there is in her fiercer sisters. Salmon of the family of Tuan MacCairll or Fionn MacCumhal or fin made cool still jump and splash in her waters, and the human children of Tuan or Fionn or fin live on her banks.

All Joyce's elemental shapes are there. I painted a picture on the south side of the river, east of the bridge and in front of a row of cottages—Coppinger's, perhaps. Shem and Shaun and a murmuration of Maggies gathered round me to criticise and admire. Soon on some question of precedence I heard a dispute. Shaun advised brother Shem, in the language of the films, to "scran" and "beat it," and Shem was banished accordingly. The Maggies I knew "war loving, they love laughing," yet when I heard Doreen laughing more than the others I wanted to know what she was laughing at. She wouldn't tell me so I asked Violet, who, after much persuasion, said in a rich Dublin brogue, "It's because you talk so funny." When it began to "darkle" I adjourned to the Mullingar Inn. Sawdust was strewn in "expectoration" and a quorum of "representative civics" already assembled to "drain the mead for misery to incur intoxication." The subject of their "conflingent controversies of differentiation" was the Irish Grand National. Mr. Keenan, blond, burly, affable, authoritative and bright-eyed, entertained us in his customhouse. He was called away, and in his absence an amiable lady served us with pints. I met no four old men, cantankerous and censorious, but then one always has the feeling that they come in at times from more distant parts. And I did not gain an insight into this "sin business" as I was not able to go into the park in the hazelight. But here, in the space of a few hours, and in their own locality, I made acquaintance with many of the elements of *Work in Progress*—river, hill, forest, human habitations, laughing girls, brothers in conflict, citizens in council, a woman serving and a big man presiding.

The whole story is conveyed in echoes of nursery rhymes, play rhymes, popular songs, catchwords, sentimental ballads and operatic airs, all mixed through near relationship with religion and history. And then there are school lessons, endlessly repeated, like games, by generation after generation of children. The Norseman's original chaos, Ginungagap, and his last day, Ragnarok, occur in all variations, and his gods, Odin, Thor and Loki, fraternise easily with their Christian colleagues. They have forgotten their old feuds and have become good mixers. Songs and nursery rhymes have become religious invocations, and the gods have become housemall and enter easily the habitations of man.

It is characteristic of Joyce that he uses for his purpose all handy devices and limits his choice of means with no doctrine. In modifying the shapes and sounds of his words he has but followed popular usage. It is not a new practice sacred to a clique and there is nothing particularly highbrow in it. The pun is as popular now as it was in Elizabethan days. Joyce uses it and all its tribe of double meanings—rhyming slang, malapropisms, spoonerisms, backslang—just as it suits him, and to all this inherited machinery of wit and expression he adds devices of his own. When the Cockney is surprised and incredulous and says, "Would you Adam and Eve it?" he slyly spreads his unbelief so as to cast a shadow of doubt on the story of creation in the first book of Genesis. "Andthisandthis" is good rhyming slang in the mouth of a drunk for antithesis. "This ourth of years"—"The residence of our lives," spoonerism, malapropism. The puns run sentence wide and are amazing in their point and ingenuity. "With harm and aches till Father alters." "The hornmade ivory dreams you reved of the flushpots of Euston and the hanging garments of Marylebone." Runaway Shem is a "fuyerescaper." Housefather calls "enthreateningly." One of the most effective of Joyce's inventions consists in exaggerating the essential expression of a word and so stressing its descriptive gesture. He does it in *Ulysses* with "love-lorn longlost lugubru Booloohoom." On the same principle thunder-fearing children in *Work in Progress* say their prayers to the "Loud," making themselves pitifully small before him with a series of long ees. "Oh Loud hear the wee beseech of thees of each of these thy unlitten ones!" Then there is the magnifying of some natural phenomenon through an alteration, however slight, of the fixed forms of the words, to give a magical sense of dream time. "Countlessness of livestories have netherfallen by this plage, flick as flowflakes, litters from aloft, like a waast wizzard all of whirlworlds." And we are always to remember that this is the speech of beings who are of our world but not in it. To this add numberless inventions where the word is a picture of the thing—the "sputing and tussing" of sick and sorry Shem, the "smuttering of apes," the "frantling of peacocks," etc. But this is no more than a continuation of the work of the builders of our speech.

There has always been a language of expression and a language of communication—one for building Bush

House and the other for building that Tower of Babel which is poetry—so that the question, often asked, "Why doesn't Joyce use the words we know, and put them in a familiar order?" is superfluous, or can be answered by asking another. Could any paraphrase of a Shakespeare sonnet convey its beauty, and if it failed to convey the beauty would the meaning be there? Let the doubter try:

> *The mortal moon hath her eclipse endured,*
> *And the sad augurs mock their own presage;*
> *Incertainties now crown themselves assured,*
> *And peace proclaims olives of endless age.*

The wonderful night piece at the end of *Anna Livia Plurabelle* is already familiar, but let the reader, sensitive to the magic of the following passages, ask himself if that magic would not disappear if the material that conveys it were altered in any way.

"Yet he made leave to many a door beside of Finglas wold for so witness his chambered cairns silent that are at browse up hill and down coombe and on eolithostroton, at Howth or at Coolock or even at Enniskerry. Olivers lambs we do call them and they shall be gathered unto him, their herd and paladin, in that day when he skall wake from earthsleep in his valle of briers and o'er dun and dale the Wulverulverlord (protect us!) his mighty horn skall roll, orland, roll."

"Liverpoor? Sot a bit of it! His braynes coolt parritch, his pelt nassy, his heart's adrone, his bluidstreams acrawl, his puff but a piff, his extremities extremely so. Humph is in his doge. Words weigh no more to him than raindrips to Rethfernhim. Which we all like. Rain. When we sleep. Drops. But wait until our sleeping. Drain. Sdops."

Or: ". . . Nought stirs in spinney. The swayful pathways of the dragonfly spider stay still in reedery. Quiet takes back her folded fields. In deerhaven, imbraced, alleged, injointed and unlatched, the birds, tommelise too, quail silent. Was avond ere awhile. Now conticinium. The time of lying together will come and the wildering of the nicht till cockeedoodle aubens Aurore. No chare of beagles, frantling of peacocks, no muzzing of the camel, smuttering of apes. Lights, pageboy, lights! When otter leaps in outer parts then Yul remember Mei. Her hung maidmohns are bluming, look, to greet those loes on coast of amethyst; arcglow's seafire siemens lure and warnerforth's hooker-crookers."

There are stranger things in *Work in Progress* than the words out of which it is made. That which continually astonishes me is its constant and even gaiety. "Loud, heap miseries upon us yet entwine our arts with laughters low!" might be the prayer of the writer as well as that of the children sheltering under the big man's roof. All the characters in the book seem to have read, marked, learned and inwardly digested universal history; that is to say, read it at a glance, marked it with their thumbmarks, learned it from back to front and digested it while sleeping. When they have it properly in their bloomstream they play it. They re-enact it "every evening at lighting up o'clock sharp in Feenichts Playhouse." Most of us, when we look back at history, see either a brave pageant or a tragic and painful spectacle, full of cruelty, treachery and stupidity, justifiable because it was inevitable, tolerable because we believe it is leading somewhere, and excusable because something in us tells us we are responsible for it all and that in any case we can do no better ourselves. Stephen Dedalus thought history a nightmare: here it is a dream—at once an essence of and a commentary on life. It is a deathdream or dreamdeath where the shades of all the makers of Ireland walk as in some more familiar

Elysian fields. Whether it is "ten O'Connel" or "Sygs-tryggs to nine" is of no consequence where no time is. But if this is history, where are the tears? These phantoms seem to have the innocence of the unborn and the wisdom of the dead. They play eternally as Odin's chosen warriors played in Valhalla, slaying one another where no death was and reassembling themselves sociably around the festive board to eat the imperishable flesh of the sodden sow and drink immortal mead. These are night thoughts but there is neither gloom nor fear nor anguish in them. They fly the lighter for being tethered to no deathdreading avoirdupois.

Chuff "wrestles with the bold bad black boy Glug geminally about caps or something until they adumbrace a pattern of somebody else or other." They just go indoors after that to be washed and scrubbed by mother. Bad boy Shem, on his beamends with the bellyache, wonders what his muffinstuffinaches are all about and concludes that it is: "Breath and bother and whatarcurss. Then breath more bother and more whatarcurss. Then no breath no bother but worrworums." The rivalry of these boys (there is no doubt in this world and therefore no jealousy) supplies all the conflict there is; but the brothers are as necessary to each other as points of the compass or complementary colours. If there were no Lucifer, Michael's occupation would be gone, and without the assistance of Michael from behind Lucifer would never reign with trident and flames over his own proper kingdom. Anna Livia, singing and dancing, is always as happy as the day is long and H. C. E. gets on with his civic and family affairs not unduly perturbed by this "sin business." Whether she is preparing for her wedding "blickfeast" or sitting "glooming so gleaming in the gloaming," Iseult enjoys her moods of all maids. The four senators, the twelve civics, the servants and soldiers, the sticks and stones, all glitter with their own peculiar serious humour. The play in the Feenichts Playhouse is presented "with battle pictures and the Pageant of History worked up by Messrs. Thud and Blunder. Promptings by Elanio Vitale. Longshots, upcloses, outblacks and stagetolets by Hexenschuss, Coachmaher, Incubone and Rocknarrag." How mysteriously friendly these otherwise dreadful agencies become when their names are adapted for the purpose of this scene!

They are mistaken who imagine that there is a gap in the production of Joyce at any point. His work is all of a piece. The form changes but the substance remains the same—the fixed vision of the world as a whole, the hard, cool logic, the humour, boisterous or impish, the personal experiences, become for him symbolic, the preoccupation with the mystery of the word. From Stephen reflecting on the football field at Clongowes that a belt was a belt, "And a belt was also to give a fellow a belt," hearing water and things speak for themselves, and on Sandymount shore translating their noises and material into human speech, to the verbal mysteries and innovations of *Work in Progress* is but a step and a step and then a step. Joyce saw life in *Ulysses* much as an atomic chemist sees the world, as a thing of myriad forms but few elements, and the same holds good of *Work in Progress*. In the latter work, however, the view is coloured with a spirit of happy reconciliation. The exile is still there but the pathos of banishment is absent. And Bloom's pessimism (he turns from his own brief life to the aged and still young stars) gives place to the genial assurance of the active and beneficent Phœnician-Scandinavian cityfounder, H. C. E., who is awed neither by the apathy nor by the long life of the stars. He is as old and as young as they. The sullen conflict of Stephen with his contemporaries is reconciled in the unity of the twin brothers Shem and Shaun.

The landscape plays a part in *Work in Progress* it never played in *Ulysses,* and that not as a passive space but as an active force. Dublin was made by the might of mountain and the quickness of water, and the genii who created the city haunt the neighbourhood. Stephen says of the barbarian ancestors, "Their blood is in me, their lusts my waves." But he abhors history as a nightmare. It would drain the blood of the living for a useless sacrifice to the dead. Yet when he descends into it in the night he finds it is peopled with friendly shades. Strangely enough they are all parts of himself.

I never heard Joyce pretend to be a Blake adept, but I knew that he was familiar with the interpretations of Blakean mysteries of Yeats and his circle. In his later years in Dublin Joyce lived in that philosophy which maintains that on the borders of our individual memory lies the memory of our race, that outside the frontiers of the individual mind lies the universal mind, and that with the "open Sesame" of symbols (words or things) the individual mind may be made a partaker of that vaster racial experience. It is an interesting fact that of the two lectures delivered by Joyce in the *Universita del Popolo* in Trieste one was on Blake and the other on Defoe. But if Joyce at one time steeped himself in Blake he never accepted the Blakean or any other ready-made symbols. In *Work in Progress* he creates his own, and these are intentionally trivial in the original, literal sense of the word. We are led by three ways to a place where the ways of departure are also three. There are, however, similarities, striking enough, between the Londoner and the Dubliner. Each aims at summing up the elements of human experience, at presenting a picture of the world as complete, having in view its changes of time and substance—the evolution of things. To this end they both work with words as symbols, and create a mythology to represent the elemental shapes and forces of the universe. Each has a native town with its surroundings which supplies a mystical place wherein the universal legend may be enacted. In the case of Blake that place is London; in that of Joyce, Dublin.

Both Blake and Joyce have a passion for locality, but Joyce has with that passion a painter's love of the natural scene in colour, tone, space, whereas Blake is graphically abstract and delimiting. The grace, the glitter, the elegance of the Liffey landscape shine out in *Work in Progress,* but no line in *Jerusalem* creates for us a vision of London's mighty tidal drudge. They seem nearest to each other in their love of place names. The names Lambeth, "Isle of Leutha's Dogs," Muswell Hill, "mournful, ever-weeping Paddington," as distinct from the places they designate, meant to Blake what Howth Chapelizod and Lucan mean to Joyce, but we do get a vision of the actual pleasant places when we read Joyce, and of the people who inhabit them, whereas the place names in Blake are abstractions only. The place names in *Jerusalem* are like the names of the stations on the old London Underground. They appear, written in big letters, through a cloud of sulphurous steam, and to the accompaniment of clanging metal. Joyce does not help out his place names with names invented for their suggestiveness in sound. There is in *Work in Progress* no Entuthon Benython, no Golgonooza, no Udan Adan. As far as he goes is to deform, according to what he desires to express, the names of existing places. Lucalizod, for example, Lucan and Chapelizod fused together, may be regarded as the world, for the world, in principle, is no more than two or more villages united.

Blake tells us of the forces that made the world. They

are creative elements for ever forging and building, groaning and howling. Whatever they are, they are not human. His material is a loud, monotonous recitative. A whole population of elemental beings appears in *Vala* or *Jerusalem,* but they all talk with the same voice. Joyce deals with elemental shapes rather than elemental forces. Things are. They are not in a state of clamorous and painful becoming. And Joyce's material has all the grace of an opera with its balance of orchestra, aria and recitative, different male and female voices and chorus. The girls in *Work in Progress* talk with the voices and accent of girls, the boys with boys' voices, and when the men talk they talk like men, young, middle-aged or old; and the observant soldiers discuss the Big Man's frailties and hospitalities as good soldiers should.

Blake invents a whole mythology with which to explain his world. Joyce shows the world (he does not explain it) in the world's own terms, its own living shapes. He takes history as present. It is now, in front of us. That which lay *nacheinander* in time he translates, in the manner of a weaver of tapestries, into the *nebeneinander* before our eyes. Whatever Blake's ancestry, he was born a Londoner, and he has all the fury of conviction of a religious revivalist. He wants his readers to do something, to believe something, to worship something. Joyce but asks us to contemplate something. His is not a revelation, a religion, a doctrine, but a picture. It is a picture of the elemental shapes of man's mind as they appear to him after prolonged contemplation of mankind in its minute particulars. The multitudes of natural shapes resolve themselves into a few elemental shapes, and for him history repeats itself to infinity. And he has made his picture with material regarded as trivial just as he made *Ulysses,* the epic of the body, out of material regarded as unworthy or, sometimes, ignoble. But as the history of our planet is written in the pebble we kick in walking, so may the history of our race lie, living but not manifest, in common words and habitual gestures. They are the body to the outline of history. It has, from time to time, seemed strange to me that a generation that has fully accepted Blake (finding him therefore, presumably, comprehensible) should quarrel with Joyce on the score of incomprehensibility.

FURTHER RECOLLECTIONS
OF JAMES JOYCE

Joyce was born on February 2, Candlemas, of the year 1882, and I on March 1, St. David's Day of the same year, so that he was my senior by twenty-six days. My book, *James Joyce and the Making of Ulysses,* appeared in 1934 when Joyce was still with us and, as some may remember, that book contained, among other matters, some personal recollections of the author of *Ulysses* designed to give the reader an idea of the man as well as of his work. Here I set forth a few more such recollections with the same end in view. They follow no plan, unless there is a concealed plan in the seemingly haphazard operations of memory. Should any of them appear trivial I entrench myself in advance behind Joyce's own doctrine, which was that a place where three or four roads meet is a good place to look and listen for talk and happenings that signify much.

As I knew him Joyce liked to talk about his work when he could find an understanding listener, and particularly he liked to talk about that upon which he was actively engaged, and I surmise that this talk served a dual purpose. It kept his mind fixed upon the matter in hand, and it provoked responsive comment which might, and often did, prove useful to him.

Understandably the talk in Zürich turned generally on *Ulysses,* and I can remember few references in that period to his play, *Exiles.* But later in Paris, in the autumn of 1933, he referred to *Exiles* in connection with my book on *Ulysses.* The reference is important because of the light it throws on the Joycean conception of sexual love (at any rate on the male side) as an irreconcilable conflict between a passion for absolute possession and a categorical imperative of absolute freedom. It occurred during a short stay I made in Paris on my way to Switzerland. I had sent the proofs of my book on in advance, and Joyce and Stuart Gilbert had begun to read them. For my short stay I was the guest of the Joyces.

There is a passage in my book in which I try to explain the motives for Bloom's conduct as, seemingly, a *mari complaisant.* Readers of *Ulysses* all remember that in the Sirens episode Bloom watches Blazes

Boylan's exit from the Ormond Hotel, well knowing that the organizer of Molly Bloom's concert tour is bound for 7 Eccles Street, and that in all probability an act of adultery will there take place. What was to be explained was Bloom's inactivity when, seeing that the drift of events is toward his wife's infidelity and his own cuckoldry, he makes no effort to stem the drift. Rather he contemplates in advance the *fait accompli* with a sort of cool, detached fatalism.

Joyce said: "You see an undercurrent of homosexuality in Bloom as well as his loneliness as a Jew who finds no warmth of fellowship among either Jews or Gentiles, and no doubt you are right. But there is another aspect of the matter you seem to have missed."

"And that is?"

"Have you ever read or seen *Le Cocu Magnifique?*"

I told him I hadn't and waited for the sequel.

"You ought to read it," he said. "Do you remember I wrote to you soon after I came to Paris that *Exiles* was to be put on by Lugné Poe, and that in the end nothing came of it? You do? Well, it was *Le Cocu Magnifique* that took the wind out of the sails of *Exiles*. The jealousy motive is the same in kind in both cases. The only difference is that in my play the people act with a certain reserve, whereas in *Le Cocu* the hero, to mention only one, acts like a madman. Make all the necessary allowances, and you'll see that Bloom is of the same family."

It was not difficult to see the family likeness in Leopold Bloom and Richard Rowan as soon as it was pointed out. In due course a copy of *Le Cocu Magnifique* was forwarded to me in Switzerland, and sure enough there was the same theme—only heavily scored for the brass. Richard and Leopold provoke and let happen, whereas the magnificent cuckold stands by with his shotgun and his *"Malheur à celui que ne vient pas."* Unfortunately it was then too late for me to make the desirable addition to my own text.

Apropos the said galley proofs: as they were read aloud by Gilbert or myself they were placed one after the other on Joyce's knees, from which insecure position they slithered, as is their way, a few at a time on to the floor. As soon as Joyce stooped to pick up the fallen ones others slipped off to take their place. Joyce's comment was: "Galley proofs remind me of the persons of the Trinity. Get firm hold of one of them and you lose grip on the others."

This theological image occurs again in a letter to me dictated to his daughter Lucia and sent to me shortly after I left Paris for Switzerland. Joyce was very interested in my working something about the *"altkatholische Kirche"* into my record of life in Zürich. He felt that a picture of that noble city would be incomplete without such a reference. The relevant part of the letter reads: "The 'old Catholic' Augustiner Kirche is a good example of a Mookse gone Gripes. It separated from Rome in '71 when the infallibility of the Pope was proclaimed a dogma, but they have since gone more apart. They have abolished auricular confession; they have the Eucharist under two species, but the faithful receive the cup only at Whitsun. I see no prayers to the BVM or the saints in their prayerbook and no images of these or her round the church. But most important of all, they have abolished the *filioque* clause in the creed concerning which there has been a schism between the East and the West for over a thousand years, Rome saying that the Holy Ghost proceeded from the Father and the Son, Greece and the East Orthodox churches that the procession is from the Father alone, *ex patre* without *filioque*. Of course the dogmas subsequently proclaimed by Rome after the split are not recognized by the East, such as the Immaculate Conception—See the Mookse and the Gripes [Note: This is of course in *Finnegans Wake*. F. B.] that is East and West, par. beginning, 'When that Mooksius' and ending 'philioque.' All the grotesque words in this are in Russian or Greek for the three principal dogmas which separate Shem from Shaun. When he gets A and B on his lap C slips off, and when he has A and C he loses hold on B. . . .' "

Joyce alluded to the split of 1871 in the course of a conversation with me in Zürich, but all that I can remember of it (perhaps the question interested me little at the time) is his final word: "What I can't understand," he said, "is, why do they boggle at the infallibility of the Pope if they can swallow all the rest." The Holy Roman Catholic Apostolic Church in its Irish form was a net he had flown by, but having won the freedom he needed, he could admire the Church as an institution going on its own way unperturbed in obedience to the law of its own being. "Look, Budgen," he said. "In the nineteenth century, in the full tide of rationalist positivism and equal democratic rights for everybody, it proclaims the dogma of the infallibility of the head of the Church and also that of the Immaculate Conception."

Joyce's attitude toward the Christian religion was twofold. When he remembered his own youthful conflict with it in its Irish-Roman form he could be bitterly hostile, but in general, viewing it as a whole as an objective reality and as epitomized human experience, and from a position well out of reach of any church's authority and sanctions it was for him a rich mine of material for the construction of his own myth. Then he was a collector displaying all a collector's ardor, a in the case of the *altkatholische Kirche* referred to above.

Little as I suppose the Anglican *via media* would have appealed to his cast of mind, he must on one occasion in Zürich have attended an Anglican service, for I remember him telling me how well a certain consular official read the lessons. Only once did I see a Catholic priest in the Joyces' lodgings in Zürich. When I called I found Joyce patiently trying to get a little Belgian priest to talk about church music, whilst the priest himself insisted on discoursing on the theme of *"une mort tres edifiante"* he had just witnessed. I felt that Joyce was not amused.

August Suter told me that Joyce accompanied him once to a High Mass at the Church of St. Sulpice, and that Joyce explained to him (a Protestant) the meaning of each action as the Mass proceeded. When asked by August Suter what he regarded as his principal gain from his Jesuit upbringing, Joyce replied: "How to gather, how to order and how to present a given material." A discipline worth possessing whoever the drill sergeant.

The cosmology, hagiology and the sacraments of the Christian religion are built into the façade of *Ulysses* and *Finnegans Wake* for all to see, but it might perhaps one day profitably interest a theologian to inquire how far the rejected doctrines of the Churches pervade the inner structure of those works. For example: Is there a Manichaean leaning in Joyce's "spirit and nature" duality? Does he in his treatment of the mystery of fatherhood affirm or deny the consubstantiality of father and son? And what of the major theme of *Finnegans Wake*— the Resurrection?

For himself, as I say, religion was no longer a problem, but as a father (and Joyce was a good father) the problem must have cropped up again in another form. In his later Paris period he told me that he had been reproached for not causing his children to be brought up in the practice of religion. "But what do they expect me to do?" he said. "There are a hundred and twenty religions in the world. They can take their choice. I should never try to hinder or dissuade them." This was certainly true, for Joyce would never have denied to others the freedom he claimed for himself. But perhaps there are some situations where no completely satisfactory action is possible.

Very skeptical at first when I wrote him from London that I intended writing a book about *Ulysses* and the days we spent in Zürich, Joyce warmed to the project as it took shape, and when the book got to the stage of reading the galley proofs, he was positively enthusiastic. In a taxi driving up the Champs Elysées after a sitting of proofreading, he kept quoting bits of it from memory. And then: "I never knew you could write so well. It must be due to your association with me." While I was in Switzerland, in Ascona and Zürich, he dictated to his friend and *homme d'affaires,* Paul Léon, a number of suggestions which he urged me to work into the proofs. Some of these I used, others I failed to make use of, partly no doubt on account of my dilatoriness, but partly also because they were concerned with music or some other subject I feared to touch because of my ignorance of it. However, used or unused, I appreciated to the full the generosity that prompted so much proffered assistance.

For about two years during our stay in Switzerland, I met Joyce almost every day. Later, during his stay in Trieste and during the early part of his stay in Paris, he kept me informed by letter of the progress of *Ulysses.* For about five years after its publication, I lost touch with Joyce altogether. Then, hearing through Miss Sylvia Beach that I was in Paris, he wrote asking me to call. He was living *dans ses meubles* in the rue de Grenelle. From that time on I saw him whenever work or some other occasion took me to Paris and also on several occasions when he came to London.

I found the Joyce of Paris and *Finnegans Wake* different in many ways from the Joyce of Zürich and *Ulysses.* The resounding success of *Ulysses* had given him an air of established authority, and the task of composing *Finnegans Wake,* often amid weighty family cares, had taken some of the spontaneous naturalness out of his manner. But observers change together with things observed, and the flight of time shows different aspects of all of us, though never what isn't there.

It was some time in the early or middle thirties, I think (I can never remember dates: only occasions) that on one of our strolls somewhere near the Etoile Joyce surprised me by starting to talk bitterly about women in general. I was surprised only because I had never heard him talk that way before, for lives there a man who has never let himself go on the subject of womankind at some time or other? The interesting thing is always the how and the why and the how much. On the first of the two occasions I have in mind, he began with a bitter comment on woman's invasiveness and in general her perpetual urge to usurp all the functions of the male—all save that one which is biologically pre-empted, and even on that they cast jealous threatening eyes. So far nothing unusual. But then he stopped suddenly in his tracks as peasants and country people habitually do when they have something especially weighty to communicate.

"Women write books and paint pictures and compose and perform music. You know that."

"Yes, I do," I said. "And there are others who have attained eminence in the field of scientific research. But where does that get us?"

"It brings me to this point. You have never heard of a woman who was the author of a complete philosophic system. No, and I don't think you ever will."

So that was it. The creator of Molly Bloom and Anna Livia Plurabelle could never of course be a misogynist. No doubt a recent sojourn among women who were laying down the law about God and the universe, or, still worse, attempting to put him right on the matter of scholastic philosophy, was responsible for the outburst. But what for me makes the incident particularly worth recording is Joyce's designation of the demesne of philosophic inquiry as the one impregnable province of the mind reserved exclusively for the male. On the occasion of the second blast of the trumpet, I listened to a similar tirade on the same subject: woman and her urge to rivalize with menfolk in the things of the mind as well as to dominate them socially.

"But," I said, "as I remember you in other days you always fell back upon the fact that the woman's body was desirable and provoking, whatever else was objectionable about her."

This produced an impatient *"Ma che!"* and the further comment: "Perhaps I did. But now I don't care a damn about their bodies. I am only interested in their clothes."

Thus Stephen's interest in the "handful of dyed rags" survives his interest in the "squaw" they were pinned around. And when Joyce said clothes I took it for granted, knowing his bent, that he did not mean those wondrous garments devised by Dior, Fath, and others for the social adornment of the female form. I understood him rather to mean those garments visible only on the clothesline or on privileged private occasions. Throughout his life Joyce remained faithful to the underclothing of ladies of the Victorian era. Readers of *Ulysses* will remember the important part these articles played in that composition whether gleaming in the gloaming under the navy blue skirt of Gerty MacDowell or "redolent of Apoponax" in Molly Bloom's bedroom. They flutter also through the nightworld pages of *Finnegans Wake*. They were to Joyce feminine attributes of even greater value than the curves and volumes of the female body itself and certainly, as appears from the foregoing, of more abiding interest. Indeed he used, in the Zürich period, to carry a miniature pair in his trousers pocket until one sad day, as he sadly informed me, he lost them. A great number of Joyce's readers and admirers I am told inhabit the United States of America, and no doubt had he visited that hospitable country he would have been right royally entertained; and yet I cannot imagine his ever being wholly at his ease in a country where the word "drawers" is applied to those cumbersome

and uninteresting male garments called "pants" by most of the inhab-
itants of the British Isles. For the word was for Joyce a word of power,
and in it lay all the magic of the thing designated by it. To witness I
call one of the pieces of advice he sent to me dictated to Paul Léon:

"As regards the Nausikaa chapter you will receive a ponderous
volume of some six hundred large pages on the origin and history of
what he chooses to call *Le Manteau de Tanit*. He believes this subject
should be treated by you with IMMENSE seriousness, respect, circumspec-
tion, historical sense, critical acumen, documentary accuracy, citational
erudition and sweet reasonableness. . . ." And on the same subject in
a further dictated letter: "St. Bernard wrote, '*Qui me amat amat et
canem meum,*' but the love philtre of Isolde is alluded to somewhere by
her in W.i.P. [Note: *Work in Progress*] with this free translation, 'Love
me, love my drugrs.' Verbum sap."

It has often been said of Joyce that he was greatly influenced by
psychoanalysis in the composition of *Ulysses* and *Finnegans Wake*. If
by that is meant that he made use of the jargon of that science when
it suited the purpose of his fiction, or made use of its practical analytical
devices as when Bloom commits the *Fehlleistung* of talking about "the
wife's admirers" when he meant "the wife's advisers," the point holds
good. But if it is meant that he adopted the theory and followed the
practice of psychoanalysis in his work as did the Dadaists and the
Surrealists, nothing could be farther from the truth. The Joycean
method of composition and the passively automatic method are two
opposite and opposed poles. If psychoanalysis cured sick people, well
and good. Who could quarrel with that? But Joyce was always impatient
or contemptuously silent when it was talked about as both an all-sufficient
Weltanschauung and a source and law for artistic production.

"Why all this fuss and bother about the mystery of the unconscious?"
he said to me one evening at the Pfauen Restaurant. "What about the
mystery of the conscious? What do they know about that?"

One might say that both as man and artist Joyce was exceedingly
conscious. Great artificers have to be. As I saw him working on *Ulysses*
I can testify that no line ever left his workshop without having been
the object of a hundredfold scrutiny. And I remember my old friend
August Suter telling me that in the early days of the composition of
Finnegans Wake Joyce said to him, "I feel like an engineer boring
through a mountain from two sides. If my calculations are correct we
shall meet in the middle. If not. . . . " Whatever philosophy of composition that indicates, it is certainly neither automatic nor convulsive.

On one occasion I stayed the night in the Joyces' flat in Paris. Joyce was ill and looked it, and Mrs. Joyce thought that an extra man in the house might come in handy in case of emergency. The emergency arose at about eight the next morning. I went into Joyce's room and found him short of breath, looking very pale with a cold damp forehead, and evidently holding on to himself very tightly in a state of intense anxiety. If I had known then what I learned later in Civil Defense during the war, I should have felt obliged to suggest first aid treatment for shock. Mrs. Joyce sent me for a doctor. Lunching with them later in the day I asked Joyce, then somewhat recovered, what the doctor had said, and Joyce replied that the doctor had asked him what he was afraid of.

"I told him," said Joyce, "that I was afraid of losing consciousness, and he said that from all the signs and symptoms, pulse, temperature, etc., I had nothing to fear on that score."

Unlike most natives of the British Isles, Joyce disliked and feared dogs, perhaps on account of his poor sight and the dog's unpredictable temper. He would never go in for his evening treatment in the eye-clinic in the rue du Cherche-Midi until Madame had doubly assured him that the dog was on the chain. But he had a considerable sympathy for the cat with its persuasive manners and its compact self-sufficiencies. One of the waiters at (I think) Fouquets gave the Joyces a black cat and on my first visit to them after this acquisition I found Joyce in the middle of the living room putting on an act of homeless despair.

"Look," he said, pointing to his chair on which François lay curled up and fast asleep. "Since this animal came to live with us I haven't a chair to sit on." I heard, alas, that François had to go. Unlike the London cat with his countless back gardens, the Paris cat has few free spaces where he can pursue his loves and wars and practice at leisure his fastidious sanitary engineering.

Once as we were walking up the Champs Elysées together, I pointed to a beautiful white goat harnessed to a children's cart and said how much I admired these courageous and inquisitive creatures. Joyce fully agreed and, stopping to contemplate the stately little animal, said he couldn't see why the goat had been selected as a satanic symbol. *"Hircus Civis Eblanensis."* There was a good deal of the surefootedness and toughness of the mountain goat in Joyce's own composition and more than a little of the relaxed vigilance of the cat.

The front that Joyce presented to the world was anything but that of the extrovert broth-of-a-boy Irishman of stage and screen, but in Zürich he did occasionally exhibit a certain impishness said to be an Irish characteristic. In Paris I saw none of this. I have known him, for example, to tell stories about me to third persons (certainly not to my discredit: indeed they were designed to make me out a bigger man than I am) and then he would tell me what he had told them and laugh gleefully, expecting me to join in the merriment. One of these stories was that I was a painter well known in court circles and that I had received an important commission from King George V himself. If I shared his merriment in any degree it was not without a mild fear that the story might get round, and then I should have to suffer the embarrassment that always lies in wait for the pretender.

Somewhat in the same vein, though quite harmlessly, he always spoke to me and about me as if I were a Cornishman, and that for the fifty per cent insufficient reason that my mother was a Cornishwoman. I told him often enough that my father was a native of County Surrey and that I was born and brought up in that County, and further that I had spent only a few months of my life in the delectable Duchy. But it made no difference. I was still a Cornishman. He would begin sentences with such openings as, "Your countryman, King Mark. . . ." Or, "As a Cornishman you'll. . . ." It was as if he wanted to rope me in to some select Celtic confederacy in which I certainly did not belong to be—as a Cornishman might say. But as Joyce himself said in one of his dictations to Léon, "We did not sing either 'The Wearing of the Green' or 'And Shall Trelawney Die?' in honor of our respective Irish and Cornish forbears." True, we didn't. But that may be explicable in the words of Calverly:

> *We never sing the old songs now.*
> *It is not that we think them low,*
> *But because we don't remember how*
> *They go.*

Joyce always held that the English never really hated the Germans, even in wartime, but looked on them as belonging to the same family, cousins perhaps, who were doing pretty well for themselves, maybe a bit too well, on the mainland of Europe.

Joyce associated a good deal with such Greeks as were available in wartime Zürich, for he thought they all had a streak of Ulysses in them. Although he knew some Greek he was not a Greek scholar by high academic standards. By chance one day I stumbled on the fact that this was a sore point with him. I told him that I left school and went to work in my thirteenth year, but that the only thing I regretted about my lack of schooling was that I was never able to learn Greek. He thereupon regretted his insufficient knowledge of that language but, as if to underline the difference in our two cases (or so I interpreted it) he said with sudden vehemence: "But just think: isn't that a world I am peculiarly fitted to enter?" As a work of reference for his *Ulysses* he used the Butcher-Lang translation of the *Odyssey*.

He joined Pearse's Irish class in Dublin, but said of Pearse that "in a classroom he was a bore." He told me that he couldn't stand Pearse's continual mockery of the English language, instancing in particular Pearse's ridiculing of the English word "thunder." This was probably the limit, for as all readers of *Finnegans Wake* can testify thunder was for Joyce a word laden with very big magic. He soon abandoned Irish in favor of Norwegian which he studied to such purpose that later he was able to translate James Stephens' poem, "The Wind on Stephen's Green," into Norwegian (as well as into Latin, Italian, German, and French). In any case Norwegian was for him an obvious choice as an alternative, for he regarded his native Dublin as fundamentally a Scandinavian city.

I have commented elsewhere on Joyce's reactions to the criticisms of Clutton Brock and H. G. Wells, but his remark when I mentioned Wyndham Lewis's criticism of *Ulysses* is worth recording: "Allowing that the whole of what Lewis says about my book is true, is it more than ten per cent of the truth?"

Joyce rarely referred to the work of his contemporaries. There is, however, a comment on Proust in a letter written to me in 1920. It reads: "I observe a furtive attempt to run a certain Marcel Proust of here against the signatory of this letter. I have read some pages of his. I cannot see any special talent but I am a bad critic." Joyce's first and, as far as I am aware, only meeting with Marcel Proust took place shortly after the end of the First World War at an evening party given by a wealthy Parisian lady in honor of the Russian ballet, then all the rage in Paris as elsewhere. The evening wore on and Joyce, having had a few drinks, was thinking of going home when in walked Marcel Proust dressed to the nines. Their hostess introduced them, and some of the guests gathered round to listen to what they thought might be brilliant conversation. "Our talk," said Joyce, "consisted solely of the word 'No.' Proust asked me if I knew the duc de so-and-so. I said, 'No.' Our hostess asked Proust if he had read such and such a piece of *Ulysses*. Proust said, 'No.' And so on. Of course the situation was impossible. Proust's day was just beginning. Mine was at an end." Poor visibility for stargazers.

Very soon after I had made his acquaintance in Zürich, Joyce and I were taking an evening stroll on the Bahnhofstrasse when the conversation turned upon the variants of the comic sense possessed by different nations. Joyce retold me a funny story told him by my friend and colleague, Horace Taylor, at that time in Zürich, and as Taylor was an Englishman Joyce supposed that it was a typically English funny story. Joyce didn't think it was funny at all, nor did I, another Englishman, for that matter, though I forget what it was—something about a man falling out of a window, I think. Then Joyce went on to tell me the story of how Buckley shot the Russian general in its original spit and sawdust taproom Irish idiom, a story which he regarded as exemplifying the exclusively Irish sense of the comic. He retells the story with baroque exuberance in the dream idiom of *Finnegans Wake,* following its manifold implications in the Taff-Shem Butt-Shaun dialogue, and the metamorphosis the story undergoes furnishes as good an example as any of the treatment the common stuff of life receives at Joyce's hands in that composition. Here is the story, in substance, in ordinary language and, in parentheses, some relevant passages from the Taff-Butt rendering of it.

Buckley on duty in the trenches before Sevastopol sights a high-ranking Russian officer coming into the open ("With all his cannonball wappents. In his raglanrock and his malakoiffed bulbsbyg and his varnashed roscians and his cardigans blousejagged and his scarlett manchokuffs and his treecoloured camiflag and his perikopendolous gaelstorms."), a general at least, and Buckley notes that he is about to obey a call of nature. ("Foin duhans! I grandthinked after his obras after another time about the itch in his egondoom he was legging boldylugged from some pulversporochs and lyoking for a stooleazy for to nemesisplotsch allafranka and for to salubrate himself with an ultradungs heavenly mass at his base by a surprime pompship. . . .") Now was the time for Buckley to do his duty as a soldier. There's the enemy. Whatever he's doing fire at him. But one touch of nature makes the whole world kin, and Buckley hasn't the heart to shoot a man in just that hour of need. ("But meac Coolp, Arram of Eirzerum, as I love our Deer Dirouchy, I confesses without pridejealice when I looked upon the Saur of all the Haurousians with the weight of his arge fallin upon him from the travaillings of his tommuck and ruecknased the fates of a bosser there was fear on me the sons of Nuad for him and it was heavy it was for me then the way I immingled my Irmenial hairmeierians ammongled his Gospolis fomiliours till, achaura moucreas, I adn't the arts to. . . .") So far, out of sympathy with a fellow mortal, Buckley has just looked on and has done nothing. But when he sees the Russian general claw up a piece of turf to make his parts clean his Irish temper boils up. He goes mad and ups with his gun and shoots the Russian general, presumably where Frankie shoots Johnnie in the well known ballad. ("For when meseemim, and tolfoklokken rolland allover our-land's lane, beheaving up that sob of tunf for to claimhis, for to wolpim-solff, puddywhuck. Ay, and untuoning his culothone in an exitous erse-royal Deo Jupto. At that instullt to Igorladns! Prronto! I gave one dobblenotch and I ups with my crozzier. Mirrdo! With my how on harmer and hits leg an arrow cockshock rockrogn. Sparro! . . .")

With regard to the language used by Joyce, particularly in *Finnegans Wake*, it is sometimes forgotten that in his early years in Dublin Joyce lived among the believers and adepts in magic gathered round the poet Yeats. Yeats held that the borders of our minds are always shifting, tending to become part of the universal mind, and that the borders of our memory also shift and form part of the universal memory. This universal mind and memory could be evoked by symbols. When telling me this Joyce added that in his own work he never used the recognized symbols, preferring instead to use trivial and quadrivial words and local geographical allusions. The intention of magical evocation, however, remained the same.

In spite of his more than semi-blindness, Joyce had a natural feeling for the visual arts. He once asked me to paint for him a salmon (an avatar of HCE) and I promised him that I would, but, alas, I never managed to fulfill my promise. My only excuse is that a whole salmon is a very big lump of fish and costs a lot of money. Besides, my family seeing me come home with one would be looking forward to salmon steaks, and in all likelihood by the time I had finished getting the noble fish on to canvas I should have had to bury it in the garden. But of one thing I am sure: Joyce would never have been satisfied with a picture of a disintegrated and synthetically reconstructed salmon. He loved and admired the natural appearance of the fish. "A salmon is a wonderful thing," he said to me, "so full and smooth and silvery." August Suter told me that when Tuohy was painting Joyce's portrait he started talking about the poet's soul. "Get the poet's soul out of your mind," said Joyce, "and see that you paint my cravat properly."

But, as is well known, the art that made the greatest appeal to him, apart from his own art of words, was the art of singing—singing with any voice, but particularly with the tenor voice, as all his work bears witness. He could admire a certain measure and some aspects the art of Count MacCormack, "the tuning fork among tenors" as he called him in one piece he wrote and "the prince of drawing room singers" once in talking to me. But his overwhelming enthusiasm was reserved for another countryman of his, Mr. Sullivan, for many years singer of leading tenor roles at the Paris Opera. This enthusiasm has already been alluded to by myself and others who have written about Joyce, but to what lengths it led him may be seen from the following description of a certain evening at the Paris Opera when Sullivan was singing the part of Arnold in Rossini's *William Tell*. In one of his letters to me dictated to Paul Léon, Joyce said: "Perhaps Léon who is typing this will shoot you off a pen-picture describing my antics in the stalls of the Paris Opera for the scandal of the *blasé-abonné*, and the ensuing story in the press." Here is the pen-picture duly shot off by Léon and no doubt checked by Joyce:

Late Spring three years ago [Note: That would be 1930. F. B.] J. J. came back from Zürich after a second visit to Vogt. [Note: Dr. Vogt, the famous eye specialist. F. B.] Sight maybe a little better. Concert of Volpi heard. Also much talk about a performance of *William Tell* with Volpi in the part of Arnold. Conversations with Sullivan establish that Volpi had the entire score cut by some half of it and the key lowered by a half note. This Volpi performance is narrated with all sorts of compliments in the N. Y. *Herald* (Paris edition) by their official musical critic (M. Louis Schneider). Immediately a letter is written to him containing a wager by Sullivan to let him and Volpi sing both the part of Arnold in the original score in any concert hall—the arbiter to be Mr. Schneider and the stakes to be a copy of the original full score, nicely bound. Naturally no reply from either Schneider or Volpi. Yet Schneider had written that nobody at present could sing the part of Arnold as had been done by Volpi.

A week later, performance of *William Tell* with Sullivan. Sitting in the fifth row right aisle next to the passage your obedient servant, next to him J. J., next to him Mrs. Léon and next to her Mrs. Joyce—somewhere in the stalls an Irish Miss, correspondent of some paper, and a gentleman, correspondent of the *Neue Züricher Zeitung*.

First and second acts pass with great applause, J. J. being greatly enthused. Third act where there is no Sullivan on the stage spent in the buffet. Fourth act after the aria *"Asile héréditaire,"* sung with great *brio* and real feeling by S., applause interminable. J. J. excited in the extreme shouts, "Bravo Sullivan! *Merde pour Lauri Volpi.*" The *abonnés* (this being I believe a Friday) rather astonished, one of them saying: *"Il va un peu fort celui là."*

Half an hour later at the Café de la Paix: great conversation in which S. joins after he has changed his clothes. At the moment of parting the *Neue Züricher Zeitung* correspondent, having been talked to all the evening about music, approaches J. J. with the following words: "Thank you so much for the delightful evening. I have some pull with my paper, and should you wish I could arrange for an article or two by you on your Paris impressions to appear there."

J. J.: "Many thanks, but I never write for the newspapers."

The Correspondent: "Oh, I see, you are simply a musical critic."

Next day an article in the Press: "Monsieur James Joyce, after a successful operation, goes with friends to the Opera to hear his compatriot Sullivan sing in *William Tell*. Sitting in a box after the Fourth Act aria he takes off his spectacles and is heard saying: "Thank God I have recovered my eyesight."

I always felt that originally Joyce was of an open, impulsive nature, but as we all know natures have a way of being modified by experience as well as of being subdued to what they work in, like the dyer's hand, and therefore I suppose that a spontaneous utterance of the natural Joyce might easily be checked and stifled by an acquired defensiveness. This is an attempt to explain in advance something that occurred during one of my visits to Paris in the early thirties. Joyce and I were alone in his apartment, and while I was looking at a book during a lull in the conversation he broke the silence with: "When you get an idea, have you ever noticed what I can make of it?" I looked up and waited for him to go on, feeling rather pleased with myself that I should have any ideas of such a caliber. But instead of going on he walked back and forth across the room, looked out of the window and changed the subject. I wish I had asked him there and then exactly what he meant, for it has cost me a lot of cogitation since then to arrive at a conclusion as to what the idea might be. Quite certainly it was an idea having a bearing on *Finnegans Wake,* and an important bearing at that—something fundamental. The words, phrases, anecdotes, snatches of song, and suchlike that he picked up every day from somebody or other were so numerous that he would have considered them hardly worth mentioning, and in any case he would not have used the word idea in connection with them. I come finally to rest on two possibilities. He may have been thinking of a talk we had in a café near the Amtshaus in Zürich. I told him on that occasion how much my dreams interested me, and explained the difficulty I had in making a written record of them. All the dream quality went out of them as soon as I turned them into a string of time-bound sentences. This is one guess. In any case I have always felt that at that session some seed was sown that later was to blossom into the dream language of *Finnegans Wake.* "That was the prick of the spindle to me that gave me the key to dreamland." It could be. Why not? There must be germ carriers also in the realm of ideas. Or it may have been a poem of mine I once showed him in which I tried to express a state of mind between sleeping and waking. I called the poem "At the Gates of Sleep," and it ended with the words "Sleep is best." If in the first guess, the suggestion was for the dream material of *Finnegans Wake,* in the case of the second guess the suggestion would be for the timeplace to be inhabited by his ". . . twin eternities of spirit and nature expressed in the twin eternities of male and female." The quotation is from *Stephen Hero.* Tracing a work of genius to its source is like searching for the source of a river. Eventually we come as with Anna Livia Plurabelle to the principle of evaporation and condensation working through the sea and the sky. But in a rough and ready way it is true that the original inspiration for all Joyce's work is always to be sought in the imaginings of his boyhood and adolescence in Dublin. The idea, of course, may have been in some word or other I let fall and forgot as soon as uttered, for, as he wrote to me during the composition of the Circe episode of *Ulysses*: "A word is enough to set me off." However, if both my guesses are wrong then Joyce's moment of inhibition must take the blame for my vain cogitations.

I talked with Joyce for the last time in the spring of 1939 when, having a little money in hand, and sensing that the outbreak of war was near, I went to Paris to see the city all artists love before enemy bombs should mar her noble skyline. It turned out otherwise, but that is the way some of us foresaw it at the time. Joyce was living in a flat in Passy. When I called on him, a copy of *Finnegans Wake* fresh from the printers lay on the table. In the course of the afternoon he asked me to read aloud to him Anna Livia's monologue as she passes out by day to lose her individual identity in the ocean whence she came. No doubt he knew every word of it by heart, and no doubt I blundered in the reading of it, but he let me go on to the end without interruption. It was perhaps the first time he had heard the words spoken by any voice other than his own. The last I saw of Joyce was his wave from a taxi late that afternoon.

I was to write an article on *Finnegans Wake* when I got back to London, but I found it heavy going with war a practical certainty looming close ahead. Later in 1939 Joyce and his family began that series of moves that were to end in Zürich in 1941. His self-exile in Europe may be said to have begun in "noble Turricum abounding in all manner of merchandise," and there it ended. He wrote me, though not frequently, during 1939 from Etretat, from Berne, and finally (as far as my record goes) from Gerard-le-Puy in the Allier—about literary reactions to *Finnegans Wake*, about his family anxieties (both his daughter and his daughter-in-law were ill), but never a word about the war, not even the most guarded reference. His entry into Switzerland was referred to in the press. Then came news of his sudden illness. A paragraph in the *Evening Standard* announcing his death was shown to me in the dugout where I was standing by to report air-raid damage. When I met Mrs. Joyce in Zürich after the war, she told me that during the day preceding the sudden onset of his fatal seizure Joyce had been to an exhibition of French nineteenth century painting. Somehow there seems to me to be an affinity there, I mean between French nineteenth century painters and Joyce, in the sense that all the work of his imagination and intellect was rooted, as was theirs, in a natural sensibility.

INDEX

Index

335

MIDLAND BOOKS RECENTLY PUBLISHED